I AM, YOU ARE, WE ARE

Into the perilous deep you dive. Trusting yourself. There's no one to see. No one to suck back a breath in fear for you. You have faith. Know. You are seal, an otter, salmon. Whale breaching. You are in the womb and buried in earth. Nothing are you not and these depths are the true reality. They are the ocean and the way of the well. You are a cave that has no bottom so we may be sure there is no center to this earth, only space. I yearn from my place of sleep. I love you for guiding me to this edge. I feel your bones in my bones. You are a line a million strong. Your lovers of a million years watch. Warrior bright. Old. Old and brazen. Young and sinewy from the long hunt. Banging their shields as this she-bear passes, fearless of them, your cubs following you into the forest. Into the future. Into the bloodline of the unborn. Into the wild woman who shakes the world off. Into the wild man who walks on all fours by your side, his hide the color of the snowline, for yet you are still winter, his eyes black as the wings of ravens, catching light. Taking flight.

You are the silence. No one sees you dive.

INITIATION | A MEMOIR

LY DE ANGELES

INITIATION | A MEMOIR – © 2016 Ly de Angeles. All rights reserved. No part of this book may be used, reproduced, stored in a retrieval system or transmitted in any form or by any means, electronic, mechanical, photocopying, scanning, recording, including Internet usage, without written permission from the author except in the case of brief quotations embodied in critical articles and reviews.

Revised Edition (2025)
ISBN 9780648502524

Cover design Lisa Engeman and Ly de Angeles
Cover design by Lisa Engeman | oCulture
Cover photography Zo Damage

OTHER BOOKS BY THE AUTHOR

The Way of the Goddess, Prism/Unity, 1987
The Way of Merlyn, Prism/Unity, 1990
Witchcraft Theory and Practice, Llewellyn Worldwide, 2000
The Feast of Flesh and Spirit, Wildwood Gate, 2001
When I See the Wild God, Llewellyn Worldwide, 2002
Pagan Visions for a Sustainable Future, Llewellyn Worldwide, 2004
The Quickening, Llewellyn Worldwide, 2005 (first edition)
The Shining Isle, Llewellyn Worldwide, 2006 (first edition)
Tarot Theory and Practice, Llewellyn Worldwide, 2007
Magdalene | Witch of the Grail Legends, 2012
Genesis | The Future, 2012
The Feast of Flesh and Spirit | Revised, 2015
Priteni, the Decimation of the Indigenous Pagan Celts, 2015
The Skellig (with Melaine Knight), 2017
Witch | For Those Who Are, 2018
Under Snow (with Serenity de Angeles), 2019
Advanced Tarot | The Art of Prophecy, 2020
Brave | For the Unclaimed People, 2021
The Changeling | From Winter, Spring is Born, 2022
Savage | Bodywork, 2023
Priteni | The Decimation of the Celtic Britons, Sonant Edition, 2023

Dedicated to all of us stolen from family, custom, origin, culture, language and community. Have courage. We cannot be broken.

We are still here.

LA LOBA – BONE WOMAN

In the long ago when the world made sense and humans didn't do so much talking, wolves ran free across the world. Then the new people manifested from some hidden old greed-land, that the badger folk forgot to close the door to, and they decimated the people of the old ways, killing their stories which were also their souls. Killing off the wolves if the wolves were their totems. Scared of everything.

There are hides and hollows and hedges in the world where the otter people and the raven people still live, keeping the stories of the long ago alive for those willing to listen.

The story of La Loba is that of an old woman living hidden in plain sight in places that everyone knows that most people don't know. Clarissa Pinkola Estés says, "She's been seen travelling south in a burned out car with the back window shot out… or riding shotgun with truckers"[1].

When she's not getting up to mischief with other animal people La Loba gathers the bones of the long dead wolves that lie white under moonlight, scattered across the ancient land, until she has a complete skeleton. Then throughout the depths of night she works her magic, finally giving her breath. Come dawn the wolf is enchanted into life, yips with laughter, licks her face, pauses for mere seconds before running, wild and delighted, toward the tree-line.

---

[1] *Women Who Run With the Wolves*, Random House, 1992

When I first learned this story I thought it just another folk tale because I didn't understand. Now I do. She has been in a desert that sooner or later we all travel. A seemingly barren place that, in truth, is not. Finding sustenance there can only happen with familiarity and through the teachings of the old people who know these stories.

La Loba is in every woman, as is the wolf, as is the free woman she eventually becomes.

The many mythic people in my story are to remind us that we are all still in the long ago. That the people in mythworld are very real and that we are being fooled by creatures not always like us. Not always with our stories or our best interests at heart. That we have as much right to be here as they do. That they should not fear us just because they do not know the way of us.

We must protect La Loba wherever in the world she turns up. Offer her coffee and a place beside the fire. A bed for the night in exchange for what's in that pouch hanging off her belt or what she's got clutched tight in that fist. Or in her remembering. Or maybe just because of the relief we feel when she comes to our door in the first place.

AUTHENTICITY

BECOMING BONE WOMAN

I have unlocked the stories in my bones. Memories of ancient primordial forests in which I hunted, making love beside a vast still lake. Remembering that my dead mother's skin still lies there, remembering running silently between towering spruce trees in the snow, following the reindeer along deep ancestral tracks. My father was born on the pelts before the fire pit in a house made of earth, his mother and aunties chanting birthing spells low in their throats, and the small wide eyed children of the horse keeping vigil until the heavily tattooed old woman bites the cord. His child is me. A thousand generations ago you and I were there. Nothing has gone. Life has changed and many have suffered an unbearable isolation because no one has reminded us of who else we are other than beyond the current skins we wear. A walking man explained the Celtic word hireath to me as homesickness, a longing, deep and inexplicable because we don't know what home is. The suffering this causes. Dispossession is in our marrow and that fear, beneath the surface we present to the world, of lovelessness and plastic and asphalt, crowding us into a corner from which we cannot escape.

Initiation is a mapped and charted experience that many people do not understand or comprehend when the experience is not on their terms. You will be woken up. When wolf mother takes us in her jaws and pulls us into the myth we must comprehend that we are helpless. Myth is not fallacy. Myth is as real as the skin that keeps our rawness clothed. Joseph Campbell, in Hero with a Thousand Faces, explains initiation as firstly a Threshold. We die to who we have been. And yes, always tragically. We cross into the Liminal World and become lost. This could last a lifetime if we lack the necessary insight to realize what is happening. We need to be on the lookout then, as we travel the days and nights of desolation and confusion, for the signs of the Return. We must keep our ears pricked and our tails bushy. There must be a Return. Someone to know us. To be met and the purpose of this new life be revealed.

When we consciously understand the place in which we currently live as the liminal world of not-life we may very well be ready to Return. We will know. We will meet the Gatekeeper. This could be someone already there or someone new. They will complement the true us. This is not like any other compliment. The person is recognized for the depth of them and how far they have climbed from that pit. Words will liberate the dark night of the soul. The Gatekeeper gives the keys to a new life. Do we have the guts to walk through? To accept the change with only courage? To leave that lost place, savage forest, mist of futility, cave of self-doubt and take the challenge of being raw, temporarily blind and furless?

No one can hold us should we choose to make this choice, to wear the next mask and to clothe ourselves in this new garment of self. We don't have to cleave to the identity that we thought defined us. Life is art. Life wants experience through who we are and what we do. Wants the lone wolf to run with the pack.

My most recent initiation took nine years and I didn't know until I reached the other side.

My birthday 2006. Five hours at the clinic in Tweed Heads while my daughter has an abortion. Arriving home to my eldest son waiting with a bunch of flowers. Them starting in on each other. Him calling her selfish for doing this on my birthday, her not defending herself, standing up to him because what he does not know is that she is bravely battling the comedown from a speed addiction. The conversation escalates to all-out screaming.

I tell them to both go away. There is no birthday. Then I sit on the chair by the kitchen window wondering what the fuck just happened. Absolutely convinced I am dead. Pointless. I don't know how long I stay there barely breathing. I walk across the road towards the beach. Then I'm sitting in the gutter of the street parallel to the ocean. Unable to move. A stranger comes out of her house bringing cigarettes. She lights one for me. We sit in silence. She must know if not the facts, the feeling.

To take or give initiation at the hands of a person is one thing. Quite another when life is the initiator. Because something is wanted. But first skin is flayed from us, brains are burned to ashes, souls turned inside out and air blown into them to rid them of creases. Bones are ground to powder and this dust is sent, by wind and water, across the whole earth seeking a home to fertilise with memory. To remember a terrible and tragic beauty to drag into now.

Year after year I stripped away the seeming-knowledge I had accrued over a lifetime—of witchery, of being woman—hunting for the pristine pools of limey water that lie silent within bedrock. A mystery successfully hidden from culture by smug-mouthed old men. Hidden in plain sight but never taught. The delusion of isolation from relationships with other species: rock, tree, sky, everything. The realization that we do live in two places simultaneously: the crass, beautiful, brutal world seen through my eyes as human, and myth world where the stories are that of forest and stone fortress, and initiation understood as clearly as an honest sentence. Where tragedy and ecstasy make sense.

Witch people, like magicians and sorcerers, conjurers, druids and hoodoo hexers, like cunning women and cunning men, kadaichas, shamans, mundunugus, manitous, angakoks, curanderas, bruxas, enchanters and shape shifters are needed in this world. We are the stories not bound by dogma or preserved in aspic, displayed as relics in a museum. We cause disquiet. We make questions but may not have answers. We are the wildness and the frightening places. The cave entrance under the ice at the base of that crevasse. Blue handprints on the rock face imprinted with an ochre of confusion by people we cannot name and from a time we cannot confirm. One must belong.

We are Once Upon a Time people. People of the reindeer. Volcano people. I know that air has feelings and that messages can be sent through the earth; that I can touch someone and their lives will be forever changed but that I am not responsible. I know the shape of that cloud is a conversation. That a forked stick can find water. That the ring around the moon warns of rain. What I might tell you can go straight to your gut or the throat, and yes that's a metaphor, but you do feel anxious because even though we are seemingly separate I can look at you and you might squirm because you know I know you are lying and are so lonely; that anything you do will have consequences. Everything has consequences. Mirrors are all around us.

Mircea Eliade wrote that *Initiation recapitulates the sacred history of the world. And through this recapitulation, the whole world is sanctified anew ... can perceive the world as a sacred work, a creation of the Gods.*[2]

The language he uses covers me with wasps. What Eliade wrote is in a dead and religious tongue steeped in Abrahamic analogy.

Initiation is occult. Hidden. Unexpected. One comes to the Threshold, passes through, crosses over or drops down the rabbit hole into the Liminal Space where one is lost within mists of unfamiliarity because the only mirror we have is who we thought we were, confounded or temporarily mad. Finally, we meet a Guide, the Threshold Guardian and the Return. That return is only significant if the newly initiated individual is embraced into the pack, the culture, held in the arms as newborn flesh. Someone auspicious now drapes you in a garment with which to clothe your wise soul.

This is the deep world. The land of myth. Where we are also other animals and the voice of crow and walrus, both familiar and alien. Where we are torn apart and rewilded.

So now, at the other side of this fearful and fearless journey, I have become La Loba—Bone Woman. I wear her skin, and my hair, once the color of night is now white. What is the garment? Not an old language but an immortal one, hidden beneath those same old men's prattles, their pomposity, dry and dusty with the verbiage of religion and class. Of schooling that does not educate but indoctrinates.

I'd written a book about witchcraft, published in the year 2000. Do I regret that? Not at all, but by locking the words onto the page I trapped brother wolf, manacled sister eagle, put the wild salmon in a

---

1 Rites and Symbols of Initiation, first edition, New York, NY Harper and Row, 1958

pond and said, There. This is what you are and here is where you must abide. I closed an open system that should remain as unpredictable as weather.

I don't know when the penny began to spin. A while before this initiation, that's for sure. My coven converged at full moons, dressed in meticulously hand-sewn robes and talismanic ritual jewelry, lit candles and incense, placed athamé, wand, chalice, pentacle, the skulls of long-dead ravens, on an ancient wooden box I called an altar, cast the circle *deosil* (east to west), invoked the spirits of earth, air, fire and water, murmured the incantations to one goddess or another, to one god or another. And deep down I was now thinking I should not be doing this. Knowing in a very fearful silence that I was dressing the wild world in the garments of predictability.

Not long after that birthday and mere weeks before we were given notice to vacate our home of twelve years, I had a dream that gave me the clues I would only interpret, fully, almost a decade later. Early morning, the hazy light of dawn twilight, I approached an old, weary, shabby weatherboard house in the company of several others. We were there to clean. A gnarled, borer-holed, sadly grey plank barred our entrance, nailed like a warning across the front door. The sinewy old man made us wait. From the tool belt at his hip he took sandpaper, cloth and oil. He sat cross-legged on the grass and transformed that plank into beauty, mirroring the day. He nailed his plank friend atop the door and we entered. Come the reds and indigoes of early evening we had travelled all the way out the back and stood above a steep V-shaped valley, leading west to the last of the sun. The breathlessness of that place. Granite escarpments, shadowed and vast, trees high upon the cliff top black against the gloaming. Ravens calling sentinel for miles in all directions.

I stood beside a young woman with a bucket in her hand. She said, what happens if we leave? Do you think we'll ever be able to find a way back? I, in my considered wisdom and certainty of experience, said, I'll be the guinea pig, shall I?

Then night. I stood, weeping, on the derelict, deserted platform above a railway track, a young girl's hand in mine. A station worker, with a broom and one of those long-handled scoops for rubbish on the ground, asked if he could help.

I can't get back, I replied.

We actually moved to that house in my dream, with the escarpments and the sun setting in the cleavage of that valley to the west. But reality was fog surrounding trees in winter.

Then in 2007 I felt myself dissolving. I was no longer whole. Life made no sense, but I kept on reading tarot and the people kept coming. Many of them also broken.

Was this what Eliade meant? Was the whole world in liminality? We were a year prior to that global financial crash, the illusion of money built on the same hollow mound as Vortigern's doomed castle. Lots of broken people that year.

We think we're the same person just going through travails. That we'll wake up safe in a few days or weeks or months and the drama will have passed. We'll be the person we were, hold the values we held previously and believe what we always believed.

Silly me, I still thought I was who I had been. As yet I had no level of insight. I thought the Byron Shire, where I had lived for twenty two years, was still my country.

In truth I had no home and experienced hireath, that dreadful longing, constantly.

In Melbourne in the winter of 2012 the fog triggered a memory. Fog thick and silent outside my daughter's kitchen window. The day Samhain-like. Closing out everything. Reminding me of a lifetime ago. When my children were babies. When I was a child. When I still had all my teeth. I hid in a back room all day writing the since-deleted beginning to this memoir, knowing beyond doubt that home was no longer home. I could no longer pretend that I belonged anywhere. I needed fog, all the many shades of grey, bone-deep cold, architecture older than me. Its history and dereliction.

When I told friends I was leaving they asked why, perplexed at the thought. If I stay, I said, I will wither and fade and have bequeathed nothing of any current value. I will become a bent and invisible old woman.

The friend who was secretly a Guide said *why don't you teach Celtic studies, history, at uni?*

I didn't understand.

I can't, I explained. I'm really stupid. I've just pretended to be clever all these years.

Rubbish, he replied. You can start with a master's if you want to. You need to meet my supervisor in Hobart.

I laughed but he wasn't being funny. The fog thinned a little and I could sense the dapple of sunlight.

Later that year I took my twenty nine year old daughter to MONA [3] for her birthday. In Hobart I met that scholar. She gave me the keys to the Return.

The man I initiated thirty-four years ago is also a Historian, one of his talents: genealogy. He asked for my biological records. What? More shredding of secret, long-held delusions of ancestral importance? Bus drivers and servants in the houses of gentry? But for me existentialism is always blended with mysticism and the curiosity to know the treasure at the heart of the Maze. I had new stories and a fledgling new language and guts.

So I allowed this goblin in.

The Historian rescued the roots of my ancestral tree and, week after week he dropped names like nuggets of dull and lead-like information. These long-dead relatives all lived in the north of England. Albion. Generation after generation. I was busy elsewhere and the Historian's morsels were boring. What a brat I can be. Then he spoke a name. A spell.

Oh, he said, quizzically. They're not all from Lancashire, Yorkshire and Lincolnshire. You have a Welsh ancestor after all. Caradoc ap Silures.

I must have looked ashen and the Historian frowned.

I did have that strange feeling one gets when one is about to faint or the sensation of dreaming and was I really clothed?

I know that name like the back of my hand. My ancestor is also my hero two thousand years into the past. Those people that never moved were indigenous to that country. Priteni'd (tatu'd) for initiation and status, Britons are named for this. Memory. Ancestral earth.

Born into a bigoted and sexist world, brought up as someone's fabricated lie, living a lifetime with no family other than my children,

---

[3] Museum of Old and New Arts. Also the Druid Isle now Anglesea.

their children and people well-trusted, the Historian gave me a core reality. At the conclusion of the initiation he clothed me in a new skin.

He handed me the keys to knowing my culture and lineage—my authentic ancestry—and I thought myself no longer lost. There's always more, though, isn't there?

About now I want to also mention that I have been haunted by what in legend and lore is the Trickster. The Trickster is an entity or spirit, puka or sometimes a god that exists within the myths of almost every culture worldwide. And this beast has sashayed and danced through mythworld, taunting and challenging me for most of my life. Always riding one man's body or another. For a while. Just like in the movie Fallen.

When I did not guess the game the Trickster moved from man to man disrupting my cool and obfuscating my liberty. Originally this character of lore presented benevolence. Even at my birth. Men who desired to control, to own, to direct, even to be protected. The Trickster sought an outlet for misbehaviour, stealing power, imposing a culturally-approved order, impoverishing.

When I refused to learn of my own choices, embody knowledge, when I have acquiesced to the cultural expectations and norms of female out of laziness or fatigue Trickster discarded the body of the man whose form he wore. Who was left behind? I don't know. The ones I allowed inside my body became daunted and weak. The Trickster sucking their strength from them and leaving me the aftermath. They all ended up the same. Fitting into some approved paradigm that didn't work for me or that was just downright ugly in the way of myth: behaviourally.

The Trickster exists within every indigenous culture and also in the modern psyche. Provides stern lessons. Whether Loki or Crow, Coyote or Puck, Bugs Bunny or Reynard the Fox, Eulenspiegel or Dr Who, what Trickster wants, ultimately, is what everyone wants. Worthy stories. So that living is an experience of granite strength but feather-light malleability. Of excitation and liberty. Duende.

The men were possessed by the Trickster until I gained all kinds of true strength. Savvy. The capacity to love without disrespecting my hard won core ideals. Without compromise.

From birth until my early adult years Trickster took upon itself the role of authority. Someone who knew better than I what was good for me. Then, when I turned my back on that archetype—took to anarchy—the tactics changed. The Trickster played the sexy card. Became beguiling, seductive. Chose handsome men to wear, for me to make love with. The Trickster persuaded men to persuade me that they loved me.

In the latter encounters I was complicit simply because I was naive to the real story. Every woman I have ever met wants to be loved. We also have—or I once had anyway—a propensity to stay, even when the relationship was rabid. Even when the Trickster had abandoned the men weak, broken and bleeding, or violent and controlling, or once again seeking domination because that's all they had left. The Trickster wanted nothing less that my cultural and gendered weakness abolished. Wanted my neediness to be in an intimate partnership, with any traditional affectations, to be the discarded skin of the python left in a mango tree. To be witch. To learn the language of animal people. To break me, see me bleed. Become bone. Allow myself to be clothed in the body of the long-dead wolf and walk freely into tomorrow.

There are others from mythworld wearing men's bodies throughout the story. Not all of them problematic. There's the Historian, the Guardian, the Gate Keeper, the Woodsman and others that I'll discuss more deeply when relevant. They are all friends to women, or are careless of the gender of any person. There's a Cuckoo in there somewhere. You know the one. Pretends to be something else to enchant us into being reed warblers and feeding another bird's chic. Until the masks, so firmly glued on in the long ago, slide down just enough for us to say *boo*.

PART ONE

We're at that time of year again. The howling night when the wolves come back to the forest from the summer hunting grounds. Calling to each for miles in every direction to gather for the stories at our grandmother's house.

They run and lope through relentless lines of birch that shed autumn leaves like a storm of dead yellow butterflies. Hunter moon lights their pelts in silvers, shadows and night. Tails like pennants, bushy and long. Sleek and well fed from the meadows and tree line to the south. The young, still puppies, distracted by everything but knowing not to stray for too long.

PUPPY PRESCHOOL

CHAPTER 1

The first initiation began at birth. The twentieth of December 1951. No suckling for me. An unnamed Trickster signed my identity away. Ripped from my mother's body and presented by nuns to strangers for purchase. Fifty years later, when seeking answers to my history through archival resources, the first four months—who I was, where I was—remain lost and unknown, despite all sleuthing.

I was sold by the nuns of the Mater Catholic Hospital in North Sydney to Jan and her husband Eric, for £300. I was to be a christmas present for their older girl—a pretend-sister—a child acquired the previous year. Eric was the second Trickster.

Home was the residence above Eric's shop. 666 Military Road, Mosman. When I became an adult I learned that Aleister Crowley, somewhat infamous founder of the O.T.O. and Thelema, was thought by his mother to be the 'beast of the apocalypse' whose number, according to the biblical revelation, was 666.

The faux sibling was nasty and her lips were a lifetime of one thin, bitter line. I didn't like her. She was always sickly and used that to manipulate the pretend mother. We were never friends. I think from the beginning we both knew there was not a breath of kinship between us. We didn't look remotely alike.

I was sent to kindergarten when I was three years old. Killarney. A school, once a private home, off Spit Road in Mosman. Rambling, magnificently antiquated with belfry and oleander gardens. I only stayed a little while on my first day because I didn't much fancy school. When I appeared at home Jan was Hoovering, my entrance shocking her. Traffic in 1954 was nothing compared to later years but I had still traversed two main roads.

Jan returned me to the kindergarten the very next day and I was told by the head mistress, Miss Laver, that German Shepherds now guarded the outside of the gates. If I ran away again they'd tear me to pieces.

Retrospectively I wonder whether she knew I was a bastard, therefore not really deserving, because I was viewed with suspicion the entire time I was there. I loved books and was reading from the infant age of three. I was in trouble several months later for being the suspect ringleader of three girls, all chatting with the door to the loo wide open. Apparently seeing each other weeing was taboo. I was punished by having to spend six weeks of lunchtimes in the boys' playground. Segregation of the sexes was strict. I was a tomboy (gender neutral) so those six weeks cemented friendships with several lads, all of whom I loved. Including Miles, the boy I almost killed. His father was building a double garage and every afternoon Miles and I covertly stole from his stack of bricks, carrying armloads into the woods at the bottom of the garden where we built a cubby house. I was really, really in trouble (I wasn't there) when the whole thing fell on him. He was hospitalized with concussion and I was never allowed back to their house.

Our neighborhood was an equal mix of protestants and catholics but Eric was quite forthright in his slander of the latter, especially the Irish whom he referred to as paddy micks, insisting large families were peasants while small families were posh. Everyone was oddly proud, however, when one Mosman catholic woman gave birth to her seventeenth baby. She received a letter of congratulations from the pope of the day. The hypocrisy was as offensive as a corpse in the attic.

Year after year in the liminal spaces, lost in nonsense, lies, cultural and religious superstition, I was shuffled from one christian denomination to another, before the age of eleven, in experiments that never lasted more than a few months. Each thought their deity was better than the others, even though they were all named God. I was asked to believe extraordinary things like hell where you burned forever. I was told at a christian Sunday school that I'd probably go there when I died because naughty children do and all children are naughty. And heaven, a wonderful eternity for the righteous was up amongst clouds. Angels sat on those and played harps and that God Almighty, an old man with a perpetually flowing white beard and who wore an eternally clean white frock, sat enthroned amidst them. His son, whom he had allowed to die in a sacredly sadistic way, occupied a chair off to daddy's side and both were technically queenless. When I looked skyward I thought heaven must be an awfully long way away, not visible to the naked eye, and how would one get there? And if that was all anyone did we should have a better option.

Each denomination demanded money. Eric gave the faux sibling and me two shillings each for the collection plate. Cults do that, I was later to learn. Nothing was taken seriously, except for the clang and resonance of hundreds of now-silent bells.

Smoke from chimneys; from fireplaces banked with wood or coal, misted autumn days, redolent with rot and air hazy from countless backyard incinerators and bonfires. The distinct nostalgia that only that time of year, and European trees shedding leaves onto damp footpaths, can evoke.

Despite Eric's bigotry, I grew up with the neighboring Carmody and Mooney kids and we rode scooters with pumped up tires and bounced, suicidally, on pogo sticks. The first boy I ever kissed, when I was eleven was Jimmy Mooney, one of the children of those detested paddy micks.

666 Military Road Mosman was called a mixed business, which meant men's haircuts and the smell of California Poppy Hair Oil and Brylcreem. Down one end of the shop was a canary and a budgie, both in separate cages, Stan the barber, who also did shaves, on occasion, for old blokes with a penchant for the cutthroat razor, worked with his unexplained paraphernalia on men seated in a leather barber's chair. Down the other end, closer to the door and the street Eric, an old man born in 1897, and sometimes Jan, took the money and penned sales in a large green ledger. They sold Russian Sobranies with gold tips – ever-so-fashionable – Pall Mall, Lucky Strike, du Maurier and every possible brand of cigarette. Audrey Hepburn-style long black cigarette holders and short, tortoise-shell ones for people with the cough. He sold cigars, pipes and pipe cleaners, fancy ashtrays and lighters. In the center of the shop was a big oval counter displaying lollies and chocolates. The desk enthroned an ornate cash register and a monstrous Bakelite phone that could kill if ever it was thrown in a temper.

Behind the door at the rear of the shop was a stockroom that led through to a laundry, outside toilet, concrete yard and a gate that opened onto a narrow lane. Inside twenty-one stairs were climbed to our residence.

That stockroom was always gloomy but not so dark I didn't know where the chocolate was. They were out-of-date but I peeled off the wrappers, their color leached to beige and chalky, covered with speckles, and ate them anyway

On weekends we children were hustled outside after breakfast—porridge, soft-boiled eggs with soldiers, cornflakes—and sometimes went home for lunch—but were otherwise not allowed inside again until sunset unless we were ill or damaged.

I knew every inch of Mosman all the way from Spit Junction to Taronga Zoo, navigated each road possible to Balmoral Beach (a mere twenty minute walk) and from there, every ledge, hand or foot hold I considered safe, depending on the tide, all the way to Chinamans Beach, named for the long shells that looked like Chinese men's fingernails a hundred years into the past.

I couldn't do that coast climb now. Scrambling and crazed leaping over barnacled, slimy, razor-sharp, oyster-shelled rocks, deep-water pounding the shallow caves, kelp to strangle if one should fall in. Deep, dark water. Perilous and life-threatening, I wonder what the parents of those of us who took the risk regularly would have thought, had they known. But they never found out. Jan said what did you do today? Went to the beach, I'd answer. End of conversation.

In the nineteen fifties teenage boys had their hair greased and slicked back and worked on their cars in the vacant lot on the weekends. The slick-back was called a duck's tail and had a special comb that poked out the pocket of every swell guy's shirt. All of them wore leather jackets or sports coats. Girls wore their cardigans on backwards with pearl buttons. They had rope petticoats under skirts cut on the bias with wide, red belts, ponytails and *bobby socks*.

Men had names like Denny and Eddy and Ray. Stanley, Percy, Archie and Rupert had become bad luck because so many with that name had been slaughtered in the war. Doo wop was not yet R and B, Elvis would become the king before the decade was over and Robert Menzies had Australia tightly under the control of the crown.

The era of the crystal-set portable radio was pressed up against the past like a threat to Monday and god save the queen. Lipstick was still war-years-red, but then coral and pink became the rage, as did cake mascara. The beehive was a hairdo worn by women who wistfully wished to be Brigitte Bardot. Hair was sprayed into submission, delicate silk headscarves often draped over them, keeping them safe from the terror of wind. Head scarves, actually, were very much a necessary item. For church, for shopping, to cover the bobby pins and curlers of the neighbourhood women when they popped out. One went to the 'rest room' to powder one's nose as shiny noses were just wrong. As was everything not groomed. We all wore gloves and those women and girls not wearing a scarf always had a hat. So did men. Or caps. Bare heads were never seen outside the home.

Eric had a corgi like the English queen did. His name was Shorty. That took a lot of imagination. Everywhere Eric went the dog was sure to be there. He knew to cross the street at the crossing. We rode trams in Sydney then and the tram stop was right outside our shop. Mosman was a village and the milk was delivered daily to the back door in pint bottles, with red, blue or gold foil lids, the gold tops being the best with half an inch of cream resting just under the lid.

We were forced to drink the stuff every day at school just before recess. The small bottles would sit in their wire crates outside the classrooms until a teacher handed them out. Even in summer. Curdling as the day unfurled its savage heat.

Drink, growled the teacher.

No, I replied.

We continued like that for a while but she was always going to win and I finally did what I was told. I projectile vomited on her.

CHAPTER 2

Jan was born in 1916 in New Zealand, the eldest daughter of Marian Potter and I don't know who else. While not a very Irish-sounding name Marian, my authorised grandmother, said she'd been born in County Cork in the late eighteen hundreds. No accent, but what did I know of truth from fiction then?

Marian, at the age of eighteen, married and moved to Dunedin where her three children were born. In 1925 they immigrated to Sydney. By the time the Great Depression struck her husband was dead, she had three teenagers, no money and like many, was destitute and abandoned by society. In the Depression years people tried to make tuppence by renting spare rooms to the many homeless men and women who came to the city desperate to find work. Marian did the circuit of houses with vacancy signs in the windows in and around Edgecliff, Kings Cross, Darlinghurst and Paddington, conning the owners into giving her a room overnight. She would promise to pay in the morning because the poor little ones needed to be bedded immediately. She was an expert at what she called midnight flits, waking her children in the wee hours and doing a runner without paying.

Jan remembers breaking into empty houses—no doubt deserted when the banks foreclosed—where they'd often sleep on newspaper laid out on skeletal wire mesh bed bases still bolted to iron bed heads. Marian put her children in school whenever she could, which wasn't often. As a result, Jan and her siblings were barely literate.

Before she came to live with us many years later Marian managed the Rembrandt Hotel in the Cross. I went there once. The hallways smelled of furniture polish. The decor was dark and art deco. The elevator had bronze concertina lattice doors on the inside and finely beveled glass on the outside. Lined with wood and mirrors. The fixtures were brass and shone like gold, a glorious paean to modernity. All down the halls hung yet more mirrors, and the arching bodies of naked, nubile ceramic nymphs supporting pearlescent globes of light. And there was Marian in her dark blue wool overcoat and a silver fox stole with its dangling feet and a sad, flattened head. She wore a pillbox hat with a black spotted veil that insinuated itself over one eye and that sprouted a weaponry of hatpins with diamante ends, glamorous despite her hunchback.

In 1933 Jan boarded a freighter, the only woman on the ship. She sailed steerage to America. She lived a couple of years around Minneapolis, Minnesota and the Rockies. She would never say what she did whilst there or how she supported herself, but she always had a noted appreciation for American men. The photos of her from the war years taken around Sydney show a glamorous vixen-like woman with bleached blonde hair and voluptuous figure. There she is standing on the deck of a U.S. warship with a girlfriend and two handsome sailors, one of their little, circular white hats perched jauntily on her head.

Back in Australia, aged twenty-five, she decided to take the acceptable path of marriage. Settle for domesticity and have a family. Two years later she wed the first of three husbands, an American seaman who drank too much and had a woman in every port. They divorced after just a year. The second marriage, in 1942, lasted a day. The newlyweds went to a hotel for the night and hubby gave Jan a list of chores she was to fulfill, informing her he was booked on a train the next day for the Melbourne Cup. She had never conceived and now, in her thirties, was desperate for children. She consulted a gynecologist. After examining her he informed her that her vagina was too long. The semen couldn't reach inside her far enough for her to conceive. She was unlikely to ever have a child, no matter how many men she married.

Eric was her third husband. A business deal. He was an SP

bookie—a starting price bookmaker for horse racing—and a poker player, a lousy one. He'd already gambled away the properties he inherited from wealthy dead parents, including blocks of flats in Kings Cross, all the money. A fortune. The right to access his remaining assets had been revoked by Muriel, his sister, who lived in Melbourne, was outrageously wealthy and managed the family's fortune derived from Cob and Co. in early Australia. 666 Military Road had been the one cherry Eric was allowed. Jan married him in 1950 so she could acquire a child to pretend was her own. She needed his signature. They bought a baby that November. The older girl to whom I was presented as a christmas present.

I don't know if the Trickster was there in Eric all along. I suspect so. But I was not warned for many years.

In the nineteen fifties women had the vote but they had no legal rights. They couldn't buy property without a man to sign the paperwork and the deed would be in his name. A woman without a husband by her late teens raised eyebrows, tongues tsking in condescending condolence. Without a husband by twenty they were either risqué, whores or spinsters. And education? A girl could have one but was not expected to be intelligent, and she learned for practical purposes only.

If she had a job she gave up when she married. Men were shamed by working wives. Before that she might be a nurse. Clerk. Seamstress or secretary. Waitress. Typist. Telephonist or receptionist. School teacher, hairdresser, ticket seller on the buses or railway or at the cinema or the theatre, usher at the movies, shop assistant. Or take up nunnery. Or become a christian missionary. And lots of people wanted to be those because Australia was a christian country. If she was gentry or her family were titled she would paint, travel, write poetry, take another woman as a lover, climb a mountain, be a spy, herd cattle or fly solo across the Atlantic. If she was not lucky she would learn the arts of the stripper. Take up prostitution. Learn the butchering skills of a kitchen table abortionist. Some, with perhaps a peculiarity or two, might have run away to join the circus while others, like me, would have learned the secrets of mediumship, of contacting the dead and telling fortunes down seedy back alleys.

A woman could not legally work in a government job, including after she was given away by her father to some agreed-to man, for legally approved sex. Either shotgun or, occasionally, for love. The kitchen, cleaning, laundry, shopping and raising kids became her sole vocation. That and pleasing her husband by looking splendid despite the sag and inevitable mistresses, were her lot until death they did part. Or until he left her. The word obey was in her wedding vows but not his. Life was servitude to the family, before abandonment.

Jan, like every woman in Mosman from the stock of a *united kingdom*, did the washing on Monday, in the copper over the fire. Hers was in the laundry at the rear of the shop. She wielded a wide, wooden paddle that kept everything moving in murky, steamy water. Sunlight soap lay half-submerged in its wire cage, hooked over the lip of the tub. She washed everything by hand and used the scrubbing brush on the grease line around her husband's collars.

When she was done washing and paddling everything was thrown into the twin concrete tubs and she reheated more water in the copper for rinsing. Same again with the paddle. Then the washing was squeezed, a piece at a time, between the two round, thick cylinders of the wringer, turned by a handle, before being hoisted on her hip in that big wicker basket, up the twenty one stairs to the living quarters as the clothesline was strung between the kitchen window and the yellow wall of the greengrocer's on the other side of the gate at the end of our yard.

Stockings were silk, with seams, gripped by suspender belts, girdles with hooks and eyes meant to force a stomach to remain flat, brassieres for pointy tits that went all the way to the waist, the days when knickers had elastic that could snap at any moment. Sneakers were called sandshoes and were always white and smelled of vulcanized rubber. We wore lace-up shoes with ankle socks, and gloves and hats on the street. We ate chops or sausages and two veg, and thought of England as home. People never talked about sex and men opened doors for women, gave up their seats on public transport for them, stood up when one entered or left the room, never sat with them at the pub (which was really a place for blokes). They could legally bash their wives and children. Pregnancy was hidden beneath big dresses, birth treated as an illness and breast feeding thought a thing for peasants. Polio had recently been a pandemic. Thalidomide, supposed to help women suffering morning sickness when pregnant, was about to destroy the limbs and lives of children and their parents. Pharmaceutical companies had assured them the drug was safe.

An era of almost no plastic. Greeks and Italians, who'd immigrated to Australia to work on the Sydney Harbour Bridge and Warragamba Dam, were called wogs and dagos. These refugees of post-war Europe slowly infiltrated Mosman in the sixties, opening fruit shops and milk bars. No Germans or Japanese though, even if their grandparents had been born in Australia, because they had been the enemy in the war.

The White Australia Policy, that preferred European immigrants and Englishmen to anyone else, wasn't fully dismantled until 1973. When I was a child there was bigotry towards anyone with any color to their skin. Unless it was a tan.

We, poor, deluded and deceived children that we were, had not yet dined on European cuisine and I had no idea I was one of them.

CHAPTER 3

Collecting wooden fruit boxes to build my own house in our back yard, a concrete slab surrounded by a high, shabby wooden paling fence. Boxes provided a myriad of cubicles. A plethora of shelves and hollows. One afternoon Jan, the faux-sibling and I were in the pet supply store buying budgie food and oh! There was the smallest fluff-ball of a tabby kitten in a cage that could not possibly stay out of my arms. Love at first sight. Jan warned me I had to keep the already-named Tiddles outside—Eric hated cats—so I made her a home in one of the fruit boxes. She was inside and on my bed within a week. I could communicate with her more easily than with people. Dogs as well. Any wandering personless on the streets of Mosman inevitably ended up in the yard. Loved and fed. Once discovered their owners spread the word of where missing pets were likely to be found.

Eric's antiquity made him an embarrassment on the occasions he walked us to school. He was excruciatingly old fashioned and usually absent. Occasionally, on a Sunday, he took the sister-person and me walking, usually through the back paddock, down Clifford Street onto Morouben Road and Stanley Avenue where his friends lived.

Mosman had fields then, and in the spring we'd gather armloads of freesias and jonquils. Their scent would drench our house along with the summer perfume of wisteria and wild mulberries.

My first memory and glimmering of magic and mysticism began with one of those walks. Dew in nasturtium's leaf. Liquid light. I rolled that sphere around and dozens of identical pearls of transparency formed for a split second before reuniting, with the speed of thought, back in the depths of the center. I drank dew. My first recalled encounter with wonder. Still in the liminal world.

I began breaking into abandoned houses. Closed up and left to rot. They were obvious, their English gardens gone to ruin, the couch grass overgrowing pathways. Dandelions, bindies, farmers' friends and milk thistle laying rose bushes low. Once neatly trimmed privet hedges exposing their true nature. I was in love with the smell of neglect.

The experience of ghosts. Haunted feelings. Shivering up my spine on the hottest Sydney summer day. Most were just sad. Lost and confused. The shades of people who had become old, trapped and forgotten. Who didn't know they were dead and looked at me with silent eyes, just wanting to know what was happening and where their possessions were. Why they were so alone. Why they had been abandoned. Women mainly.

I frequented one particular house month after month and thought of us as friends. Partly furnished, the floors initially strewn with the detritus of hurry and negligence. Daddy longlegs swung in terrified circles as I passed and mouse droppings, like licorice, stuck to the soles of my shoeless feet. A two storey house with narrow stairs to upper rooms, with abandoned beds and flyblown tobacco-colored lace curtains. Polished wood banisters and still-shiny parquet floors. The kitchen separate, not far from a little outside, chain-pull loo. Charles Dickens *Oliver Twist* in a hard green cover had been left open on the floor under the stairs. Rat nest material. The first book I read from cover to cover with no illustrations. Along with that were two old 78 albums, Slaughter on Fifth Avenue and The Dream of Olwen. The latter was the 1947 soundtrack from a movie called While I Live about a girl in Cornwall composing a piece of music under the repression of a dominating older sister. I could relate. She never completed it. She walked in her sleep, fell off a cliff and died. Twenty five years later a young woman, claiming to have lost her memory, came into the house and finished the composition. The plot was that the dead sister was born into another body to complete the music.

This was my introduction to something other than the commonly held ideas du jour that when you die, you either just die and rot, or you go to heaven or hell. The first concept was terrifying because rot was not understood then to be compost.

I held my first séance in that house. With my friends, twins Suzanne and Annette. Planned. The twins' mother was a practitioner and they had spied on her so knew what to do.

Afternoon. Sad, pale grey blinds pulled down. We lit a candle. We had no proper ouija board so we made one on a left-over mirror, letters of the alphabet written on paper and cut out, as were the numbers one through ten. Yes and No. All were placed in a circle. A glass was upturned, each of us lightly touching the base with a finger. Movement. Frightening and exciting.

Spirit of the Penny, are you there?

We waited in a state of nervous seriousness, possibly committing an evil but not caring.

The glass did a little shudder. We held our breath. In a slow, stilted screeching across the mirror that glass, haltingly, like a newborn blindly heading for the teat, moved to the Yes. We did not squeal. We did not bolt. We looked at each other accusingly, to wide eyes and shaking of heads. No. One. Pushed. The glass.

Q: What is Annette's middle name, asked Suzanne.

A: Edna.

Q: How old am I?

A: Ten.

We conjured the Spirit of the Penny every Saturday after the movies until the glass began to spell out terrible things, calling us cunts and insinuating that one of us would soon die. When the ouija spelled out that Eric was going to kill Tiddles I stopped using it. For a while. Bright copper pennies became an omen of change throughout my incomplete life.

What happened to the people that disappeared from those houses? Places built in the time of Queen Victoria? Sydney was still populated by survivors of the Great Depression and two world wars but was also a city awakening to the dawn of an economic boom. The young did not understand the old.

Some of those houses must have contained the wives of dead soldiers, those women inheriting the places and perhaps even those before them. Or men who today would be understood as suffering post traumatic stress disorder. Alcoholic because of what had been seen and done abroad. Flanders Field in Ypres. Along Kadoka. Prison camps. When they came home... What then? They bashed their wives and their children, drunken schizophrenia. Lost in dreams that left them screaming.

They eventually got old. Were moved out of the way by offspring reveling in modernity but crippled, somehow, by the parents of war. People can be like that. Need denial. Need to not see the faces of those they cannot understand or forgive. These once-children committed their elders to the infamous geriatric hospitals. One way doors to the coffin. I know. I worked in a couple much later. Night shifts when my firstborn was a baby. A horror of bedsores and rejection. We raced cockroaches down the corridors at three in the morning just to keep ourselves awake. Young epileptics housed amongst old women whose bodies would not bend so they were washed and changed—because they were invariably incontinent—and tied to chairs in the same position as they lay in their beds.

    I clocked on at five thirty one morning, and after breakfast, worked with a man in his sixties. He'd had a mild stroke. His face drooped a little on the left and his left hand closed claw-like around a handkerchief to prevent his fingernails digging into his own palms. He was from Orkney, north of Scotland and he was proud that he'd fought in two world wars for crown and country. He showered himself, embarrassed at the thought of any young woman seeing his nakedness and still sufficiently able. I shaved him, though. As I did so he happily informed me this day was his birthday and that his family was coming to take him to lunch. We dressed him in his only three piece suit. Tweed. Over a clean plaid shirt with a tie of olive green. His cap was jaunty. I polished his good lace up shoes and tied the laces because he couldn't. Then I handed him his cane and assisted him to the sunroom where he waited. When I eventually brought him a lunch tray he refused to catch my gaze.

    He sat there for my entire shift. Until three thirty in the afternoon. They never came.

    Those few empty houses with the ghosts of old memories were later torn down to build the blonde brick flats that invaded the era with ugliness. No one to say stop. No heritage listing. In 1967 a tornado wreaked destruction all along Spit Road from the marina to the junction where we lived. That was the excuse developers had needed to raze history to the ground and line the road with four storey boxes. The fields went. No more jonquils. The nostalgia and smells of those old haunted and abandoned treasures alive only in isolated memory.

CHAPTER 4

Even though Australia had TAA, Ansett ANA and a very local Qantas, hardly anyone flew, and people were considered very chic and sophisticated when they did. People dressed in their finest clothes for flying.

Overseas destinations, however, meant travel by ship. Suitcases and trunks stamped with exotic labels that made us curious about the world.

We went to the dock at Woolloomooloo the day Eric's sister, having come by steam train from Melbourne, boarded the ship moored to the dock that would sail her to Europe and then around the rest of the world. When the gangplank was pulled away, and before the horn sounded the departure, friends and family stood about, left behind to wonder. Everyone's necks were craned cruelly backwards searching the decks above until magnetically drawn to one set of waving hands belonging to their relative. Those of us earthbound held rolls of colored paper streamers and, hanging onto one end, we madly flung the roll towards the ship, hoping the loved one would catch hold. They often did. The length of ocean liner to dock beribboned in airborne stripes of color.

And me falling in love with the pungency of maritime fuel, barnacles, iron chain dragged from deep water and the sea-wet wood planking of wharves.

The great blaaarnnt of that horn and ropes the size of thighs, being unwound by strong men with their sleeves rolled up, from anvil-like bollards bolted to the pier and painted grey; the whoosh of water as the ship pulled away.

We waved until the ship was out of sight. We had to. Something terrible would happen if a hand dropped too soon. The vessel would sink. The beloved would die or disappear forever. Any one of several dreadful outcomes would be the result. Deep in our DNA is the knowledge of Viking and Phoenician, of gales off the Arctic crushing the fishing boat under a mountain of black waves, of being smashed to pieces on the rocks along the coast of Cape Horn, the burning armada and the suffocation of lungs rapidly filling with sea. Of being eaten on the way down. Every one of us has an ancestor drowned sometime, somewhere.

That day on the dock was the year before Jan banished Eric back to Melbourne, the marriage a finally-acknowledged lie. He beat her. She cowered in the corner of the couch between the cushions, her legs pulled to her chest and her arms protecting her face. He slashed at her with a dog's lead growling "You didn't just dump one bastard on me, you dumped two."

There was the Trickster. Waiting years to drop the dad scam. To let me know what I was and just precisely what the man whose skin he wore was capable of doing. Eric stormed from the room a look of disgust at me. Jan pleaded that I say nothing to anyone about what I had witnessed. She pretended confusion when I asked why he said what he'd said. He meant something else, she lied.

For over twenty years she'd kept up the pretense of biological motherhood to both the sister and me.

When Muriel returned by ship from her world tours she stopped at 666 for a night. She bore gifts. A fan from Spain, biscuits in a tartan tin from Scotland and a doll dressed in a bra top, a grass skirt and lei, from Hawaii. There was a kimono in the mix somewhere as well. When Muriel asked Jan if she needed money Jan had told her to go fuck herself. She could raise us without the old woman's charity. The significance of this only becoming apparent decades later when Muriel died and her will was read.

This was the year I began to menstruate, the advent of the blighting of my face by acne. Marian resigned from the Rembrandt Hotel and moved into 666 to provide Jan with emotional support. She made her money from the house interpreting cards and tealeaves.

By then I had a relentless hunger for reading. At that time mainly Poe, but really every tale of what I understood as the supernatural that I could consume, and everything on ghosts and what happened after death.

I shared a bedroom with the sister-person. The first room along the hallway after climbing the stairs to a landing. A meter square of old wood that could not be trodden on without creaking. Around the corner from the top of the stairs were the bathroom and the linoleum-floored kitchen, up two more stairs, beyond our bedroom, was the master bedroom and a sitting room.

Months earlier I'd stolen Bodie, a one year old female, black cocker spaniel-collie mix. From Lorraine, who lived down the back field and who was apathetic and neglectful now the dog was no longer a puppy. Bodie and I became inseparable.

My bed had broken on this particular day and Jan hired a camping one for overnight or until a new bed could be sourced. Bodie woke me. She was part growling, part panting but shivering all over. She'd been curled up with me but right then she put paws to the ground and crept under the stretcher. The night was moonlit. The enormous silhouette of a man in a top hat and overcoat filled the doorway. Should have scared me but didn't. The sister-person slept on.

Turn the light on, Dad, I said, some still-sleeping part of me forgetting that he'd gone. The apparition moved out of sight, to one side of the door frame and towards the landing. I waited for the creak. Silence. I pulled on the light cord and looked, guileless and rather naively, around the corner. No one.

I went back to sleep.

The following morning, I remembered the visitation. Probably the night watchman, I thought. Very rarely Jan would forget to lock up and the watchman came into the house, woke her and got her to secure the premises after him. I am creeped out when thinking of some strange man wandering through the house with his torch and me sleeping so deeply that I could have been murdered in my bed. I suggested him at the table over breakfast.

No one came in, Jan said.

I told her what I'd seen. She suggested I had been dreaming. Bodie woke me, I explained. The man wore a top hat.

Was he big? Marian asked. The little hairs on the back of my neck stood up.

Yes, I replied.

Stop that, said Jan, her eyes a threat.

Marian pushed back her chair. We'll talk after breakfast, she whispered.

You'll do no such thing, Jan warned.

The look Marian gave her could have sliced a face open. Later when I asked who the man was she said she didn't know. She'd had the same experience in her young years while still living in New Zealand. All she knew was that her talent at foretelling he fiture began not long after. I only ever met one other person who has seen him. Many years later. A seer in the Victorian high country. She also read tarot. So accurately she hunted me down to take her weekend clients. She was my sole living inspiration. Poe was, unfortunately, dead.

From his home living with Muriel in Melbourne, Eric sold 666 and paid Jan out with £11,000. She bought a large house in the same suburb. Marian took the back veranda as her own because of a separate entrance for her clients. We had hardly any furniture because much of what we'd owned had been sold to make the full deposit.

In some unspoken desperation Jan applied to the Post Master General's Department (PMG), responsible for mail and telegraph services throughout Australia, to be a billet for their trainees. All young men. The PMG funded the furniture for the house and paid her a stipend. The young men paid rent to her. They were aged from their late teens to early twenties and they came from around the Pacific. Māori lads and Fijian, from Malaysia when still called Malaya, from India and Papua New Guinea. They came to Australia to do their apprenticeships in telecommunications. Their cooking skills were the beginning of a lifelong taste for exotic and unusual spices. And experiences.

Garry Wilkie-King was the only Anglo-Saxon. What was interesting about him was that he was an advanced student of White Crane Kung Fu and he trained in our back yard. I loved to watch him and mimicked the katas. The martial arts were to have a continuous, if sporadic, effect on my life, helped along, in later years, by the 1972 television series Kung Fu that starred David Carradine. Garry's brother lived near Goulburn in country New South Wales. I'd helped him erect his illegal dwelling beneath the overhang of a cliff. He called himself a witch and the locals knew him as such. He was shot twice but lived. Their mother had a mole on her leg that her doctor ignored, calling her a hypochondriac. Many months later she sought a second opinion. Losing most of her leg was the first time I heard the word melanoma.

The Cuban Missile Crisis pulled the world to the brink of a nuclear war, Marilyn Monroe overdosed and in South Africa Nelson Mandela was about to spend the next twenty seven years of his life in prison. Here in Australia the government backed the USA in the beginnings of the atrocity that became the Vietnam War. This was the year I read Greer's The Female Eunuch and knew a mirror.

A momentous cracking zeitgeist of change. Now that Eric was gone Jan announced that she had always been catholic. The faux sibling and I were thrust into that religion and were sent to the Sacred Heart primary school. I don't know if I was ever baptized. I probably was but I have no idea what or where. If I wasn't, the nuns and priests in Mosman abruptly had me on my knees. I had to learn a catechism off by heart like a parrot and to confess all my atrocities. That was supposed to confer purity as long as I knew the spells to exorcise the demons and the chants to summon atonement. I was taught the difference between venal and mortal sins, that I never spoke back to a nun, that I wore a silly white dress and veil and took communion four years older than all the other children. I had to agree to eat the body and drink the blood of a long dead man and to believe in the reality of the delusion. I was also to be confirmed and to take a saint's name as my extra middle name. I got in trouble with the nuns because I chose Francis of Assisi. I was not allowed to. A girl could not be confirmed as a man. I agreed to pick the usual Therese right up until I knelt before the bishop and he asked me my name. I told him Francis. Assisi or Xavier? he asked. Sort of an initiation I suppose because he then daubed my forehead with oil in acceptance. We ate fish on Friday from then on.

    I was also initiated as a *Child of Mary* and wore a blue cloak and was in with the elite girls allowed to enter the church by a door near the altar.

Evocatively ritualistic. The christian bit was irrelevant. I felt chosen. Possessed by a power awoken because of the experience of something that ancient.

I learned to kiss properly and to understand what petting was because all the girls in my sixth class would gather in secret in the washrooms and practice. We touched and examined each other's breasts and genitals, learned what felt good. We practiced what we knew of how the French used their tongues. The boys in the playground next door, controlled with an iron fist by the jesuit brotherhood, began to look better with every passing month.

I didn't know the truth of that institution then. Its cruelty. Its history of bloodshed and persecutions, its denial of women's rights and anyone not considered fitting. Its torture, assault and theft of children even up to the present day. I experienced something else; something decidedly mystical.

John D, in the world of myth would have been the Alchemist seeking to turn lead into gold but in this world he was a catholic priest fresh out of seminary college who lived at the rectory of the Sacred Heart Church, Mosman. I had a crush on him. He was young and approachable. I spoke with him as often as I could. I once asked if considering myself to be witch was possibly sinful. He'd asked if the question was rhetorical. I'd said no.

Do you conjure the devil to hurt people, he asked, trying not to laugh. I said no. He said he didn't have a problem as long as I said confession and took holy communion. I asked if I had to confess witchcraft if I didn't think it was a sin. He said as long as I didn't think so then no. That was the logic. It was him first told me about the King James English version of the bible and that the quote thou shalt not suffer a witch to live was a mistranslation. The word was Greek for a pharmacist. Subtle way to kill a king, I figure, is poison. Is that why tasters sat at the downwind side of a banquet table?

He had a specific philosophy about religion that singled him out from everyone else I have met in any kind of clergy.

What's god? I asked.

Love.

No, what's god?

Love.

What about the catechism and Jesus and the crucifixion and vows and stuff?

He shrugged.

But you give out communion and do all the masses and take confession.

Yes. But I'm a priest because I was called.

By god?

Yes.

What's being called like?

Clean on the inside and being in love, all at once.

He became a regular visitor at our house and a very good friend to Jan. Years later when I'd returned from England in my twenties, he arrived at a party Jan threw. He was in a wheelchair.

What happened? I asked.

I've got spinal cancer.

He'd done a couple of significant confessions and needed to talk about them with another priest because of implications. He was working both the Block in Redfern and maximum security at Long Bay Jail. He had an Aboriginal woman come to him pregnant with her sixth child. One she didn't want. She could hardly feed the others. Her husband was an alcoholic and spent their welfare at the pub. She was going to get an abortion, but she went to confession first to ask if what she was doing was a sin.

What'd you tell her?

That god is love.

Did you find out what happened?

No. Because in the same week I heard the confession of a man who was in prison for the term of his natural life who'd fallen in love with another man. They were intimate.

Why was he in confession?

Because he was catholic and he'd been told homosexuality was wrong even though he didn't think of himself as homosexual, just in love. I couldn't absolve him because to do so was against the laws of the church.

Just told him god is love?

That's right. So after talking with that other priest, a snitch it turns out, I was transferred to Pymble.

Oh no.

Rich people, who sinned till Friday, went to confession and got absolved, went to church on Sunday, socialized and examined who was wearing what. That's when I got sick.

That year, 1962, I had my first close encounter with an entity. In a dream. I was pursued by people intent on my death and I ran into a blind canyon. The cliffs were made of chalk. When I turned around to see if I was followed the entrance was no longer there. I was corralled by hundreds of feet of white chalk walls impossible to scale. Panic. Above me, on a ledge, was a man or a woman, dressed in rags the same color as the chalk so that he or she morphed with the landscape. He or she talked about life, its mysteries, and its wonders, everything that was going to happen. He/she spoke in rhyme. I attempted to wake myself up many times so I could write down what I was being told but every time I was sucked back into the dream. I awoke to full daylight and remembered nothing of what was said but Chalk person was the Gatekeeper and I became fully conscious that I, too, had been called. Just by whom or what I didn't know.

I was confused. Flooded with love but for no one and nothing. The experience of a rapture bubble at six in the morning in an empty church. Before the first mass of the day when the nuns prepared everything and lit candles. I had to be alone because as soon as people arrived the rapture bubble evaporated, the exquisite feeling deserting me. I'd sit for a while at the rear of the building in the dark, right beside the graphic, lifelike and humanly proportioned statue of a tortured, bloodied, crucified man, wishing only that I could symbolically take him down. I should have known I was about to die.

CHAPTER 5

Death. I've been dead or very close more times than I can count. And the so-called dead hang around so what is death? I get them in tarot sessions often. Peripherally. Usually at the right shoulder of the client. They can be tricky because they don't always give straightforward information, and they can take a while to get their point across. Many have been lost for quite some time. Desperately seeking to communicate.

Recently I had a young woman sitting opposite me and before we even opened the cards a name rang loudly within my brain.

Rhetorical question, I explained, but who's George?

People know they're not to talk to me until towards the end so she said nothing. Death was all through her cards. Past and future. When we finally came to question time she shuffled, asking, Am I insane? I took a bit of a double take because she was lovely. I laid out the spread but I just got that kid in the Bruce Willis film, The Sixth Sense, so I leaned over her phone and whispered, I see dead people.

She almost had a seizure. Then she explained. First about George. She'd had a fascination with death and graveyards most of her life. When I'd asked who George was she'd kept a poker face but told me her legs had felt like rubber. When she was in Scotland she explored Greyfriars kirkyard. She'd wandered about looking at the stories and was stopped in her tracks. She was compelled to turn and look at a gravestone she hadn't noticed. The name was Sir George

Mackenzie, also known as Bluidy Mackenzie, who imprisoned twelve hundred protestants in 1679, had at least four hundred executed and allowed most to die of starvation. On top of that she regularly wakes in the wee dark hours to the image of a man with a clown's head sitting on the end of her bed, or another glimpsed hiding behind her door. This had happened since she was a child.

How do I get rid of him?

Welcome to my world, I replied, you don't.

She worked in Brisbane as a bank teller. Now relieved. People had told her there was something wrong with her, poor woman. She simply has a curious nature and rather psychic, if unfortunate, gift.

During my eleventh year Jan, washing dishes, asked me to bring her the toaster so she could shake out the crumbs. I stuck my hand in. It had been plugged into the wall socket and switched on. My hand was wet. She resuscitated me. I'd stopped breathing and my lips were blue. She'd covered me with a blanket and stuck a rolled up towel under my head. She'd phoned our doctor because in those years they actually came to the house. He didn't hospitalize me, just suggested a couple of days in bed, confused that I had no burn.

The second time was only weeks later. I was at the Balmoral Baths, a wire enclosed swimming area of ocean, and a whole mess of us kids were in the water larking. A boy pushed me under and kept me down. When I knew I couldn't hold my breath any longer I put my hands over my nose with the genius notion that this would form an air pocket. I'd remembered that upturned boats have them. And I breathed in. Then I was on the boardwalk spewing water with someone pumping up and down on my ribcage. It was decades later that I understood that someone, intentionally or otherwise, tried to murder me.

Those first two experiences of my own death, coupled with the death that being born and rendered motherless had caused; opened something of a door between what we think we know and what we most certainly don't. The closer the calls the wider the opening.

Death could be thought of or observed to be occurring but technically that's not true. The recognisability of the person as we know them changes, that's all. We weep when that person, that probably had eyes, ceases to see us or the world in the way we've come to expect.

And the Return? Complete with acknowledgment? The first writing competition I ever entered was Book Week of the Year. I wrote an essay on a story I'd read called A Child of China in which a young girl carries her even younger brother all the way across country during the revolution because their parents have been killed and she knows of relatives a long distance away. The original essay was lost on the cut-off day, but a nun called Mary John sat me in a room alone. She demanded I write something to hand in. She didn't believe me when I explained that I'd already done it but that it had disappeared the night before. And I was yet to fully comprehend how far the sister-person would go to get her kicks.

I won. My prize was a dictionary that I read. I had my photograph taken with the mayor of Mosman that ended up in the local newspaper.

CHAPTER 6

1963, the British had been using Australia as a nuclear testing ground since I was four years old. This was the year they finally stopped. In the meantime, the Maralinga Tjarutja people were exiled from their ancestral home and the place bombed to smithereens. Movietone News showed footage of pipe-smoking officers with big smiles, along with hundreds of common soldiers, turning their backs to the mushroom cloud and the fatal blast of wind that followed a split second later rendering most of them doomed to the lethal cancers and diseases caused by nuclear radiation. Of course everything was to have gone so spiffingly well and everyone thought this exciting destructive force was ever-so jolly and clever and weren't we lucky that Mother England thought us such a special place that she would deem us worthy of these important events?

The Beatles released Please Please Me and I began a love of all things rock and roll, rhythm and blues. Then. On November twenty second. A man named Lee Harvey Oswald assassinated John Kennedy and I, others—my neighborhood—went into some kind of community shock and grief.

In an era of an unprecedented push for collective liberation, on so many fronts, being alive buzzed with a breathless anticipation. My concepts and ideals around freedom, an idealized belief in human good and that an age of enlightenment from *god save the queen* was immanent, filled my creativity with poetry. Life was adrenaline-fueled. Everyone was awakening to a new era of music. Both rock and roll and politically driven folk songs. Local people, the boys in the house and all of us at school discussed politics. In particular Bobby Kennedy and Black emancipation in America. Then he was shot. No one knew what to do anymore.

Lyndon Johnson issued the order for the U.S. to enter into the Vietnam War which would, very soon, drag Australia along, introducing conscription in the form of a bingo-style birthday lottery.

That war. That useless, terrifying, senseless slaughter of young men uniformed and weaponed, their newly-long hair cut against their will, changed warfare from trenches and a recognizable enemy to jungle and urban clashes where maybe that six year old girl or that ninety year old man could shoot and kill you. That kind of suspicion resulted in madness culminating, five years later, in the My Lai Massacre: the murders and mutilations of hundreds of adults and their children by U.S. military personnel. Afterwards they burned and destroyed whatever was in their way.

During those years the U.S. military sent its troops to Australia on R and R, rest and relaxation, transforming Kings Cross into parts of America, another reason for protests because many of us feared we'd become a new star on that country's flag. Not destined. We belong to an imposed *united kingdom*, ruled over by a queen and her hidden minions. Don't we? But, my goodness, war is such a cash cow.

On the streets of every major capital city, in what is commonly known as the west, protest marches demanded the war end. When that finally happened years later, for the first time in known history neither the people nor the press glorified the returning soldiers. They were vilified.

At twelve, I was enrolled in an all girls' high school in Cremorne. And I crossed the next Threshold while that first initiation was only just complete. No time to breathe in between. The acne that began when I was eleven was now terrible and Jan took me to a skin specialist. A dermatologist.

Now is when things get blurry to a degree because the Trickster had left Eric's emaciated body and had taken over this man, the doctor who was going to save me. To cure my acne.

After having my blood and urine samples tested he prescribed three things. First a course of the newly available contraceptive pill because I had a rather high levels of testosterone and that might have been the cause of the zits, then a monthly dose of infra-red ray treatment to eradicate scarring, and thirdly a cocktail of Amytal, Librium and Largactyl—three tablets, thrice daily—because I had an artistic temperament. This alone could also be the reason for said pimples. I had no idea what these pills were and the treatment was not explained. One did not question a doctor's opinion.

Jan paid him month after month for ray lamp treatments, each time burning my skin a little more. For over three years, until he broke me. He eventually decided the drugs I was taking were not sufficient. It was suggested I was resistant to what he had earlier prescribed. I was moodier than ever. There was a better brand on the market. He took me off the medication I'd been on all those years and replaced it with Valium.

Amidst social upheaval, where the lines between gender behavior and appearance blurred for the first time in recorded history, Anglo Australians began to openly express affection for each other, a thing unheard of just a few years earlier. The petals of a revolution against imposed cultural paradigms were unfurling.

Prior to the sixties holding hands in public was unacceptable. Way too French. Kissing in public was also taboo. Making out on the lawn at the Botanic Gardens? People finally began doing this. The Summer of Love was still years away but we were already exploring open sexual relationships and casual encounters of intimacy, while still being raped and called sluts.

I am vague about the first years of my teens. Drugged, and with no insight into the consequences or the effect. My once raging appetite for knowledge and learning disappeared. My first experience of sex was when I was fourteen. It was rape. Balmoral Beach, late one afternoon up in the dunes. A man named Dennis. I had a crush on him but didn't understand sex. He was thirty four. I said it was my first time and to please not hurt me. Sand rubbed me as raw as his penis. I thought that if I just let him do it he would love me. It was like a piece of wood was inside me, leaving splinters. When he finally pulled out he looked down at my bare lower half and smirked. Fuck me, he said.

The first one? I was confused. I didn't know I was supposed to bleed. I was embarrassed and ashamed. Nobody had ever told me about a hymen.

With the plus side of acne being enforced contraception there was no need to worry about unwanted pregnancies despite being utterly uninformed about a) how uncomfortable and one-sided sex actually was because blokes knew nothing of nothing except pleasing themselves and b) syphilis and other sexually transmittable diseases. I sigh with relief, now that I am older, at having dodged those bullets.

By the time I was fourteen I was very definitely witch and expressed that through both clothing and attitude. I'd been holding séances for a year. I'd been to see the Beatles at the Stadium and screamed my head off, progressed to Bob Dylan, Joan Baez, Buffy St Marie and the Rolling Stones. And all this need was coursing through me. These were the sixties, the years of release from the cruel guilt of a repressive religious ideology. I craved touch, thought sex was the answer. I was wrong.

In high school all I cared about was poetry, literature, the theatre and speaking French. Slowly dropping out.

I rode pillion with a Hells Angel one Saturday afternoon at the Royal George Hotel on Sussex Street in Sydney, now gentrified and known as The Slip Inn, where the Push, a motley group of artists and intellectuals, left wingers, homosexuals, journalists and jazz musicians, and that included Germaine Greer and Clive James, led a revolution of their own towards our social freedom. I had my first rum and coke in that pub. I wore tons of pancake makeup and black eyeliner. I think I looked much older than my years because the barman never questioned my age.

The mystical awakening that I'd experienced in primary school was still with me but now shared equally with a wildly carnal interest in all things sexual, outrage at the Vietnam War, the vagaries of being drugged, the writings of Poe, Wilde, Yeats, Shakespeare, Wordsworth and unfortunately, Dennis Wheatley, a novelist writing exclusively occult novels. Crap that sold.

The trend towards feminism was not yet a political one but by now I understood inequality. The word slut did not apply to boys. I rejected the still-standard ideal of femininity outright. I was angry. I was still excluded from so many rights, because of my genitals. Made no sense. I was still expected to behave like a lady. What was that? A lady was supposed to learn to walk with books on her head, to be eloquent, to talk small talk, to cover much of her body most of the time. A lady didn't smoke cigarettes or listen to loud music or have casual sex or ever admit to rape.

What was I? Even then I refused those tired terminologies. I was bohemian, a child of the Beat generation, I identified as witch and thought I was a woman. I was proud, a little foggy, very moody, confused by a culture to which I could not relate. Rebellious. Angry. Sing *god save the queen* in assembly? I refused. That landed me detention weekly.

Television was changing history, journalism presenting official propaganda of events happening around the world, as was the steady popularity of plastics, the use of petrochemicals in more and more insidious ways and the introduction of additives to food that would prove poison to future generations. For now, the consumer was informed of their health benefits. In the U.S. the struggle for equality by the African American Civil Rights movement had taken a new turn with thousands marching to Selma Alabama and television cameras capturing police thuggery and the use of dogs to terrorize. Radio Luxemburg was joined by other pirate radio stations in giving British youth rock and roll. Nothing much at all came from behind the Iron Curtain. In 1962 the Aboriginal people got the vote and in 1965 a voice, in Charles Perkins, who led the Freedom Ride. Conditions were, and still are, deplorable. Treaties and constitutional recognition just someone's courageous defeat.

Both nuclear proliferation and the arms race were now savagely on between several countries and the U.S. had accumulated—what? —about ten thousand nuclear warheads.

Marlborough, Benson & Hedges, and Viscount, were cigarette brands. Teachers smoked in classroom, doctor and patient in the surgery. Every seat in every cinema and on every bus and airplane had an ashtray as did the bedside table of every person in hospital. Cigarettes were considered manly if one rode a horse or sexy if smoked through a long black Breakfast at Tiffany's cigarette holder. Everyone smoked just as everyone drank alcohol. There were no coffee shops. A doctor prescribed me Camel for asthma.

Heroin was big business, smuggled in the body cavities of dead soldiers being shipped home from Vietnam to the U.S. or Australia. Timothy Leary began experimenting with LSD. Cooked up in labs all over the world and taken by seekers of mystical experiences everywhere. And the military somewhere. These were the years marijuana claimed the spotlight as the drug of choice amongst troops in Vietnam especially after Bob Dylan shared a spliff with the Beatles.

I was not interested, although I most definitely experimented, even though most of my friends were users. I was still a book junky and still writing deep and meaningful poetry, all long since burned.

I was also, without my knowledge, a pharmaceutical drug addict.

On Saturdays my friends and I busked at Circular Quay to try to make enough money to entertain ourselves over the weekend. I played guitar—badly. Bob Dylan's Hollis Brown was my sole contribution: a very long story with only two chord changes. We spent the money on Cokes and hot chips, and then hung out at Suzie Wong's dark, downstairs café in the heart of Sydney where the Easybeats performed before anyone knew who they were.

Teenagers had been mods or rockers or surfies. My friends and I were known as beatniks but fast on the heel of the new word: hippy. On Sundays we caught the ferry into the city, first to the National Art Gallery, then amok in the Domain where soap-boxers ranted about armageddon or peddled a christ and how to be saved. There were others though. Some political, some deeply certain of aliens among us or, in the case of followers of Anton le Vey and his early satanic church, graphic descriptions on how to have very good fun indeed because there really was no such thing as sin. The photographs of him were stupid. Simply christianity in reverse. Certainly not witchcraft.

Then there were the marches. People in their thousands, in protest against a great many wrongs. Initially against the atomic bomb but then the adversity of the war in Vietnam and also for equal rights for women. My friends and I walked in them all. The backbone of a generation.

I was the only Australian in my peer group at high school and my best friend was Judy Schwartz. Her family was from Poland and Romania and her parents Holocaust survivors. She was a consummate artist (I say *was* because she died young).

At some stage during my early, drug-addled teen years I'd learned to ride horses. I rode so well that I was given a job teaching younger kids every Sunday with Chalice Riding School in Randwick, at Hyde Park. I'd go to Judy's house after. Her mother made lunch. A culturally glorious blur of gefilte fish, tahina, chopped liver and sauerkraut, black bread or maybe matzos and latkes.

Many of my friends were Jewish. I was invited to all their parties. I had no religion but I looked like a young Barbra Streisand so no one thought to question what I was doing there and Judy never told. My other school friends had last names like Keig, Larsson and Piezak, and even though we attended a high school in the snobbish suburbs of northern Sydney, Europeans were still frowned upon and thought of as those people. My clique wore black. Black berets, black tights, black jumpers, black eyeliner, tons of makeup, and moods. At fifteen I shaved my head and pierced my ears.

CHAPTER 7

Between twelve and seventeen I wandered the mists of the liminal world and amidst the despair and loss of self, I delved deeper into mystery, reading Lewis Spence and the Tibetan Book of the Dead. I read as many books on witchcraft that the local library held on its shelves. Most of which dealt with demonology, satanism or European inquisitional witch trials. My friends and I challenged the ideas of right and wrong, good and evil and intentionally walked beyond the bounds of a consensual acceptability. We were introduced to the ideas of reincarnation. I read The Search for Bridey Murphy about a woman in Texas who, under hypnosis, recounted a whole other life in Ireland, including her birthday. I was infatuated because hers was the same birthday as mine. The dilemma over what happens other than a body death was compelling. I was open to spirits, demons and any other apparitions or wandering fleshless entities.

I held my séances on Saturdays after the cinema, even during high school and the drugs. We'd darken a room, light candles, attach ourselves to the glass, I'd summon the Spirit of the Penny and always something would come. Always there was a sad, if bitty story to tell and always whoever or whatever they were they proved themselves by answering a question that one of us asked. I invited some, they invited others and we'd often have between seven and ten people at the table. A teenage girl with a shaved head, big hoop earrings, spots and a drug habit. Mistress of proceedings. I was, about then, shunned by christian people in our neighborhood. I was rumored to be doing the devil's work. Jan enjoyed all the visitors and pretended to know nothing of what was whispered. For the time being anyway.

I became suspicious of the ouija once again because the person asking the question always knew the answer. What was that? I was older by now and almost compulsively curious. I didn't know about the egregore, the collective unconscious or subliminal influence at the time but I wanted more proof. I asked the visiting sprite for the first name of another friend's mother, something I did not know because we always called other people's parents missus something or mister something. The thing got nasty and called me names. Again called me a cunt and suggested several ways I could get fucked. That I would die soon.

What not my cat? I thought.

Then one afternoon when a question was asked I answered mentally, and the glass spelled out what I'd thought. This was repeated several times. Somehow our mere presence made this happen. I was really confused but impressed with the breakthrough.

I ran séances a few more times, despite my secret. But then the board turned. The glass spelled out threats, caused fear, touched the core of dread in all present, insinuated. Toxic. I admit I was afraid. I stopped using the ouija board, again, at fifteen. From then on those gathered held hands. I went into trance and spirits spoke through me because, despite what else was wrong in my life through those years, the mysterious was not one of them.

Intellectual and spiritual fruit were politics, freedom, justice, music, sex, theatre and art but most of all the occult and the so-called supernatural. Witch. Something within the word invoked fires though winter mists on hillsides, spells to cure and the cursing of wife-bashers of which there were legion. Freedom from orthodoxy, liberation from religion, connectedness to other than my own species, a way of being that was outside the restraints of cultural definitions of woman. Unique and clear. Owned by no one.

Since that dream when I was eleven I had felt connected to a something. In the company of the unseen but nonetheless real. Still the presences of sad or disturbed ghosts but this was different. This was potent and there was an indescribable freedom and intelligence in the connection. Awakening also, was my sense of communion with plants. Like a canyon of cool, autumnal air, like phosphorescence in the river, we began communication that had no need of a voice.

New Age bookshop Adyar was in the heart of Sydney and presented us with an entirely unrealized selection of writers who were also practitioners, experts and authorities on all things occult and metaphysical. Wheatley, Crowley, Blavatsky, Bonewits. Um... Everything written about magic came with the concept of high and low, and with a bigotry towards witchcraft, portraying the practice as a thing for peasants. Golden Dawn, Rosicrutianism, Theosophy.

Women were considered necessary as altars, mediums, channels and fortune tellers but never anything but secondary to men. Gerald Gardner insisted witches perform rituals nude. In England? In winter?

In the sixties, in Australia, I had not heard of Maud Gonne, neither did I know that Pamela Coleman Smith was the artist of the Rider-Waite tarot and what befell her through neglect. When I found her story, I was offended at the cover up. I was so deeply engrossed in hunting that the deep disquiet and unease I felt around Trickster, posing as a skin doctor, was dulled by three years of the effects of heavy medication to which I was addicted to the point I still thought I knew what normal was.

When I was fifteen he left me under the infrared, acne-treating ray lamp for way too long because he was busy on the phone in another room. Nothing showed until the following morning. My face was so burned I was in agony. Like the most severe sunburn ever. At first my face blistered and then, over several weeks, the skin peeled. My face continued to peel for a very long time. Trickster had done well. Those were the days when doctors were lesser gods and considered sacrosanct, so Jan didn't sue for negligence. At the end of several months I still had acne. I never went back to him, stopped taking the Valium and fell to pieces utterly. I knew nothing of the withdrawal affects. I was destroyed.

CHAPTER 8

Searching Balmoral Beach at night. With the police because the sister-person has disappeared. Is feared drowned. Me feeling responsible because we'd fought about her towel which she'd left at the baths. She wanted me to go back and get it. I'd said no. She'd stormed off. Hours ago. She'd ended up in the house next door to us, partying with the English boys living it up under the ten pound scheme and I got a beating for not getting her towel.

That faux sibling was dragged out our front gate by the cops for running away, often, and often for things as simple as not liking dinner. Using epilepsy as an excuse. Threatening to not take her medication. They took her to the station and scared her with the threat of Girls' Home, common for adolescents in that era, kind of like prison.

I had a crush on a Canadian boy who dumped me after two weeks. A was also experiencing agony in my muscles and joints that had no seeming source. I could not ride and the poetry was dead. Jan brushed aside my complaints but the trauma intensified to the point where I could barely stand. Jan concluded I was a hypochondriac. All in my head. The nausea, the exhaustion, the insomnia. The depression. That was the worst. The impossible depression. Was this the artistic personality disorder that I had been diagnosed with? So bottomless that I downed a whole bottle of Valium one day. I woke up in hospital the next, after having my stomach pumped.

Jan was appalled that I was a basket case. Utterly at a loss to understand why. As was I. This was not something she could handle at all so again she sought medical advice. With the wisdom of hindsight one would think she was beyond saving for again putting her faith in doctors, but she did. And she continued to do so her entire life, analogous to sexual pleasure, I am sure, because a doctor was the only person she could trust with her most intimate parts and secrets. Or so she believed until her brain no longer worked.

I was packed off to North Ryde Psychiatric Centre and locked in an observation ward. The night I arrived I was made to take medication for sleep. I must have dropped like a stone. In the morning nursing staff demanded I get up. I couldn't. Whatever they had drugged me with had been too much. Two of them got me up. I could hardly see. They slid my feet into someone else's slippers and a towel was slung over my shoulder. I was half carried, half dragged, to a public shower block where several pairs of legs were all I recollect because I could not lift my head. Then the arms let me go. When next I woke up I was really awake. And in pain. I had fallen flat on my face onto the concrete floor of the shower room. My front teeth, always a little buck, had broken. My head ached all over. I wanted help but I was in the observation ward. I was not allowed any outside contact. I didn't know what to ask for.

I was in the facility for twelve weeks. Jan visited twice but had nothing to say. I sat in a psychiatrist's office once. He asked what I felt for my father. I told him I didn't have one. He was angry at that. He got up from behind the desk, opened the door and bent his head to avoid looking at me. I left. I knew. He didn't. If he did—if it was in his notes that I was trafficked—he hadn't read them or didn't care. I attended group therapy sessions and asked the other patients deep and meaningful questions so that several of them thought I was a young staff member. I still shaved my head, wore tons of makeup and big silver hoops in my ears, all of which was allowed, but now I was even more self-conscious because of broken teeth and I was not taken to a dentist at all while there.

I fell in love, properly, for the first time. He was a fox, his name was Ces, and he was a morphine addict. He was seventeen, beautiful and mutual in his feelings towards me. The first person to tell me they loved me. We spent all our time together and at night I slept with his sweater. He shared speed with me, after getting hold of several tablets while on weekend leave. I sat up all night writing what I honestly believed to be the most epic and amazing poetry ever. Cathartic. Magical and deep. Utter rubbish.

I sat alone one night out in the gardens up on a grassy knoll, smoking a cigarette. I wasn't sure about life, still, at that stage, despite

Ces. But right then and there, clairaudience kicked in. Unsought and in a non-schizophrenic way. What I heard was both inside and outside my head.

Not your time to die, the Voice said matter-of-factly.

This shocked me in a way that words cannot adequately explain. But something changed. Because I was clear. That was the very moment when, retrospectively, the withdrawal symptoms of the last twelve months must have stopped. This was the Gatekeeper and the keys I was handed were to another life, the garment of witch and the art of theatre. I was sixteen years old.

Within days Ces was released into the care of his parents and I went banging on the psychiatrist's door.

When can I go home?

Are you ready to go home?

Yes.

Then go. There's nothing wrong with you.

I moved into my owner's house. No choice. Nowhere else. So often throughout life, nowhere else. So I kept running once I got the chance.

I was in contact with Ces for about a year but in a strange way. After a matter of months' release he was caught doing drugs again but this time he was sent to Emu Plains prison farm. I visited him with his mother every weekend. He escaped. I saw him twice before he was again arrested. Drugs were everywhere by then. Candy. In our faces. Offered as treats on the streets. Ces took anything.

He was sent to Gove, a correctional facility in the badlands, Northern Territory. Six hundred miles into Yolngu country, as far away from the Sydney drug scene as the law could have sent him. His father had begged the court to do this. He wanted to save his son. That didn't stop Ces hating him. He ranted in the one letter I had from him.

I heard nothing more until, along with several other guys, he turned up at my door in a battered old Holden station wagon that they'd picked up in Queensland. On the journey down the coast they'd stopped at a cattle paddock, the dung gardens to gold-top mushrooms (psilocybin) beyond counting. They had gone on a picking frenzy, were tripping off their heads and still had plenty of mushies left over when they arrived at the house where I lived. There was no air-conditioning in cars in those days and the damp, flaccid things were melting. They reeked of dead animals. Ces offered me some but the smell made me retch. I asked if they wanted to come inside. He said no. He kissed me, got in the car with the others and drove away.

That was the last time I saw him. He died of a heroin overdose not long after. His father phoned to tell me. I was so shattered I refused to go to the funeral.

From 1968 everything changed. I was no longer in the nightmare of pharmaceutical addiction and hormone insanity. I awoke to a glacially clear life and to an indefatigable determination, I also experienced that deep, seemingly-bottomless but necessary, grief that I didn't even attempt to stifle. I was not depressed, just sad. I cried for dead foxes, and I cried, also, that day in April when Martin Luther King was assassinated. I wept at the injustice of the world around me, for what had been done to me and taken from me so far. I was strong again and Jan had my teeth fixed. Almost.

I devoured books on magic and mysticism, the new science of parapsychology and I joined the Psychic Research Society. But there was also drama.

I could still smell backstage of the Town Hall in Mosman where we performed our end-of-year dances while I was in kindergarten, so I auditioned to study with the Independent Theatre in North Sydney. I was accepted, and began the three year course. I also tried, as a dropout, to study philosophy at Sydney university. I got in. I was out again my first semester because I questioned of the works I'd read by Nietzsche and was told I hadn't learned sufficiently, yet, to be audacious enough to have an opinion. So I left.

Drama seemed more forgiving.

In 1968 the school was the bauble of Doris Fitton. but its principle architects were Gillian Owen, Robert Levis, Colleen Clifford and Bunny Brooks. They taught everything from voice production to Shakespeare, from acting for screen and television to directing, my personal preference. We trained in stage presence and dance at the Bodenweiser Studio on Broadway and within the smaller studio, a converted house.

At the year-end eisteddfod my class had small parts in a play called A Man in a Tree about a druid in the branches of an oak in Hyde Park, London, doing nothing. I played an office *bird* on a lunch-break with my friend. My partner in the play was struck dumb with fright from the moment we went on stage until the last of the applause died down. I spoke both our parts.

On the final day of the performances the prizes and winners were awarded. Everyone in my class earned a certificate except me. Some were snide, others heartbroken for me. I did know, though. Something. When Robert Levis called out my name he was laughing. I had won comedy actress of the year and as he handed me my prize, the Complete Works of Tennessee Williams, he chuckled and said he hadn't laughed like that for years. Tears, he said, fall down laughing tears. I think I'm offended, I whispered into the microphone. That only made him laugh more.

My best friend in those days was fellow student, Margot. Her younger sister had died from a heroin overdose at fifteen, a couple of years before. When her family found her body she was still in possession of a small baggie of smack laced with Ajax, a powdered all-purpose cleaner. The pusher had never been caught.

Margot and I and several others conducted a séance. Her sibling came through and gave us an address in a lane in East Sydney.

We caught the bus to Wynyard where a giant roll-over map showed us the address was real. Margot phoned the police. When they asked how she got the information and she said her dead sister told her.

I continued orchestrating the occasional séance and now had card and tealeaf readings from Marian. I had staunch friendships among the theatre crowd and the art, music and bohemian community from Kings Cross to Cremorne.

In the early months of my seventeenth year I told Marian I was a witch and could she help me meet others. She said the daughter of an old friend lived in the Cross and called herself the same. She'd telephone.

So I met Roie Norton. Witch and an artist who had once been accused of painting pornography. Marian and her parents had been friends in Dunedin and had emigrated to Australia at the same time.

She lived in Potts Point in a pokey, smoke-filled, dimly lit flat. Art, mess, an altar. Statues of Pan and Hecate. Masks. The paraphernalia of witchcraft everywhere. The place reeked of magic, paint and ashtrays. Roie made us tea and came from the kitchen just as the phone rang. She seemed worried and distracted. She waved us to sit down and took the call. When she hung up Marian introduced me, embarrassed. Why? Roie seemed a sad woman. Thin-faced and bucktoothed with pointed black eyebrows and a small but generous smile.

When Marian finished her tea she left us, saying she was going to buy cigarettes and run a few errands. That she'd be back in an hour or so. Roie smoked.

So what makes you think you're a witch?

I can make things happen, I said. Know things before they happen. I feel the spirits of places and things. And I think I've been called.

Roie said she'd ask around. See if there was a coven that would take me.

About a month later a man who said he was friends with Roie phoned and would I like to meet some people? So I went to the address he gave me.

An almost empty warehouse in Edgecliff and I was greeted at the door by Wil, a girl/woman about my own age. She was coven high priestess, her dyed red hair almost to her bum. Inside was dim. Concrete floor. The windows taped with sheets of newspaper. Smelled of frankincense. Damp, but not dirt. Charcoal, stale red wine and beeswax. The mustiness of an old building in which wind is unknown. The roof above us tin, the beams stained with age. A glass-partitioned office down one end next to a tiny lunch room with an urn. I sat at the table smoking while she brewed us mugs of instant coffee. A man crossed the empty space, heavy boots making echoes. Black jeans, black t-shirt. Thirty-something, long blonde hair tied in a ponytail, small silver earrings, light eyes, broody, cocky.

He kissed my cheek and introduced himself as Thor. This was his coven. He put milk and sugar in his coffee, and I was asked what I thought about witchcraft.

I poured out my story except for the bits about being drugged and the psych hospital. He asked if I'd heard of Dion Fortune or Aleister Crowley or Robert Flood. No. Golden Dawn? Yes.

Rosicrucians or Thelema? Yes. Did I know about the Inquisition? Was I okay with the idea of ritual sex? He wore Aramis cologne.

I was initiated in November 1968. During the years I trained with them I also trained at the Independent Theatre, moved out of home and into a flat in McMahon's Point with a girlfriend named Jill and worked odd jobs. There was no point becoming attached to any of them because being with the theatre meant quitting when I scored a part in a production.

Sidetrack: Even though gold top mushrooms were used ritually and often by the coven, I also took LSD. Only three times but they were three times I will a) never forget and b) think I'll never do again, but won't say for sure.

Jill and I shared that flat with Patty, a girl who had a problem with gingivitis, whose body odor was rank and who never washed her clothes. A one bedroom flat, by the way, with three single beds. The first time I took acid was at a party in Edgecliff. They were called four-way trips and they came in tablet form. Someone gave me a whole one and I remember lying on my side watching and listening to an impossible neon electric sound and light display deep within the wall. I reared away like a brumby when some guy tried to touch me up, walked out into the dead of night and stood on my own at a crossroads, in the rain, waiting for a cab. I'd look in one direction and a taxi would pass from the other, I'd turn around and the same thing would happen. That went on seemingly infinitely until I finally hailed one. I have no idea how I managed to sound normal when I gave the driver my address and the rain on the windscreen and the swish/swosh of those wiper blades were wonderful but the experience, on the whole, was horrid.

The second time Jill coaxed me. She had met a policeman and he had invited her to be his companion at a wedding. The man was six foot four inches tall and was built like a truck and the last thing she thought she could do was put up with his relatives for an entire evening. We took half each. We had a massive wall-to-wall wardrobe and she wanted me to help her choose her look. The experience of trying on different outfits just got funnier and funnier until we were in paroxysms of laughter. Then he knocked on the door and, afraid that he would know she was tripping, we closed ourselves in the wardrobe but that was even funnier still, so we finally emerged. I hid in the bathroom while Jill let him in. She must have chosen clothing at random because within minutes they were gone, and I was left tripping off my face.

A little later I sat watching Ricardo Montalban playing the part of a priest on a television show about tenement bosses in New York, and the squalor of the occupants of their properties. At the start a boy handed Montalban a large paper bag, the contents hidden from the viewer. He eventually confronted the tenement lord in his penthouse office atop a fancy high rise building and demanded that the man provide safer conditions and to fix things. The boss said no so Montalban unscrewed the lid of the huge jar he has been carrying around in that paper bag and upended it onto the Mafioso's desk. It had been full to the brim with cockroaches.

Those things swarmed over his desk, out of the television and across the floor of our flat. In my direction. I pulled my legs up onto the couch, preparing to scream when Patty came home. And the flat was just a flat. I didn't want her to know I was tripping so I asked her to play poker. She agreed. I'd learned in a school holiday job one year when I worked as a cashier for a butcher shop. Those men taught me tricks I will never reveal. She'd brought home several bottles of cider, Strongbow being the drink du jour in the early seventies, and I proceeded to get roaring drunk to cover my tracks.

We wore bellbottom jeans or miniskirts with white lace-up boots, maxi skirts in a semblance of *hippydom*, hot pants with spandex lacy tops and ankle-length coats with faux fur collars. Huge earrings, pale lips and tons of eye makeup. Teased hair and huge sunglasses. We were Carnaby Street in Sydney. The era when an entire ensemble got away with performing naked in the top selling musical Hair.

The last acid trip was also with Jill. We were working a part time job, in the evenings as go-go dancers, at the Cheetah Club in Kings Cross. On this particular night, Jill had the loan of her cousin's car. We'd again dropped half a tab each and, let me tell you, if anyone had asked me that particularly rainy night why this drug had been invented I would have replied dancing! Until we left the club.

I can't possibly drive, said Jill. You'll have to.

Okay, I agreed.

I didn't have a license and I hadn't learned to drive but I got that car into gear and bunny-hopped for a few blocks before I got the hang of it. Jill gave directions and we cruised down to Woolloomooloo and turned a corner headed for the Cahill Freeway. We hit a massive oil spill. The car rolled three times and into a parked motorcycle. That stopped us ramming the garage section of a smash repair shop. Oh the irony. Luckily for us a police patrol unit had seen the whole thing happen and came to our aid. When they realized we were unhurt and when we adamantly refused to go to hospital the lovely men drove us home. Jill told them not to worry about the car, and because this was 1971 nothing more happened.

That initiation was a ritualized one. Done at the hand of a man and threatened at the point of a sword. At night. I lost track of time because I'd been fasting for three days. I took the bus to Kings Cross then walked the rest of the way. I arrived at sunset and Wil was the only one there. I stripped in the little kitchen and dressed in the black robe I'd made and sat and had one last cigarette.

You ready? she asked, proffering a scrap of cloth.

I was blindfolded and my wrists were bound in soft cords. I was fed something heavy with honey. Her chair scraped back, and I heard her sit. Heard her light another cigarette. Heard the door open and people cross the concrete. Was stood with hands on either arm and guided through the building and outside. Helped into a car.

When we eventually parked I could hear the surf and smell hot chips.

We walked a short distance along a street then onto steps. We climbed steadily but by that time I was nauseous and deep in the forest of another world. Being loved by sound. In the belly of an animal mother but also being her. Smelling vast smells. I'd been fed goldtops. Brought partway back to the world of wind and water by the sharpness pushed into my chest. Then Thor's voice. Clean and clear. Kindness. Seductive. Viking with a London accent. Asking me to swear oaths of loyalty and secrecy. Telling me my ritual name. On and on, more and more, There and in some grove, trees higher than could possibly exist, old. I wanted to stay.

They removed the bonds and blindfold. I was given a silver pentagram on a chain. We were high above Bondi in a stone circle on the cliffs. The nausea was gone and I was ecstatic. Everyone kissed me. Wil completed the words of the ritual and scattered the circle of salt. They did all the work, gathering everything up. I needed to sit down. Thor passed me the wine bottle and I took a swig. He laughed, pulled me to my feet, asked where I was. I couldn't talk for the life of me. We piled into cars, headed back to the covenstead, got very drunk and all had lots of sex.

Sex magic was usual. For summoning power, for spell-casting, to gain what one wanted, to curse the man who'd slapped his wife, and for whatever Thor suggested. Wil's body was the altar for most rituals. Ritualized sex, chanted to by the rest of us. We took it very seriously. And do not misunderstand me, it was beautiful. It was never vicarious. In my second year I had my turn. Thor was high priest. A coven still very much a man's world. Women, even the coven high priestess, were thought of as vessels that a female deity, Aradia, possessed.

Many of our rituals happened at that Bondi circle, always in the small hours of the morning.

Men positioned themselves at intervals along the track leading up. Homosexuals, in the days long before anyone accepted them, who had their own secrets and never would have told about us. They were the days when male prostitution got a man bashed or imprisoned. Or killed.

My experience with the first Sydney coven included the study of all those people and groups mentioned at our first meeting, the myths and magic of Egypt and Greece. Robert Flood, Thrice Great Hermes. The Book of Thoth. Writings on alchemy. Kabbalah. Nostradamus. Leland's Aradia, Gospel of the Witches. Did I enjoy this? Yes, and No. While the work was new to me the language was dated, stilted, male oriented and way too religious. I read Regardie's Golden Dawn and Crowley's 777 books both tedious and, in retrospect, irrelevant. The White Goddess and The Golden Bough. Lots of Dion Fortune. Gerald Gardner's The Meaning of Witchcraft. Learned rules and tables of correspondences. When to work what spell, its colors and planetary associations. Great to know. Then. Rubbish now I know how contrived it all was. Got to start somewhere though, right?

We gathered at the solar solstices and equinoxes. Full, dark and new moon. The fire festivals of the ancient Celtic year. Most of the rites dedicated to Aradia and Pan despite not one Italian amidst the bunch of us. And so, even then, I was indoctrinated into dualist theism and the worship of human-like deities.

We trained in astral projection, astral spying; experimented with telekinesis, had lessons in spell-crafting and scrying, trance and contact with the spirit world, banishing and hexing. I was taught not to think in terminology of right or wrong, rather right or other. Tried like a mad woman to move objects with the power of will. Never happened. Not then.

I was taught to really hear and really see and not just think I was doing so, or react, or respond in predictable ways. These were powerful tools for keeping streams of consciousness and experience untainted by mediocrity. One of the many things that were never answered, though, was what the astral realm was or the spirit world. There was always a sense that they were passing information along a string of beads. I taught myself to use the same language. I had lost my own in an attempt to fit in. Long ago learning to mask a true self. The flowering of a lifetime of 'imposter syndrome' along with a solar system of other unacceptable traits and behaviors by which I could remain alive.

This is not initiation I was to ultimately understand. This was capture. Free thinking and questioning and challenging were stomped. I was not in charge. If I wanted to learn I would do as I was instructed.

Not long after her birthday in the February of 1969, Marian predicted her own death. She was feisty and herself even then, in her eighties. She'd taught me a bit about the cards and the information she gave was never wrong. She also taught me about freedom. She lied to me. The lesson no one taught me: question even the nice ones.

Thursday was when she predicted her death. I drank my tea, upended the cup and turned it three times in the saucer she examined the dregs.

Your mother is going to be really upset between now and next Tuesday.

Why?

Everything will be alright.

After a pause she handed me back the cup and said, I like violets.

A statement.

What?

Nothing.

I came home in the wee hours of Sunday morning after a night out and her reading lamp was still alight. I looked in on her because she took sleeping pills and occasionally fell asleep with a beloved Western novel open on the covers, her glasses still on her nose and a cigarette still glowing between her fingers. I'd often worried that she'd burn us all alive. But not that night. She looked strange. I woke Jan.

Nan looks weird.

She'd mumbled something from deep within her covers.

Her mouth's hanging open.

That's normal. Go to bed.

I did.

Next morning Jan couldn't wake Marian. She was alive but unconscious. Jan called an ambulance. Marian died that day of a massive cerebral haemorrhage. But that was not all.

After her death Jan was distressed. Still at the hospital. She phoned Joan Carmody to beg her help arrange the funeral. She then asked the staff when she could organize to take the body.

Ah... mumbled the nurse, you'll have to contact her doctor.

There's a problem, he said over the phone.

What? What bits?

Silence. Dumbstruck. I was there.

What do we bury? she asked.

Silence.

Oh...

Marian had donated her body to science. The legal document was with her medical records.

An empty coffin was cremated on Tuesday. Hundreds turned out. A few relatives but mostly strangers. Lots of strangers. I asked someone who they were. I asked another. The answers were the same. Clients. I'd had no idea. So secretive. Poesies of violets covered the coffin.

I thought I was in love with Thor and he was nice to me, but in truth he paid me the same attention as he did everyone else, always seductive, knowledgeable. But magic and mysticism were his total focus. His true love.

I'd asked Wil, once, about who he was when he wasn't with the coven.

He's married and has three kids, she said. His family moved from Norway to England when he was a boy. He came to Australia on the £10 scheme and stayed. She didn't know anything else. Just warned me off my infatuation.

You're in love with what he represents, she scoffed. It's all glamour.

None of us ever met outside the covenstead and I knew next to nothing about any of them. It was never meant to be a social club. I stopped going when I got pregnant to Thor.

CHAPTER 9

On the whole, so-called bastard children were as unwanted in the early seventies as were the mothers of babies so described. Consensual sex was still not generally acceptable outside of marriage. Not really. Well for most people. But a pregnancy? If you weren't a long-term girlfriend or engaged? To men this was a woman's fault. A way to entrap a man into marriage. Not alright that they might be held responsible. Abortion in 1971 was most commonly done by other women on kitchen tables through the insertion of an unwound coat hanger. Quite often summoning death.

When the pregnancy was confirmed I was terrified. I didn't know what to do. I only had Wil's number. I wanted to let Thor know. I didn't know what he would do but I have no doubt he would have been pissed off and likely deny responsibility. I tried her number time and again but only ever got the answer machine. I left a message saying I was pregnant and could someone to please phone me. No one ever did.

When I sat Jan down and explained she was excited. A reaction I had not expected. That little bubble of something exquisite erupted inside me. I was then booked into the Royal North Shore hospital for pre-natal visits. From the onset I was hounded by social workers demanding I sign my baby over to them for adoption. They were determined to shame me but by now I was an initiated witch and a hippy. In a world of enlightenment. They were bitches.

You'll never be able to look after a child alone. You'll have to abandon it sooner or later. What will its life be like without a father? How can you do this to a child? You'll never get a man. This will tar you your whole life. What will the child think of you when it realizes that you had sex without marriage? It will hate you. I'd spat at them saying "he".

They were wrong. The lifelong unconscious knowledge of abandonment, of having no heritage, no aunties or blood-anyone is unspeakable. What is a society that ostracizes under morality clauses based on religion? I spit at you.

Graduation took place with the Independent Theatre and I continued to work at the insurance company, as an accounts clerk, right up until the eighth month.

Jan was really happy and I should have been afraid because of that but I didn't have the guts to ask what the cheeriness was all about. Didn't guess she would want to control yet another child. That she had a plan.

Into the groove of pregnancy, she dove like a junkie scoring a baggie for the first time in days. She still had not confessed to not having given birth but I hoped her excitement was genuine. Never having had a child this was the closest she would first get.

Eric came to visit from Melbourne and I told him. He was disgusted.

Don't you give the bastard my name, he huffed and wheezed. Ya slut. Apple doesn't fall far from the tree after all.

I passed Jan a look that sought permission to kill him.

Call it Jones or Brown or Smith. Call it what you like but don't you dare give it my name.

Nasty, nasty Trickster.

We never spoke again. Nor did I attend his funeral.

I had yet to learn that my Lancashire grandmother's last name before she married was Brown.

On the eighteenth of February 1972 I birthed Adam. I'd been told I was overdue and that the unborn infant would by now be in fetal distress because I had high blood pressure. I was admitted to hospital and induced. Made to walk up and down the corridor for fourteen hours because every time I rested my contractions stopped. Finally I was allowed a bed. I was forced to lie on my back with my legs in stirrups while strangers in sterile masks, white gowns and green gloves probed my vagina. A doctor, mumbling something unintelligible from behind a white mask, sliced my perineum muscle with a scalpel. Women were not allowed to squat so babies could slide out easier. Didn't really know anything.

After twenty two hours labor he was born. He weighed one and a half kilograms, so I presume they got the dates mixed up. I had fourteen stitches in my fanny. The umbilical cord was cut and my baby taken away until he had been cleaned and swaddled. I was terrified. Only then was I was allowed to hold him and feed him. I was in love, unable to look away.

Julia and I had tea together once a month after prenatal checkups at the outpatients of the Royal North Shore Hospital. She was tall and beautiful. From what was then known as Rhodesia. We became the best of friends. She was also single and due to give birth around the same time I was. When I began labor I phoned her, and she told me she would make me a kaftan for when I was released from hospital.

The day after Adam's birth an orderly came to my bedside at around six in the morning. He said, Miss Gerhart is outside and wants to see you.

I experienced a moment's confusion wondering why she was there so early, then I realized. I hobbled to the corridor.

She was on a gurney, grinning between contractions, hand-sewing my kaftan. She birthed a baby boy a few hours later. They cut her as well. Later that evening I was allowed to visit her. The staff had provided an infra-red ray lamp to help heal her stitches but instead, she was sitting up in bed tanning her face.

Months later, when she and I needed to wean the boys through the necessity of work, we rented a cabin in the woods in the middle of a pine forest at Blackheath, top of the Blue Mountains. Open fires and damper with jam, and magpies on the kitchen table every morning.

Eventually she returned to her family in Rhodesia. We determined to keep in touch so our boys could be like brothers. Letters continued regularly. Then stopped. That was during the years of bloody conflict and I have often wondered what happened. I never heard from her again.

The sister-person had married and by then, also pregnant, had her first child in June and not long after that Jan came out. Now that she was officially a grandmother the secret of our origins was her monster. Too huge a burden to wear in isolation, the guilt and responsibility dark clouds on her horizon. Biologically-inherited health problems became an issue and she felt the overwhelming necessity to confess our illegitimacy and adoption and provide us with rudimentary information.

The day Jan told me was painful. For her. I sat in the kitchen. She paced, cried and wrung her hands.

I have to tell you something. And you have to promise not to tell your sister until I've had the chance to explain this to her myself.

You've killed somebody, I said.

What? No, worse.

Pacing, wringing hands, by now weeping quietly.

You're having an affair?

No.

You're dying.

No. Oh dear.

You're leaving the country again?

You're adopted.

Pause. She stopped pacing but kept crying. Waiting for the confusion and condemnation.

How is this news? I said.

She was utterly shocked. To be some strange woman who had bought shamed women's babies. To live a lie for that long. Her pretending had been creepy but I didn't let on. She told me the whole story then, about talking Eric into the deal, about how she just went along the line and picked a newborn because there was no waiting list in those days and no ethical criteria. That they'd paid three hundred pound sterling. That there had never been any other choice but that she wanted me the moment she laid eyes on me.

Like chocolate, I thought.

She told me the name of the woman who bore me—well, technically a girl because she was only sixteen years old—and that she was English. That was all she knew. She made me promise not to look for her while she lived.

As for searching, I wouldn't have known how. Not then, anyway.

CHAPTER 10

Towards the end of 1972 Jan agreed to look after Adam so I could have a night out. I met up with a Jill and we took a cab to a wine bar with a live band. We danced together as women often did and we'd just sat down at a table when I was brought a glass of red by a young man with dark brown eyes. He asked if he and his Mancunian pal could join us.

Jill studied the other guy and said sure, why not, when I, a fledgling back in the social game, had already fallen for the Aquarian charm of the deer-eyed man sitting himself on the bar stool beside me and leaning close. Here was the Trickster come to feather his nest in the form of a twenty one year old Englishman. Flown out by the British ten pound scheme. There was chemistry. I let him know I had a little boy.

You're married?

I'm not, I replied.

He said he wasn't bothered, and could he have my phone number. We began dating.

After several weeks we had sex. Really, really interesting sex.

I talked about witchcraft. Casually, just to get him in the loop. He asked about my son's father and I'd smiled, choosing not to answer. He seemed to listen when I filled him in about life and my philosophies. I chatted about Shakespeare.

He also admitted disinterest in everything except our mutual politics, sex and love of music. When he eventually met Adam they got along.

He'd seduced me utterly. After several months I suggested we live together.

He was mortified.

What if my mother found out? She'd never forgive me. How could I tell my family? No. I couldn't do that. But if you marry me...

A woman became a wife when she married. I knew it was both ownership and sanctioned (legal) sex. My opinions have always been clear on what that is. A married woman does her husband's bidding. Obey remained in wedding vows. They had children whether they wanted to or not. Housework, cooking and cleaning? Theirs. All unpaid. Women got an allowance from their husbands for food and clothing. We did all the shopping. Women in Mosman still did their washing on Mondays and cooked a roast on Sundays. Most did not have cars. Marriage is a contract that usually does not work in a woman's favor. Women are put in geriatric homes after the fall, retaining no one and nothing.

We lose individuality. Get mummy tummies and scared. Demands and expectations manifest in unacceptable but necessary ways. We take up wine o'clock. The happy ever after stories fed to us in children's books about princesses found and saved by princes is cruel. Love is love, wonderful, but love is a feeling and never for the whole of a lifetime. It very often conceals cruelty. A Walking Man once explained the Mars cycle to me. That after approximately two and a quarter years the cracks show. A person has to exhaust every enticement to stay in the company of the object of that love.

I was young and knew nothing of this. And I wanted to be with him. Believing him to be a real man I eventually said yes.

Whoever my mother was I was glad she couldn't see me say that word.

A straight Englishman, no matter how pleasing to look upon, no matter how good the sex, is a straight Englishman. He liked a beer but was not an alcoholic. Loved food and cars and soccer. He wanted a speedboat. A two-tone Valiant. But from the first night I knew I faced a disaster. In bed he turned his back on me and slept. He did so the next and the next. For two weeks.

Why? I finally asked.

What? he answered, indifferent.

Why the cold shoulder?

A long, protracted pause. Him leading up to the answer.

We're married now.

And?

There's no more screwing till you learn to be a good wife.

I sat up. Switched on the bedside lamp.

And what the fuck is that supposed to mean?

You know.

No, I don't know, actually.

The whole witch business is ridiculous. And my washing. And the cleaning and stuff. And you can't work. No wife of mine is going to work. Makes me less of a man. So you have to stop. And for fuck's sake, learn how to cook.

I'm not going to go on about this overly much. We were never going to last.

There is a power to anger. A tangible, visceral thing.

Affection is natural to all species I can think of. Discipline, yes. Response. Defense. Just not anger. I don't even know what anger is. I know the experience, though. I'm really angry when someone is being cowardly, petty, pretentious or taking what they have no right to. That includes nations, corporations, governments and bureaucracies.

Anger is really the same thing as depression, just its opposite. At least anger is an expression. Far safer than the burial of feeling because of fear. I also knew that fear. The terror of rejection if one disagrees, if one goes against the expectations of the majority. The fear of being cast out is primal because we are a pack animal and a lone beast will not survive long.

Anger and depression happen when the attacker is subtle or when they, in avid righteousness, imply that your weakness or your failings make you a lesser being.

Depression happens when there is no way back up from how far down the rabbit hole one dives to protect oneself from whatever aggression one is enduring. Like post-traumatic stress, that beast wants you dead. Isolation. Depression because too many layers of accusation, shame, guilt neglect or demand drive self-esteem into the ground and buries the true self there.

When I was young I knew anger. Red rage that never lasted long, whatever the cause soon smothered. I always found a way around the offending obstacle or thought. Any distraction would work. Wallowing in moonlight or smelling. Olfactory senses my strongest: cooking, rubber, dog fur, cut grass, the sky.

Anger turned to depression through those harrowing years of medication when I had no outlet. When I finally came up for air and could again breathe in and out like some tidal thing, I did get angry. Very angry. At our species. At the very idea that a man could even consider dropping bombs, let alone actually do it. Over and over.

I learned, then, two techniques to diffuse the rage. First, the hot-water-bottle-with-the-hole-in-the-bottom-on-the-nail-on-the-fence-with-the-broom trick. Recipe: fill hot water bottle and screw in lid. Hang bloated subject on nail on fence. Beat with broom till until flaccid.

Second was break-a-plate-save-a-baby. Wives' tale remedy that says more than words. Recipe: buy a stack of cheap plates from a thrift shop, sit in kitchen on solid chair, and crack each on the edge of the table. Clean mess only when mission accomplished.

As the years turned into decades I discovered a kick bag and fighting wraps.

I really tried with the man within whom the Trickster had taken up residence. I didn't want to be that failure that society said a woman was when a marriage became a cold war. But we separated time and time again. I loved him but this self-righteousness was ingrained. He'd come straight from his mother to me. She'd washed, cleaned, cooked, healed, toadied to his every whim. Him being the only son. An institutional family. No wildness ever allowed. Not in his quiet little home village in the heart of the Midlands. That his behavior was the norm there certainly didn't make me any less mortified.

No, the final rage happened over a seemingly innocent incident.

Your tea's ready, I yelled from the kitchen of the ground floor flat we rented in Neutral Bay.

He came from another room, grabbed up the mug and took a sip. He made a face and looked at me in disgust.

Where's the sugar?

Here, I replied, spooning sugar into my own mug.

Fuck you, he said, upending the sugar bowl. Now clean that shit up, I'm going to have a shower.

I sat there, my knuckles white as my hands gripped the edge of the table, my jaw clenching so violently my teeth hurt. Unseeing, straight ahead, burning.

I faced the wall between the kitchen and the lounge room. To my left was a curtained doorway that led to the bathroom. To my right was a built-in solid wood pantry such as is not made anymore.

The shower was one of those old fashioned jobs above the bathtub.

The rage was a burning sensation blinding the edges of my vision. I even momentarily saw the neon under that second skin. Then I was calm.

And the Trickster fell out of the bathtub, through the doorway, across the kitchen table to land naked, his head banging into the built-in pantry, dripping wet, dazed and confused.

What the fuck just happened? he said.

Even I was surprised.

You did that! he accused.

Adam and I moved back with Jan. One for witch. Entity nil. This was not the end of the game, however.

At three years old Adam was enrolled in an international preschool run by a forward thinking young French woman who only allowed three children of any one nationality at a time. Every Friday the opportunity to share food, customs and traditional dress occurred. The three Anglo-Australians, including my boy, had nothing to share. That was just wrong. I knew zero about our tribal Celtic lineage in those days. If I had I would have sent him painted blue. We'd take the bus, kiss him goodbye and I'd go to work.

In the two decades after the war jobs were in abundance. A golden age. Education didn't matter, just enthusiasm and a desire to learn. We were taught when we were hired. I wanted the job of my choice and the employment agencies reeled off one after another begging me to take what was offered. Great pay. Secure future. Mine for life if I so desired. I began working at an appliance rental company as a troubleshooter because I believed I could do anything, and the pay was great. This was before computers when vast hordes of women worked in accounts all over the city. Typists, receptionists, telephonists, record keepers clacking away at calculators and recording monthly figures. My job was to go from department to department and learn there in case someone was off sick or quit, was fired or took annual leave. I could fill in. I learned the entire company.

Then technology. The bosses needed someone to run them. Someone who knew all aspects of the firm. I was sent to a private class of the programming language called Basic, how to work with the IBM systems—huge, in-house, white behemoths that required a steady climate and spotless conditions—and trained up in the now long-dead art of the printout.

I was provided a staff of six women. Much of the work in those early days was transferring the mountains of manual information into bytes. Within months we became indispensable.

By then I had made new friends with several other mystics and New Age practitioners, mainly through the New Awareness Centre in Lindfield. None were witches. They seemed to have oddly gone underground. I couldn't find any, and I did hunt.

Julie and I met there, a professional naturopath. In her early thirties but already with silver hair. Happened overnight. In her teens. For no reason. We were both members of the Psychic Research Society near Wynyard in the city and after being paired on several occasions, discovered we had a knack for ghost-busting.

We were on the final-desperation-call-list with Lifeline. When people phoned in claiming they were possessed by something satanic, or their kids by demons, or there were poltergeists or other assorted phenomenon in the house, and Lifeline couldn't talk them into some state of seeming rationale, they gave Julie and I the phone numbers. There were the occasional inexplicable occurrences or situations that required a physical callout, but we always went in pairs because very often people claiming these things were quite unhinged.

The Exorcist had been released in Australian cinemas the year before and was still causing chaos. Possession was now at a premium. Extraordinary publicity for the catholic church. Those months were our busiest. Every second person had the devil or some other entity attempting to take over their lives.

I studied indigenous people's histories and lore; as much research as I could get my hands on, specifically that of Britain and Ireland and ancient Mesopotamia because Joseph Campbell's Occidental Mythology had come into my life. So did The Book of Hopi by Frank Waters and, for a psychological perspective, Gestalt Therapy by Frederick S. Perls. That book revolutionized my thinking because other forms of psychology involved blame and backward-looking. These were the times of seeking oneself, wanting to throw off the chains of outmoded morality and bureaucracy, to work without borders. To love utterly. Kahlil Gibran's *The Prophet* joined my treasured library. I don't know, today, if I agree with him.

Then I read Dee Brown's 1970 edition of *Bury My Heart at Wounded Knee*. That story began a lifetime of questioning authorized versions of history and the effects on indigenous people by worldwide cultural misappropriation. I wanted to know whether the Arthurian myths and whether the legends of Merlin had any historic relevance and I was to discover that they did. Many stories. In difference to several other versions, however, Geoffrey of Monmouth, in his *Historia Regum Britanniae*, crafted his Arthur from a flesh and blood activist named Caradoc, or Cradoc (Caractacus by the Romans), a Catuvellaun chieftain who united several tribes against the Roman insurgence almost two thousand years ago. They hid out in the mountainous terrain of what is now Wales and harried the Romans as the latter forced their way inland. The Romans could erect a fortress in a day. Caradoc's guerrilla forces burned them. "Fight and fight and run away and live to fight another day," is attributed to him. Cartimandua, client-queen of the Catuvellaun is written to have betrayed him to Rome. He was shipped there as a prize of war. In a bear cage.

I trained in archery with the Lindfield Archery Club. Many years later taught both my sons.

CHAPTER 11

I have read tarot for many celebrities over the years. Read tarot for them or been the curiosity at their social events. I've had a dozen cops in my little tarot parlor while they went through my diaries looking for the name of a suspected murderer's ex-partner—a client—after a cold case in Victoria was reopened with the introduction of DNA evidence. They knew she'd been to me and they had hoped I'd kept copies of the recordings. Which, of course, I didn't.

Tarot has shown me everything from the Grim Reaper in the Bowling Alley ad on telly, warning people in the early days of HIV/AIDS, to the devastating climactic challenges facing the world in the present day. The dumbing-down of our culture occurring because of media, the internet and social networking that, whilst an important tool for grass-roots revolution and the exposure of corruption in government and corporation, has its downside. Stifling conversation. Language is being decimated by sentences such as gr82cu. Writing by hand and the personally delivered letter are rapidly being relegated to obsolescence. This should be worrying. Archives have exposed jewels by way of old footage, photographic negatives, letters and journals. Written records were kept that have survived for centuries. My deep fear is of an Orwellian culture that can change history with a digital swipe or photographic deceit or even vote-rigging. And if the internet crashes and never recovers? I shudder.

Prophecy.

Cassandra was the tragic seeress who predicted the fall of Troy. Her fate was abduction, rape and finally murder. No one believed her. To their downfall. More to the point, no one wanted to believe her because who readily accepts lousy news?

Tarot defies logic and rationalization.

On the thirteenth of January next year your life will change forever, I sighed, while that Brisbane lawyer shuffled. He just looked at me. A what the fuck? Look. This was November and he'd already bought his one-way plane ticket to Sydney for that day. He'd fallen in love with a woman other than his wife and that was the day he was flying to Sydney to live with her. There is no explanation for this. I don't know. No one reading this will know. There are the cards, made of paper that for millennia were a forest and before that who knows. And then there's me, or that lawyer, who have been mammals for as long as mammals have existed and before that who knows. And then there's tarot and other than an ancient forest its existence is the communion between us, a giant, wise entity that chose to play with me many years ago because I didn't, initially, care about anyone who crossed my palm with silver, thinking, I'll never see you again anyway. How can what I say matter?

That was the key that eventually broke the spell of the Trickster. A quote from a disembodied voice that came through a kabbalistic ritual I worked over ten weeks in 1990 with three other initiates. That writing came through Binah. A deep woman's voice, and not particularly pleasant. Hardly any of those voices were pleasant. Mainly because whatever they are this is also the world to them. And this world is being harmed.

I am well beyond attempting to box these concepts into predictable paradigms because if that was to happen the door to possibility would close, replaced by dogma, even religion: two things I despise because I know what they do and what they have done across history. Abrahamic religions delude the human animal that we are apart from the earth and from all other species. The rules tell us we have other skills and that we are better and that only man is rewarded or punished by an external omnipresent male deity. That deity, in his omnipotence, rampantly and willy-nilly, causes fire, flood, famine, disease, deformity, war, genocide, terror and bigotry any one of many different destructions and divisions. People pray, in some teeth-grinding delusion, for god to fight mother nature.

Religion is a closed system. There are no questions, only statements. That is a lie and results in war and desolation. Mysticism, on the other hand, is inherently personal and cannot be shared or taught. An inclusion that involves love. Not love for anyone or anything but the experience. When Peanuts, the adult male gorilla, touches Dian Fossey's hand. That was love. Acceptance and belonging.

The nineteen seventies dripped with the nectar of new-won liberations, the wildness and sexiness of free animals. The music, the politics, the philosophies of freedom, human and environmental rights, spiritual emancipation, insight and enquiry. Women claimed their places in the new society that had the old bowing its head in shame. In Australia this was the era of Gough Whitlam. The overthrow of a twenty three year long, vice-like grip by conservatism. During his prime ministerial office we had free university, he brought the troops home from Vietnam and ended our involvement in that war. He lowered the vote from twenty one to eighteen (yes, that's right, men had been old enough to fight and die but not old enough to vote), ruled women be paid the same wages as men for the same work, ushered in multiculturalism and no-fault divorce.

Both the anti-nuclear and anti-uranium movements gained momentum but France went ahead with atomic testing at the Mururoa Atoll in French Polynesia anyway. They set off one hundred and ninety three underground explosions in all. None of us could see the sense. All of us knew the danger. The destruction of Hiroshima and Nagasaki should have sent such a wave of unmitigated terror throughout the world that that Pandora's Box would be slammed shut forever. From the nineteen fifties and well into the twenty first century, like strange puppets or greedy children, governments around the world have clamored for the technology. By the end of this race nuclear-armed warships and submarines cruise the seas with their mega loads of destruction. America's use of uranium depleted bombs (dirty bombs) litter Persia. With devastating effects on its own troops, the people of Iraq and the descendants of both. News of bone cancers and birth defects are gagged by governments.

But not yet. This was still the seventies and a time of joy. Of summer in the sand and the sea off Lady Bay Beach—bare, brown bodies without the scare of the ozone hole. Melanoma a rarity. And skin cancer? What was that?

We listened to James Taylor, sang John McLean's American Pie whenever a guitar was brought to the fire. Pink Floyd, Black Sabbath, Led Zeppelin, Joni Mitchell and the Velvet Underground. AC/DC. The Rolling Stones. Sergeant Pepper's Lonely Hearts Club Band. Steeleye Span and Jethro Tull. The music was still deep and vinyl. We had the bardry of Robin Williamson, Rick Wakeman, and the poetry of Cat Stevens. Tina Turner. I was enchanted by Cher, Bette Midler and Barbra Streisand. I thought them the most beautiful women in the world. I think I empathized with their profiles.

CHAPTER 12

In 1976 I learned numerology from visiting American practitioner Jacqueline Robertson-Swann. I trained on friends and their friends and the dead. Until I learned. I thought this was to be my spiritual career choice but there were no computers and programs then, so every chart took about thirty pages to type. Every Monday night I met with Julie at her house in Gladesville to work ritual and experiment with parapsychology. I connected through trance with an entity called Ariel that had a profound effect on my life with its wit and wisdom. Julie wrote what was said through me. I recalled nothing afterwards. I was always freezing cold and very hungry, often in the trance for up to three hours. She filled volumes.

I taught kabbalah at the New Awareness Centre in Lindfield and wrote articles for Nexus magazine, mainly on behalf of endangered, imprisoned and traumatized species.

I worked with the precursor to later computers called electronic data processors at the rental company. At twenty six I was senior manager. I lunched with corporate heads and my staff often took entire afternoons off. My immediate boss, young Englishman, sent out to update the company, hired people based on whether they could sing the first few bars of Elvis Presley's Jailhouse Rock.

I've learned things from almost everyone I've ever met, and he was no exception. His office, lined on three sides with glass, including a glass door, was way over the other side of the accounts department, a staff of approximately eighty women. I was confused, one month-end, at how the financial figures on one printout didn't agree with data on another. I phoned him in his office. He hung up on me, opened his door and screamed Ly, think, over the head of every staff member. Determined never to be so embarrassed again I learned to be the fastest and most accurate person I knew. I also did this because I was—am—intrinsically lazy. If I do a thing quickly and well I have all the time in the world to do other things. My job put a lot of people out of work. The workers there all knew me as witch and I did their numbers and read them rudimentary tarot. This was an era of intense interest in parapsychology and canteen talks were either about sex, love or what was, then, termed the *occult*[4].

Lily worked in the department next to mine. We were close friends and I knew all about the drama she'd gone through, including a court battle for custody of her son after coming out as lesbian. Her partner, Margaret, was involved in the early establishment of the Women's Electoral Lobby. She was in Queensland engaged in a custody battle, breaking down legal apartheid by gender.

Meanwhile Lily had rented a house owned by friends who, until recently, had been together happily for years. Bond Street, Mosman. Within a month of moving in they began arguing. Turned violent. They'd split up and rented the house for a pittance.

Lily also had a psychic reading from a woman I knew and respected who lived in Balgowlah. She'd predicted the abduction of Lily's son by her ex-husband and her own death by suicide within six months.

What rubbish, I said.

Come for dinner, tonight, she asked.

I took a bottle of chardonnay and sat on the floor in an almost bare room—a mattress for a temporary couch, a coffee table, a four bar electric heater cranked up to full heat and a bookshelf filled with her son's books against the wall opposite to where I'd plonked myself. Lily cooked dinner in the adjacent kitchen. Her son was staying with his father for the night, so we had the place to ourselves.

I began talking. I don't remember what I said but I do know I did not shut up and was aware that I couldn't. I talked all through dinner until eventually Lily asked me to stop.

Waves of malevolence, evil, radiated towards us from the opposite wall. While I had babbled on I had somehow protected us. I felt sick. There was something radically wrong.

---

[4] Occult means *hidden*.

One psychic says bad things is one thing, said Lily, but two of you? What do we do?

We get out of here. Come back to my house till we can work out what's going on.

She packed a duffel bag with whatever she thought she'd need for a day or two, threw her keys on top and zipped up the bag. She switched off the heater and the lights and we were dashing down the hall when I twigged that we had to get her son's bookshelf out of that room. So we went back. And in the dark we dragged furniture into the first bedroom off the hallway.

I was out the front door ahead of Lily. Without warning I was pushed hard from behind. I flew through the air and landed on the path at the base of the veranda stairs.

What the fuck was that for? I whispered.

I didn't touch you.

She was pale in the dark of the night as she helped me to my feet, and we ran to her Volkswagen.

She unzipped the duffel bag to get her keys but they weren't there. She upended the bag onto the nature strip. But they weren't there.

What's happening?

We have to go back in.

We went down the side of the house to the living room window where water pipes snaked halfway up the outside wall.

I'll go, I said.

I took my nail file from my bag and cut the fly wire. Then I climbed onto the pipes. The four bar heater in the room glowed orange and I was terrified. The window was open an inch and I was seriously fucking terrified. I pushed up the window and climbed in and felt the whole house go, *Oh, well, maybe next time*.

Then the telephone rang.

I helped Lily scramble through the window and I raced about switching on every light in the house, my heart pounding somewhere in the back of my skull. The call was from that Balgowlah psychic. She'd picked up that something awful was happening. And I knew a murder had been committed in this house. I had the disturbing image of a woman standing over a man's dead body, a knife in her hand. Everything was drenched in blood and she was grinning. A rictus of madness.

I'm okay. Lily spoke with the other woman while I switched off the heater, unplugging the cord from the wall.

Ly's with me, we're going back to her house.

Then I knew.

Check your bag, I said, when she'd hung up. The keys were on the top of everything. We left all the lights on, ran, scrambled into her Beetle and drove. We made tea and sat in the front room, me with a notebook and a pen because I was doing automatic writing at the time. I went into a trance and felt my hand moving across the page.

Not until Lily said, oh fuck, over my shoulder that I opened my eyes to see what I'd written. The whole page was covered with DON'T GO BACK DON'T GO BACK DON'T GO BACK.

Lily phoned Margaret to let her know what was going on and Margaret told her she'd had a nightmare the night before that someone had killed themselves.

I fly back tomorrow, she said. No way do I want you and Ly sharing the same bed for more than one night.

They stayed for just over a week until they could find a place of their own and I gave them my bed. The first morning after Margaret arrived I went into the kitchen where Jan arranged two lots of coffee and toast on a tray.

What's that for?

Our visitors.

I followed her up the hall and she knocked softly on the door.

Come in, Lily called.

She and Margaret sat up in bed. Jan handed Lily the tray before climbing between them.

So, she began, what do lesbians do?

That same year I joined the Women's Electoral Lobby, a staunch feminist and activist. In thanks for a tarot reading Lily gave me Horses by Patti Smith. I was organically influenced by her poetry.

Mother-of-Dogs offered me a green cottage in Cremorne. Now way too small for her purpose in life. Bottle green walls. Two bedrooms. A hundred years old. Adam and I moved in. Why did I keep leaving Jan? The televisions. She'd accumulated them like toys, and they were everywhere and always on. She also fed my son junk food that neither his body or his mental health could handle.

Mother-of-Dogs is so called because she accumulated quite a pack, all of whom had been on death row at one shelter or another. One was a Doberman, but we'd fallen in love even before I'd moved in. Her name was Shadow. She trusted me but was severely timid. A frightened dog is a dangerous dog. She bore some vicious scars and Mother-of-Dogs hinted that perhaps she had been used for sport. Shadow hid her despair in savagery towards most people and especially men but before she was put down she taught me about turning away, about soft eyes, about leaning over her to make her feel safe; that she did not need to be the alpha dog, I had that covered for her.

I'd been working the Saturday she died. Mother-of-Dogs took all the hounds for a run in Hyde Park. Shadow had thought she recognized the man in the distance. She had pulled free of her leash and taken the two hundred yards flat out, attacked and ripped his calf off before she knew the mistake and cowered. The police shot her.

Ray Buckland and Alex Sanders were by now presenting wicca to the world. Starhawk was on the scene—a political activist, social psychologist and witch—but was not yet published. I wondered why they were whitewashing witchcraft with a new word. I understood about the need for inclusion, but the rhetoric was rather more religious than mystical. Hierarchical rather than heretical. At the very least, I suppose, the knowledge of a spirituality far removed from monotheism was a giant leap back from the void. Or so I thought at the time.

Wicca seemed to be a way of being acknowledged but the problem of vilification was still there. Witchcraft was still considered a dirty word, something to do with the devil, something evil and misunderstood. Something that women did and got killed for. I understand. People need an enemy.

I was invited to talk with a group of computer technology students at East Sydney Technical College because Valerie, their teacher and a student in my kabbalah group, wanted them to learn to think laterally as well as logically. I stood in front of the class and asked who believed in witches.

Go on, raise your hand, don't be shy.

Not one hand lifted.

Okay, I said, who here is christian?

Most hands went up.

Really? I asked, pausing for effect. Well I don't believe you exist.

There was confusion for a few minutes. What I had said made no sense.

I went on to discuss witchcraft 101 for an hour and a half.

I joined a group studying reincarnation using a technique called the *kristos* experiment during which the individual lies prone on the floor, has their head and feet rubbed and is lead through a series of imaginary exercises that end in an experience of another life or another time. Seemingly very real.

This group was led by a woman in her late forties known only as CJ and there were ten of us. One was Colin. A Welshman. A Mage in the world of myth. He had both the good looks of Sean Connery and an accent that entranced. We had an affair. He taught me to cook the perfect scrambled eggs and took me out on his friend's yacht in a race out past Sydney Harbour's Heads and into deep ocean. I puked the entire time. He'd suggested I have a big breakfast, his idea of funny.

We both suspected that CJ had a crush on him and this proved to be the case when she psychically attacked me. I was living at Jan's house again. I paid half my wages to do so. I had been busily practicing astral projection when a high, mercilessly shrill whistle shocked me to full awareness. I stumbled to the door to the hallway of the rest of the house, but the noise was less outside my room. I went through to my glassed-in veranda and poked my head out the window, but the screeching was less there also. Was only loud in the middle of my room. I quickly and pointlessly—after the horse has bolted so to speak—cast a protective circle around myself to no avail. Then I saw her face in my imagination.

Silly old fart, I thought. So very, absurdly funny was the attack that I laughed. The noise got worse. I went into paroxysms of uncontrollable belly laughter, tears pouring from my eyes, my cheeks aching. The whistle stopped abruptly. CJ phoned the next day and told me I was not welcome in her little group anymore. Colin received no phone call but he never went back either.

We'd been indulging in each other for several more weeks when the Trickster phoned.

Listen, I've been thinking—
Wait, I've got something to tell you.
Silence. What?
I've got a lover.
The muffled sound of sniffling.
Are you crying?
I wanted to ask if maybe we could try again.
You're joking.
No. I still love you so much. I'm so sorry. I was such a prick.
What was I to say?
Please. Do you love me at all still?
I did, actually.
Well...
Please?
Okay. I need to think.

I thought long and hard and decided to give our marriage one last chance.

Colin was upset but was very understanding. Perhaps if he'd fought a little harder? But men didn't if the Trickster couldn't ride them. No, all that happened was destiny. Trickster moved back in and we stayed together another year. He seemed a new man. A lie.

He had never stopped being homesick for England and he asked if we could all go there to live close to his family for a change. I thought about that long and hard as well and eventually said why not?

That was February of 1978. Adam was seven and I was twenty seven. At some stage after making the life-changing decision to move to England a group of us from my work went along to a tarot party—wine, crackers and cheese, a psychic in a quiet room. When my turn came I shuffled the cards. I looked away as she spread them out as I could read rather well by then and I did not want to influence or be influenced by that.

She lit a cigarette, coughed and cleared her throat.
Two weeks of shit, she said.
What?

Coming up soon will be two really shitty weeks then you'll be right for the rest of your life.

What?

Yep.

That's all?

Ten bucks thanks.

I mumbled as I handed her the money.

Not long after the Trickster announced his grand plan. He would to go to England first and acquire a house. All Adam and I then had to do was move in. We would come two weeks later.

He flew home in late March.

Is this the two weeks? I thought. I certainly had a very gnarly feeling.

Within those two weeks I'd given notice at my firm and received a gilded, four-page reference from my boss, along with a letter of introduction to the managing director of the world international offices in the city, close to our new home in a sleepy English village near to the city of Northampton.

Adam and I were staying with Jan in the interim and an unusual visitor changed the way I would think as I aged. The sister-person's very catholic family had a great aunt who ordinarily lived in London. She visited our house one afternoon. She wore a tweed jacket and trousers, a man's white cotton shirt and a deerstalker hat. She was seventy two and walked with a pair of trekking poles. When we were alone she sat on the couch opposite where I was reading.

I used to be a nurse, but I was put out to pasture at fifty five.

Pardon?

I was supposed to go quietly.

You didn't?

Of course not. I applied to the University of London to study medicine.

And did you get in?

Of course. But I changed my study after a year.

To what?

Archaeology. Mastered in Egyptology.

So what are you doing in Australia?

I'm on digs, dear.

Really?

Seven chaps and I. Off to the Pilbara.

I shut my mouth.

Single mother, I hear.

Yes.

Brave of you.

Thank you.

I also run a half-way house for single pregnant women in London. Prenatal of course. Hardly anyone keeps their babies.

Then she wandered off to the kitchen, passing my prone mother on the way.

Your telly's very loud, she condemned.

I'm a bit deaf, replied Jan.

Do you watch a lot of TV?

These are my shows. Can you talk when the ads are on?

A moment's silence.

Can I be so bold as to ask how old you are, Jan?

Sixty one.

Oh, dear.

Why?

What if you live to be a hundred?

What if I do?

Is this what you want to do for the next forty years?

Are you making tea? Yes, thank you, I'd love one.

Summarily dismissed in favor of Days of Our Lives. But I sat frozen in thought. I would not forget this. Ever.

As I stood in the queue to board the plane I had an overwhelming and dreadful question playing out in my head. What the fuck am I doing?

Baker Street by Gerry Rafferty had one of the hottest saxophone solos ever. The Granville Rail Disaster happened in January of that year, the worst rail disaster in Australia's history killing eighty three people. Chiron was discovered and, rocking the world in October, was Elvis Presley's death.

I lasted two weeks in England. That tiny provincial village was buried in a stale, pasty mediocrity where the men all drank at the pub every night and the wives were supposed to make pâté and get their hair done.

The crunch was when I met up with the managing director of the parent company with whom I had shared lunch back in Sydney. I was offered the position of managing the computer department and training staff at a very generous salary. The Trickster had taken a job the same day. For twenty pounds a week less.

No wife of mine gets more money than me.

He was outraged. This was April. I had never been so cold. Wind with razor sharp teeth.

Then he told me he was having an affair with Patti, his girlfriend from before we'd met. I phoned Jan in Sydney.

Who died? It's three in the morning.

We're coming home. Can I borrow some money?

How much?

Just our airfare.

Who's "our".

Me and Adam.

When?

Now.

Okay. I'll call you back.

Then, a few days later: We're leaving, I said.

What?

Poor Trickster. Stupid Trickster was confused.

Will you please drive us to the airport?

What are you talking about?

This afternoon. We fly out this afternoon. The tickets are on the desk at Heathrow.

Why?

I stared at him.

I can change again, I think.

I packed. When we landed in Sydney Adam and I, once again, moved back in with Jan.

The Trickster had racked up a debt of which I knew nothing. Bankcard and a bank account in joint names. See how foolish a girl I was? Still indoctrinated by the culture that had warped women, was I? Had not learned what the Trickster wanted?

I went to work with two computer programmers, freelancing.

I'd go into a small company, transfer their manual data to computer, train the staff and get paid large sums of money. I was rid of that debt within three months and bought my first motorcycle. I needed another coven.

CHAPTER 13

A woman riding a motorcycle in those days was rare. I didn't do so because I am an extrovert. I'm the opposite. Expediency. I wanted to get to work during peak hour without being caught in traffic. I trained with a crew of men, over three weekends, in the back streets of Artarmon. They set obstacle courses meant to pre-empt any emergency. The guys—a bunch of talented, ratbag, wild colonial boys—laid down everything from brick rubble to oil spills to fire hoses whipping water across the road. Fun. After our final training session we cruised all the way up to Gosford and back on the old Pacific Highway, with its merciless hairpin bends. When I applied for my license the fifty-odd year old man doing the testing had me ride beside him in the vacant lot out the back of the Road Traffic Authority building.

Don't put your foot down, he'd warned, smiling.

He moved like a sloth. My foot touched the ground once.

He failed me.

Why?

No control.

You're kidding.

You're a woman, he said. Dangerous enough for a man, let alone a woman.

Arsehole.

When can I come back?

He was, by then, behind the counter beside another man, who was maybe seventy. He overheard the conversation.

When you learn to ride, said my judge.

When can I come back? I asked the seventy year old man.

Three days.

I rode to the Milson's Point police station. Met with the motorcycle cops. I walked up to them at the desk in my leathers.

I just failed my driving test because I'm a woman, I said. They laughed. We cruised up the old Pacific Highway again, for over an hour and when we eventually got back to the station the cops shook my hand.

He fails you again you give us his name, said one.

I was tested three days later, assigned to the seventy year old man. He walked at a brisk pace out back of the building and passed me, wishing me luck for the future.

In June of 1978, in Sydney, a Gay and Lesbian Solidarity March was planned for the next month to honor the tenth anniversary of the Stonewall Riots. Five hundred people turned up. The night started out okay but later transformed into one of terror when the cops withdrew their protection halfway through the event. The protestors fled back towards Kings Cross in an attempt to avoid attacks from gay-hating blokes, but an all-out brawl ensued with arrests and blood on the streets. Those fighting for their rights didn't give up though. This was just the beginning. One year later the first Mardi Gras took place, the festival that, thirty five years later, attracts hundreds of thousands of visitors who line the streets for the spectacular parade and fill every event venue.

I was still on the hunt for another coven. I heard through the network that Roie, the witch who had arranged the meeting with the first coven, was ill with some unspoken ailment and had become something of a recluse so I didn't contact her.
    I tried in vain through the Adyar Bookshop. Run by theosophists. Who still considered witchcraft a thing of evil. Even though they sold them they kept Aleister Crowley's Thoth tarot pack under the counter for the same reason. So they were useless. The New Awareness Centre notice board yielded nothing. In 1978 the only thing even resembling a coven were a scatter of people calling themselves wiccans. One particular group, the coven of Phoenix, put out a small monthly magazine, the Wiccan Newsletter, in which they published information on Egyptian, Greek, Roman or Mesopotamian deities and mythology, the who's who of modern magic, spells, recipes and an advertising and contacts section. I bought a few copies before I decided to phone the publishers about a coven.
    The woman on the other end of the line was Copperhead a.k.a. lady Sybil, high priestess of the coven called Phoenix and editor of the newsletter. Her husband Blackadder was lord-Someone, her high priest.
    Upper case titles were and still are very big in the occult scene.

From lady and lord to magister, exemplar and ipsissimus. Hard core, old fashioned traditions of hierarchy. Deities being paired together like mustard and corn flour. Fixed systems. How was I going to get my rebellious head around accepting this? I was doing ritual on my own. Lunar rituals of full moon, dark and new moon, sabbats of solstice and equinox as well as the four fire festivals, a few healings, a bit of hexing, that sort of thing. I was comfortable with my work both in the shallow world and that of myth. I was now also teaching the *kristos* experiment at the New Awareness Centre. And kabbalah.

When I went to that first meeting with Sydney's hierarchical self-proclaimed authorized wicca folk (I'll call them Copperhead and Blackadder) I was flummoxed. Wicca, by the way of explanation, was not a word I had come across before. It was explained to me that it was the real word for witchcraft and that everything I thought I knew was wrong. They lived in a second storey flat in Lane Cove that had statuary from Pan to a winged Isis and everything in between. They wore ornate, gem encrusted silver ankhs and explained over the course of the initial meeting that this was the symbol of their high priesthood in this particular coven's tradition and that all "their" witches wore ankhs as they were also members of a group calling themselves The Fellowship of Isis that operated—of all places—out of Ireland.

I told them of the previous initiation. but they said, Oh, no. That doesn't count. You'll have to forget everything you learned there if you're to train with us. You'll have to initiate again if you're accepted.

I mumbled under my breath, but I doubt she heard or I'm certain I would not have been invited back.

They were known as Traditionalist British wicca and were descended through an unbroken chain of initiation to a man known as Old George Pickingill—a person responsible, so they claimed, for many, many covens throughout England. Crap, but I wasn't as informed then as I am now. Was he a cunning man, who knows, but what was introduced to the modern world as a tradition? Shameless plagiarism, hodge-podge, this goes with that; a mix and match monster that drew its sources anywhere from Doreen Valiente and Dion Fortune to freemasonry.

I was invited to meet with their coven in two weeks for afternoon tea.

The Sunday rolled around, and I brought the musician named

Pete along. A musician friend. A stoner, but they all were back then. Another Sagittarian.

The coven? Including Copperhead and Blackadder there were ten of them. Men and women. Couples, mostly. Straight. Not the kind of people I would smoke a spliff with. Was I a bigot? My friends were artists, poets, social and political activists, actors, musicians. They were heterosexual or gay or any variation thereof. Many were hippies or called themselves a newly misappropriated word, shamans. Or mediums. Most were extravagant or bohemian in some way. The coven of Phoenix was none of this. They were mums and dads. They all wore the ankh of the initiate of that sect, and one fellow who smoked a pipe, the young Slug, informed me he had been a hari krishna before becoming wiccan. Only Lynden was at all interesting because she was a professional tarot reader and worked clay.

What was I doing? The chatter was all banal. Were they behaving so on purpose to check me out? Was this a test? No mysticism. Not one magical hint. After three hours of pretending to be likeable I had to get away.

Downstairs I turned to Pete. What the fuck was that?

You're not considering them, are you?

You kidding? I shudder at the thought.

Copperhead phoned me within days. I had been discussed.

I'd like to formally invite you to become a member of the coven of Phoenix and to take initiation at the time of the full moon this coming August.

Okay. Uh. Thanks. Um—

We have traditional robes that denote rank. Brown for first year initiates, green for second year and red or black for high priesthood. Hand stitched, of course. There's a pattern in this month's Wiccan Newsletter. You must also acquire an athamé—a traditional, black-hilted knife, double-bladed of course—and a boline, that's a white-handled knife. Oh, and a goblet that we call a cup. You must also make a pentacle. They're traditionally of copper, quite thick and about five and a half inches across. Fit into your hand. Do you want to know what they're all for?

What was I doing?

You must also bring a meter each of red, green and blue cord, a white candle and a bottle of good red wine. Come to the covenstead at 7 o'clock. That'll be the eighteenth. Any questions?

Ah. No. Thank you.

You're welcome and blessed be.

I tried to find another coven. There was nothing. Where had all the witches of the sixties gone?

I navigated the bone ladder down into the deep ochre-red dark of my cave in mythworld. In that place I understand bears and owls and the wolf couple curled around their puppies against the winter snow higher than their bodies; too high to hunt. None of the chatter mattered. Not the clothing, not the objects, not the rules. I had a conversation with the cave—that mother—and one-sided because she refused to answer my need to validate the masks and dress-ups. Hypocrisy. I had to find the deeper meaning, or I would walk. I would not be able to acquiesce. I am a hunter, so I left that country and dove even deeper down into utter blackness.

After days of this I understood. Beyond the dogma all is art and curiosity. Wanton. The trappings were talismans, patterns. They had simply forgotten or did not know how to explain in the seemingly lost language. I also understood that the mystery represented by the sword is who matters. Some archetypal Arthur, you see. Disney did us a great disservice by giving us the visuals of a young unruly boy yanking a ready-made sword from a lump of rock in front of a lively, if not resentful bunch of courtly men and women. That's not the truth at all. The magic is in the first person to know that a lump of ore differed from its mother rock, on the inside of that cave. That when extracted and heated to red within the coals of a searing fire, beaten, thrust into the flames, tempered in brine, heated, beaten again, over and over until a length exists instead of a blob. Magic happens. Shaped and sharpened, hilted and adorned for use by another in defense of tribe. That's initiation. That journey to become other. That's what the sword represents. Not only in this rite but of itself.

The smack in the face realization that I would be in the company of that coven for a potential three years and three days was despairingly something to come to terms with. There was no one else.

CHAPTER 14

I eventually managed to afford to move away from Jan. Adam and I shared a terrace house in Paddington with Pete. One Saturday he was visited by a couple of old friends and he introduced us. Her name was Sandy and her partner Paul Tree. His family was rich and had disowned him when he became a stoner and a hippy and dropped out. Sandy was quite pregnant and she and I talked in the kitchen while the men went off somewhere to smoke bongs. She and Tree lived between Nambour and Gympie in Queensland and if I was ever up that way to please visit. They had a big old house on the farm Tree's father had given him to disappear.

They were twenty five miles from the nearest town, down a dirt road off the Old Bruce Highway. Pete's band secured gigs at both Nambour and Gympie. On the phone Sandy assured us that he, Adam and I could stay with them but not the band because the baby was due and she was having a homebirth and that their midwife, a guy, was living with them.

We loaded the equipment into a big old green Holden panel van and drove there.

We arrived and settled in and ate a meal prepared on the wood stove, drank wine in the firelight. The men went outside to smoke joints, including the midwife.

The following morning Sandy's contractions started. By mid-afternoon they were stronger. The midwife, probably suffering dope-induced paranoia, said he couldn't stay. If something went wrong he'd lose his insurance. He ended up under the table in a corner, only going outside to smoke another joint. Then he drove off in the only car left at the farm.

Pete and the others had driven to the gig on the coast. They wouldn't be back until later that night. Tree had gone down the hill to the old cow bales, a little cottage covered in sweet peas, to drop some acid, enjoy the wilderness and play his djembe to the nature spirits, heedless of Sandy.

Oh for fuck's sake, said Sandy. She reached for the bookshelf and opened Ina May Gaskin's *Spiritual Midwifery* at the back section.

You'll have to do it, she said.

The rush that passed though me was instantaneous, even as I read. I was entranced at the thought.

I made coffee, read quickly while also getting the massage oil ready because she was laboring in her back and her bum and thighs were in agony. Adam was there the entire time. He chose to stay.

She howled and grunted well into the afternoon, wearing only a fringed silk shawl. Most of the time she was on all fours, or squatted with me, or pushed deep into the dozens of cushions and pillows. Later waddling around the room, yelling and swearing, with me warming towels in the stove for her to hold under her belly. Around sunset she pushed out an enormous, lovely baby boy. We woke the midwife and at least got him to cut the umbilical cord and put the afterbirth in the fridge to be buried later. I just cried and cried. I was so elated that I hadn't killed anyone and so sad that I had not had this experience birthing Adam.

When Pete finally arrived back with the car, Sandy, the baby and Paul Tree all bundled in and drove the nearest hospital to get checked and register the birth. The doctor said she'd done magnificently and asked if there was anyone at home who could help her with breast feeding and chores. Yes, she said, another mother. The baby weighed eleven pounds and Tree wanted to name him Apple. I said nothing when they told me.

We went to Gympie for the gig the next afternoon but towards nightfall I had the very weird sensation that something was off kilter at the farm.

We have to go, I told Pete, frantic. He grudgingly drove us back.

What was strange was that when we got there the happy hippy new family were in bed and the baby was suckling contentedly.

Later though, when the rest of the house was sleeping I could not. I sat, restless, on the overstuffed sofa before the slow combustion stove while I waited for the kettle to boil. I made tea and crept out onto the small veranda, overhung by a massive mango tree and with a naked yellow light bulb socketed just above the door, to think about everything and nothing. The moon was fat but not full, so I everything—although monochrome—was easily visible. Python insinuated from within the mango tree and slid along the branch, defying gravity to suspend a length of its body in front of my face. I merely stood there. In the moment. Then Python coiled back onto the branch and began ecdysis. A stripper who didn't like to work an empty bar. I sipped my brew, a captive audience. The process took ages but was the second most exotic experienced in a mere twenty-four hours.

When the unclothing was complete Python took the nearest branch to me and sashayed, glittering and vivid with new color, up under the eaves and into the roof, likely home for the coming winter. I delicately gathered the shed skin and went indoors. I laid the gift out along the floor. Easily seven feet long. I cut the head from the body for myself, wrapped the talisman in cloth that I stuffed carefully in my backpack. The remainder I offered to Sandy who was awake, feeding Apple.

For you, I whispered.
Where'd you get that?
Just now, out in the tree. Magic medicine for the child.
She cried.

Just before driving back to Sydney the following day Pete and I argued because he went to light up a joint in the car. I said no. Not around Adam. He'd laughed, called me an anal fucking cow.

Again my son and I moved back to Jan's house. I sewed the shed skin into a long, thin black velvet tube and attached braided leather to make a necklace.

A month before my initiation I phoned Copperhead.
I'm sorry, I said.
What for?
I can't do this.
What?
I can't do this. I've changed my mind.
Stunned silence.
You realize you'll never get another chance in this lifetime?
Really?
Not until your next incarnation. There are astral rules about this that are very clear. This is an insult.

Where can I learn about astral rules?

She hung up on me.

By the end of that year I still had not found a coven, so I called Copperhead again.

I've changed my mind. I'd like to take that initiation.

That's not going to happen. I warned you. She was dramatic.

You also said that everything to do with someone wanting initiation had to be decided by the entire coven.

I did.

Then please ask them.

Mumble.

Pardon?

I will. But I know what they'll say.

Okay.

She phoned me back after the next esbat. The coven, with the exception of one person, had all said yes.

I was in. Then came an invitation to come to the covenstead because a young blacksmith, calling himself Wayland the Smith, had wares to sell. He was a big, hairy Viking of a man who worked with traditional pattern-welding techniques. Strong knives and swords that also happened to be beautiful, the tradition of which came out of Iron Age Celtic Britain, Ireland and Europe. Different metals forged together to form patterns from feathering to fern along the length of the blade. I bought a hand-made athamé from him that day. A long, thin tapering leaf-shaped blade with the tang passing right through the rowan wood hilt and ending in a pommel in the shape of a dragon's head.

Embarrassingly dull brown robe, hand stitched? Tick. Solid copper pentacle, engraved with the symbols of pentagram, moon and the horned god, using a hammer and chisel? Tick. Silver goblet sourced from an antique shop and lined with sealing wax because the inside of these old vessels is toxic? Got it. Boline with a white horn hilt from the camping store, the wine, the candle and the cords, done.

I was actually and delightedly nervous. I kept reminding myself of those places in the deep and the silence of its learning. That the Mystery would initiate me, not this husband and wife. I had fasted. Drunk only water for three days. I felt clear and unfettered from the world of daily life.

Adam was still up watching telly with Jan. He knew what I was doing. I kissed them goodnight, filled the panniers of my bike with what I had to take and rode through the darkness, along the deserted back road through the Lane Cove River Park. Twenty second of August 1980. Cold. Thick fur-lined leather gloves not preventing the tips of my fingers from tingling. Smells of stone and eucalypt and fern, the dampness of late winter and thick undergrowth. The perfume of the mud at the edges of the riverbank down the slopes to the right of me. I rode through the wraithlike mist that so often attends river valleys. Riding in peace. Glad of my decision. When I eventually re-entered the flow of traffic I was prepared.

Panniers over one shoulder, removing my gloves and blowing on chilled fingers. Then knocking on the flat door. Blackadder ushered me into the lounge room where the coven sat around eating snacks and sipping wine. I unpacked the panniers and all my prepared ritual things except the robe were taken from me. I was escorted to the bedroom to robe and prepare. The door closed and I sat on the bed, eyes drifting to a line of green and brown robes hanging from the curtain rod. Where was the ritual to take place? Were we to go elsewhere? Was there a secret room? Was I experiencing their first secret thing?

After what seemed ages the door opened. Copperhead and Blackadder entered with the red and green cords and a black cloth. I was asked if I wanted to change my mind: "What was done could not be undone," and my life would be in forfeited if I betrayed either oath or coven. People were not yet publicly willing to come out and claim witchcraft. It could still get a body in trouble.

Ah. Okay. No.

Blindfolded with the cloth, my wrists bound with one cord and an ankle tied with the other they left me sitting as the door closed behind them. I waited. To the susurration of my own breathing. Then the door creaked open again. Within moments the room was full of the sounds and smells of people. I could hear the rustle of clothing. Then I was left alone again.

I heard muffled incantations and invocations through the walls of the bedroom and understood that the ritual was happening in the sitting room. How? I thought, recalling all the furniture.

People re-entered and took my arms. I was spun around on the spot several times. To disorient me, I imagined. I was led into the lounge room, smelling of joss sticks. Despite all I can tell of my experiences I can't speak much of this. I swore a binding oath. What I can say is that with the point of a sword against my skin I was asked many questions and I answered them honestly. Kept firmly in mind was that I was here for the Mystery. I was warned that my weapons would turn against me and a thousand other terrors befall my family if I betrayed my oaths to Phoenix. What? Threat? I shoved my grizzly bear behind me when she reared on hind legs.

The ritual was short, the blindfold and cords removed, and I blinked. Four candles in candle-holders were on each of the corners of the coffee table. Incense sticks burned in a holder. Statuary was everywhere and the other coven members, holding photocopies of their verbal responses in the ritual, were all secret smiles of conciliation and pride. Copperhead and Blackadder, known as lord and lady within the circle, were dressed in ornate red robes and jewel-encrusted ankhs, the others in brown or green.

At the conclusion of the ritual the circle was broken, I was kissed on each cheek by each person with the catchphrase, Merry meet and merry part and merry meet again, before more food and wine was consumed and I was given the gift of a small silver ankh necklace. I was informed that the god and goddess have many names and are from many pantheons (misappropriated from non-Celtic cultures). Blackadder quoted the Dion Fortune line "all gods are one god and all goddesses are one goddess..." The expression is utterly untrue, of course, and puts wicca within the same basket as any religion and—almost—monotheism, just with many names from many stolen lands thrown together. In denial of the indigenous past of each individual European and Near Eastern sovereignty and that the names refer in the most part to natural forces: earth, animal and other species' behaviors and totemic symbiosis with individual, tribe or clan, weather and human beings' relationship to them all.

Do I regret what happened? Absolutely not. Was my time with that coven a time of learning? Absolutely not.

That night I was informed that my training would happen in three stages: first rite was for a year and a day during which time I would acquire my book of shadows a bit at a time, which turned out to be photocopy sheets handed out at sabbats and esbats, attend their rituals, learn the rudiments of spell casting and be a thoroughly good, straight girl. Then I would undergo the initiation of second rite and could wear a green robe. There would be various duties I would be told of when the time came. Second rite was for a year and a day and was the priest or priestess in preparation for the third rite, high priesthood, at which time I could remain an elder with the coven or hive off to form my own, but that Copperhead and Blackadder would be my overseers for yet another year to be certain I didn't screw up.

Once I then trained people to high priesthood they would hive off to form their own covens. Like beehives. When I had three of these 'hive-offs' I could officially claim the title of witch queen. I went along with the hierarchy at the time.

In my teens with the first coven I'd been instructed that witchcraft is made up of three interwoven threads. One green: learning to deal with money, securing a home, learning herb lore, animal husbandry if applicable, weaving, sewing, even pottery, how to look after myself and others, how to grow a garden. Variations of that theme. I was already adequate with a bow so if a time came to shoot dinner I was your go-to person. All the above to ensure survival. The second is red: most witches have an artistic nature and red line witches pursue talents accordingly. The third thread is black. This is the way of prophesy and divination, mysticism, study and scholarship, trance and the art of clairvoyance. We learned about all three but were told we would probably only excel at one. A natural talent. I was lousy at green line witchery until many, many years later.

With Phoenix there was no instruction.

CHAPTER 15

I was with the coven for a year. Copperhead and Blackadder despised me. I asked too many questions and wore leathers. I challenged why they presented coffee-table decoration, and statuary on shelves, as witchcraft. I questioned why we were using Doreen Valiente's invocations if our book of shadows was so secret. I questioned the photocopied rituals that never varied, like a dogma, like a sledgehammer. I couldn't help myself. They only went outdoors to go to the shops. Never wandered a wood or forded a brook. Never spoke of them, only chanted love of them, like a dirge to something that had died. Of our symbiosis: *I am the beauty of the green earth and the white moon among the stars—*

Writing the book of shadows was optional. We could just as easily keep the bits of paper in the ring binder. I wrote in calligraphy, in a book I hand-made and bound in red leather. I added all the rituals as I was given them, including the first rite initiation but not second or third. We were not permitted, as brown robers, to know what happened on those secret nights. Copperhead had us all sewing little cloth spell bags. By the hundreds. Supposedly so we would become really familiar with the practice. They were filled with herbs and trinkets and sold to help her pay for costs.

Through that coven I expanded my connections with other occultists not only the Sydney scene but around the world. They certainly were networkers. On the phone in their flat I spoke to Doreen Valiente in England and Carl Weschcke when Llewellyn Worldwide was a small, American New Age publisher.

Whether aloud, or within the sanctuary of a mythic inner cave, I challenged and questioned and yearned for intelligent conversation. For one year.

Then I was told I was to take second rite.

Okay.

What had I achieved to deserve advancement? Nothing. Catchphrases. I bought the green cloth, stitched the plain garment, tied thread around a white candle, bought the red wine, placed all in the panniers of my bike and took that same road at the same time of year.

Once in the flat Copperhead and Blackadder took me into the bedroom and shut the door.

We've changed our minds.

What do you mean?

You're to go all the way through tonight.

What?

We want to bestow high priesthood on you.

Why?

The time is appropriate.

Oh. Okay.

You're sure?

If you think.

We haven't told the others yet, so please don't say anything until we make the announcement.

Sure.

We then pretended to socialize with the others as though nothing was afoot. As the night wore on the circle was cast, the candles on the coffee table lit, the incense was smoking and the guardians of the watchtowers to the four directions invoked. Even though I had the blindfold over my head and my wrists were tied, I was in the circle throughout the full moon esbat. I was again at the point of a sword. Again asked questions. The blindfold and bindings were removed. I was declared the high priestess *lady* Rowena.

That's all really. The candles were snuffed out. But there was still coven business to conclude and that was always done before the circle was broken. Copperhead and Blackadder then made the announcement.

As of tonight the coven of Phoenix is taking sabbatical indefinitely. We apologize to all of you and sincerely hope you are not too disappointed. You have two choices. You can work as solitaries until we re-establish ourselves in the future or... You can join lady Rowena when she establishes her new coven, if she agrees.

Silence.

Do you, lady Rowena?

What?

Agree?

Yes. Of course. Anyone want to join me?

Every hand went up except one. I looked at the Slug and sighed. Copperhead and Blackadder unexpectedly stood, crossed the floor to their bedroom and slammed the door. We sat in stunned mutual understanding that they thought their initiates were so devoted that they would prefer to work at solitary wicca, indefinitely, on the off chance Phoenix reopened. The following week the newest edition of their newsletter was published. In the advertising section towards the back of the rag was a notice. A newly formed coven run by the Lady Rowena, late of the coven of Phoenix is open for business. They listed my phone number and suggested anyone seeking initiation hook up. In those times one's ritual name was never spoken outside a cast circle. They had their revenge and I changed my name.

They weren't done being pissed off at me yet, however. I took a phone call from Copperhead asking me to pop by for a cup of tea. I did. For criticism.

You know you can't dress the way you do anymore.

What?

No one will respect you as high priestess if you don't act the part.

I put the cup down, stood as languidly as I could and took up my leathers and helmet.

Acting? If I have to dress like a monkey to gain respect I don't need the circus anywhere near me.

Wait, I'll open the door.

A tradition they'd invented that meant the person leaving would always come back. I pulled the door open ahead of her.

I was done waiting for the walls to fall in on me. Life was difficult enough and they had no idea how sad it was. And angry. Just not like they wanted. Enough to stop some unseen but seriously violent monster from jumping on my back and devouring me alive. The person Jan and Eric had paid for me to be was long-dead.

Problem was, there was no plan B.

CHAPTER 16

Saturday morning. Jan and I were in the kitchen. Adam was glued to the cartoons on telly while he ate his breakfast.

Read my cards, she said.

I went to my room to gather the pack.

She shuffled and I laid them out on the table. There, in the center, was the sun card crossed by the ace of pentacles.

You're coming into money.

When?

About now.

I was doing the trance work at Julie's house the following Monday night but Jan was so pissed off she phoned.

You're a lousy tarot reader, she said.

What's happened?

I bought a Lotto ticket.

And?

I didn't win.

She hung up.

The following Saturday I woke from a very lucid dream. I'd been in the room of an old woman. I got her out of bed and into a lilac chenille dressing gown and a pair of slippers. We left the nursing home by an outside staircase. I got her to a railway station and to the ticket office.

Destination, and how many travelling? the ticket guy asked.

Hampton. Two please.

Only got one. You pay for hers and you pick yours up at the other end. So you can get back

At the halfway mark the train pulled into a station for a bathroom break. I helped the old woman into a cubicle and shut the door. Then I woke up.

That morning, with coffee in hand I went towards the garden, almost passing Jan on the veranda. But then I stopped. I told her the dream.

The Hampton bit's funny, though. Must have something to do with Northampton in my unconscious.

I dreamed you gave birth to an old woman, she said.

Moments later the phone rang and Jan went to answer. She was pale when she returned.

What?

Muriel's dead.

Oh.

Died in a nursing home yesterday. I've got to go down to Melbourne for the funeral. Then she looked at me, her eyes like a shark's, only blue.

The funeral parlor's in Hampton, she said. Suspicious, despite wanting what I could tell her. She booked the train to Melbourne.

Three weeks later she was a hundred and thirty five thousand dollars richer.

Why? She'd asked when the solicitor read out Muriel's last will and testament.

You told her to fuck off both times she offered you money after you and Eric separated. She had respected that.

Jan was beginning to change. She was still obsessed with her "shows" but her life had become smaller and smaller, her main contact with the outside world usually the sister-person, usually to babysit. She was becoming repetitive and angry in general. Retrospectively these would have been the early-onset years of Alzheimer's that eventually put her in a nursing home.

I was offered a job at Harper and Row, the publishing company, transforming their manual system to computer and training the staff. Friedel interviewed me for the position. Word had spread about my work because not many did what I was doing. We liked each other that first day but then she introduced me to the managing director, Merv Watson, a man in his eighties. He said Hello Ly. I said,
Hello Merv.

He blanched visibly, walked into his office and slammed the door.

What? I said to Friedel.

You have to call him Mister Watson.

I snorted but she was serious, so I left.

As far as I was concerned that was the end of the matter but the next day Friedel phoned and said I had the job. I paused, saying nothing. Yes, she answered my silence. You can call him Merv.

The money was enough and the hours my own. Friedel was my boss and that of the entire accounts department, a meek and suppressed group of eight women. They sat at a very long table, with erasers and pens and rulers and all the office equipment of the era, were so polite to each other that I was afraid to say boo.

Friedel was a screamer and if someone annoyed her she'd get right in the face of the offending woman and yell. Her belittling of the staff during my first few weeks there was something I initially just observed. When she screamed in my face, however, I yelled right back, don't you ever fucking-well do that again.

The other women cowered, watching from behind their hands, waiting. But Friedel laughed.

That was really fun, she beamed. Let's go do lunch.

We all went. The tension in the office evaporated. Some people just need a good enough reason to change.

We became friends. When I bought an A4 poster in a news agency that said When God Made Man She Was Only Joking, we printed out twenty copies before work one morning. We snuck from office to office, placing them on the desks of the most chauvinist of the men. Women, remember, even then, were in the accounts department while the blokes were in sales and all positions of management.

Months later I had a vivid dream about that snake I'd encountered after helping Sandy give birth at Kin Kin. I dreamed I woke up and in the bend of my knees was Python. He was ragged. I could communicate with him.

What are you doing here?

Visiting.

I got out of bed, showered, woke Adam and made us breakfast, got him ready for school, urged the snake into a large round wicker basket that I dreamed I'd borrowed from Julie, and went to work.

Once in my office I opened the lid and showed the women what was inside. They were all *ooing* and *ahhing* when Friedel came in. It's poisonous, she said.

No, I protested, he's a fucking python.

Go home, said the dream Friedel.

I was angry and sad but I slid Python back into the basket. I walked up the road. On the other side was a stairway between shops with a sign indicating a serum laboratory. I climbed the steps and asked if someone could have a look and tell me if Python was poisonous. A white-coated lab man obliged by slithering out of the basket and lying full length along the bench with his mouth open. He did an examination and said that indeed: deadly.

Tell them to take my fangs out then, Python thought at me.

You serious?

Take 'em out.

Okay.

Can you remove the fangs, please? Will that solve the problem?

Sure will.

And he did.

Python, none the worse for the extractions, slid back into the basket. I caught a bus for home. All the way he laughed low and grunty. Other passengers heard and must have thought I was schizophrenic. I hissed at Python to shut up and was ignored. When, alone in my room, I took the lid off the basket he glided raggedly onto my carpet and looked at me with lidless, black eyes.

People are silly, he said.

I know.

You'll figure out our relationship and why I came, when you work out what my name means.

Not Python then?

Charochawtakwa.

Can't you just tell me?

No.

I woke up clutching the snakeskin talisman around my neck. Not long after that I received an invitation to the first-ever Gathering of the Tribes, a collaboration between a group calling itself the Bear Tribe (years later denounced as a con) and a coven named Y Tylwyth Teg, from Wales. They would accommodate me if I paid my airfare. I could not afford to go but I wrote to Wabun, an official of the forthcoming gathering, and in the letter I told the story of the birth and the snake. She wrote back saying *chawtakwa* was their word for a storyteller who wanders from tribe to tribe with news and wisdom but that she didn't know what *charo* meant. The first part of the name, I know now, was to be an aspect of my destiny.

Twenty third of December, the day after midsummer solstice, and work was closing for the holidays in the early afternoon. One of the women in our department had offered to gather lunch orders for the entire staff so that we could concentrate on the last of our work before a three week shut down.

    Late in the morning a bearded man popped his head around the door and said, Who's the lunch girl?

    Fuck off, I suggested. There is no lunch girl, you rude man. Jodie has volunteered to take orders.

    He snorted and walked out mumbling.

    Nevill Drury, anthropologist. An editor there. The following January he asked his secretary if she knew anyone in Sydney who was an expert in tarot. She'd worked with me when I set up the system at UPS Copiers and we were friends. She told me later she'd smiled as innocently as she could when she'd said she did.

    Who?

    Downstairs.

    What?

    Ly, the computer woman.

    Isn't she—?

    Yes, my cohort grinned.

    So I went to his office. He was in the middle of creating a pictorial tarot book and wanted an opinion on the images that he'd commissioned for the major arcanum. We talked for ages, neither of us mentioning the snit at the end of last year.

    As I was leaving he asked, are you wiccan or a kabbalist.

    I'm wicked, I replied, having misheard him.

    He laughed.

    We became friends.

Three significant events, like threads in a tapestry, wove together that year to form a new picture of the *who* of me, what destiny would reveal and where witchcraft was leading me. Mike Harner released The Way of the Shaman through Nevill Drury's U.K. affiliate Unity/Prism, and Mike came to Australia to teach the Native American technique. Nevill attended his workshops and later asked whether I would participate in the trance experiments with him. I said sure. Through Nevill and these shamanic journeys I met Moses Aaron, a professional storyteller.

Moses, in his scarlet vest with the little mirrors embroidered along the hem, ragged jeans and colorful cap, with his most Jewish of families and his capacity for remembering, vast. He conducted storytelling workshops at a center in Paddington and, years later, had several books published. Nevill had arranged for us to meet. He wanted to see fireworks; thought we'd hate each other. Fight. We became lovers instead.

In the summer of 1980 Nevill, Moses and I presented our shamanic workshops at one of the earliest Mind, Body and Spirit Festivals in Australia. There we met Liz, a.k.a Tree Lady, who, in ex-army gabardine cammo pants, and naked to the waist, was to become my second initiate. She studied with us for a year but had, before meeting us, been accepted into a chiropractic college in California. We kept in touch for a while and tried to find serious witches in the States but failed. Last we heard she had gone onto a Hopi reservation and was studying with teachers of that culture.

The second catalyst was Lynden, one of the initiates I'd inherited from Phoenix. She read tarot through a group called Fortune Fair. They hired oracles and prophets of one technique or another, from palmistry to astrology, and set them up in plazas and shopping centers, sitting at little card tables with shiny cloths or velvet draped over them; were asked to dress exotically, to only do ten minute sessions to keep the queues moving, to keep the shoppers shopping.

Fortune Fair's main office and reading rooms were right across the way from Barry Salkield's Star Goddess, a ritual supply and book shop, in the Royal Arcade. He was the ipsisimus of the magical order called the Golden Phoenix. He and I had become good friends by then but most of his initiates didn't know that, with the exception of three mutual friends, Tim Hartridge, a leading figure in the movement since the seventies, Tony Mierzwicki, author of Graeco-Egyptian Magick and Andrew Polis, an initiate of Barry's at the time, who eventually came to disdain the pomp of the good old boys' club, dogmatically hierarchical-, or *magickal*-anything and went to live with, and be initiated by, the Oglala Sioux.

I was on Pitt Street in the heart of the city. A busy Saturday and I'd spent hours sitting in the gutter of a side street replacing my bike chain. Harem pants, a slip of a tank top and covered in grease.

I'd finally arrived at the Star Goddess to purchase incense supplies. Barry brewed up some thick Turkish coffee in the back room before joining several men at the big round table that dominated the center of the shop. No one except Barry knew me and I was ignored as they continued a conversation about all things *high magick*.

The Order of the Golden Phoenix's member began a conversation about kabbalah. Such a god-bothering bunch of drivel and I interjected with some comment about plagiarizing Dion Fortune. This began an epic argument with him quoting one tome after another and me cutting him down.

Can't you ever just speak for yourself? I'd asked, eventually.

There's never been a decent woman magician, let alone a kabbalist, he spat, so fuck you.

He banged his chair back, quite theatrically, and stormed out. Barry thought the whole was the funniest thing he'd seen and heard in a long time even though I'd just lost him his best herbalist.

He's a wanker, I said. He never once mentioned Maud Gonne. She'd been Yeats lover and an initiate of the Golden Dawn. worked with MacGregor Mathers and his wife Moina, also an initiate, in their exploration of the Celtic magical tradition.

The third event was the Identity Hunter. The first person I would initiate into my first coven. A genealogist, eccentric and fellow Sagittarian.

CHAPTER 17

Time is such an agreement. And does not exist in three dimensions. And yet we seem to have too much on our hands, on our side, kill time to enable us to have more time. Never have enough. The excuse we give to not do a thing now.

We spend time.

We live time, little or long.

What time seems to me to be is either memory or possibility. Perhaps also observance, the being 'in' of life. The illusion of a linear intellectual construct, nothing more. The theory of time does not describe the seasons of reds or greens, nor when to pick wild strawberries or to watch for the birth of the lambs. Its fantasy certainly does not define us or our seeming mortality. No time has passed since I gave birth to my children and yet forty summers and winters have unfolded. I have not aged but my body has.

Time is one of the components of contemplation in all my tarot classes. Students are encouraged to crack the notion open like a prison door and to remember what we learn. To remember is to give a body to that which seems to no longer exist and, therefore, to give life in some other fashion. To recall is to invoke into manifestation someone who may have hidden an eternity ago, someone like a knowledge spirit.

Time nudges us like an elephant in the room. Exciting us if an anticipated event creeps closer or terrifying us if representing doom or the concept of loss. We are patronizingly informed that time heals all wounds and that when children are eccentric they are sure to grow up and settle down. It's in synergy with music. When an Irish fiddle plays a jig I tap my foot in time. An event that brings relief from a problem is said to be timely. In time. Sometimes. In the nick of time. About time. Ironically, the expressions are seemingly endless. It's a thing some think they can kill, or bide.

Memory is fickle; an impossible to trap animal. Might need nudging from where the stories languish in the vast spaces of the mansion of the mind or within half-forgotten communities with legends passed down, or else hidden amongst the religious texts, rolled and covered with dust in some stone monastery. Even disguised in plain sight within history books that extort what really happened until some anarchist researcher dares to challenge the lie. But nothing is gone once known.

Forgetting can lead to the sleep of freedom and the destruction of things we have no right to destroy. That's never truer than in the twenty first century. Answers are at the click of an app. Letters rarely written. Photography and film are digital and could disappear in the blink of an eye should some despot introduce censorship and erase what they deem fit.

Ancient film footage, photographic negatives, hidden and preserved in deep archives or the cellars of the dead, can reveal events not realized. Revelation.

Martin McKenna, known as the Dog Man, left his home in Limerick, Ireland, because his father was a brutal drunk, and Martin had had enough of hurt. An admitted hyperactive, Martin lived on the streets of Limerick with a pack of dogs from when he was eleven. He is a famed dog whisperer and lives in Bangalow, Northern New South Wales, with his wife, an author, and three children. He came to my house one day at Willy McElroy's suggestion (lead singer of the Wild Zinnias). I thought I might make a documentary of his life. That didn't happen but he fertilized my mind.

Martin is intelligent. He is also non-literate. Has been diagnosed with ADD but he doesn't think that. He said it was a handy label. He is proud of his memory. We went from sunlight to twilight discussing Celtic legends, in particular those of Ireland. I've gained most of my knowledge from books whereas he'd been told by old people and he remembered. He'd later been given the opportunity to learn to read and write but he was afraid of wrecking his memory.

Reading makes you lazy, he said. Why remember when you have your books to refer to?

At the end of our conversation he shook the back of my neck. A sign of friendship in dog language.

Forgetting seems encouraged by mindless things. Like advertising. Like scrolling through pithy social media feeds. Like a LAN game played in dark rooms by boys and men who have never seen bloodshed and kill to unwind from a day at the office.

In 2005 a series of riots erupted at Cronulla in Sydney. A sectarian thing. According to some reports a group of teens of Middle Eastern appearance, presumed to be Lebanese, allegedly attacked a group of life savers, an icon of Australian beach culture.

A week later a crowd of around five thousand Anglo boys and girls, many wearing the Australian flag draped over their shoulders, went after the Lebanese youth or anyone remotely Arab-looking. A bloody business. And not one of those white boys or girls understood that the parents or relatives of those Lebanese-Australians had fled their homeland to survive.

Adam and I were on a plane in 1978 on our way to England. We stopped over at Beirut airport to refuel and several armed soldiers boarded with their rifles at their shoulders. We had a gun in our faces for an hour. A mass exodus of a million people happened because of that war. There were an estimated one hundred and twenty thousand fatalities. No wonder these kids were angry. They had traumatized parents and grandparents. They were not asked why they were angry. No one talked about post-generational trauma. The deepest cut, in some way, was the use of a flag as a symbol of that hooliganism as though we were a nation. As though we had an inherent right to be here.

We are not. We do not. While the butcher's apron emblem still sits in the corner of the Australian flag we are a colony. We may have a federation and we may seem a nation, but we are not. Neither do we have an identity. People are trying to create one in the twenty first century; a bogun country that has relearned to spit on the sidewalk and considers ockerism to be cool. I don't. No one said sorry to the First Nation people until 2008. Still, many years later, conditions for most Aboriginal people are appalling. To drape that flag is to razorblade their plight with even deeper cuts.

Tarot predicts. Knows things before they seemingly have happened. Has taught me to live in the now and I do. Like there was a choice. The philosophy? What is today about? What do I do? What is important? What is next? I rarely look back for three reasons: I deplore nostalgia and would that, in the criticism of this work, an axe be taken to my words if there is even a trace because one cannot undo history, and because regret is pointless. I consider retrospection to be self-indulgence and yet is the opiate of many and can be used to justify all manner of blame.

Two things seeded this memoir: Camille, my next door neighbor in Brunswick Heads where I lived for two years was a screenwriter. She bought the option for the screenplay of a book written by a man who discovered his dead mother's diaries that she'd hidden between the ceiling and the roof of her home. She'd been the mistress of Eduard Roschmann, known as the Butcher of Riga, an S.S. officer in Prague during WWII and she had documented all of his brutality, both to her and others, including the murders of many. He'd thought his mother lived and died without incident.

The second was a client, Irina Baronova, who came to me for a reading in her eighties. I hadn't known who she was at the time, but tarot was clear she was going to be published and tarot was also clear that the publishers would find her. Some stories need to be recorded if for no other reason than to pass on to one's family. Everyone has a story.

You'll be gifting someone, I say to clients when ask why they should keep a record of their lives.

Memory. And things worthy of remembering. And the farce of those who do not know or do not remember, or else choose not to ask. The grief, as with dementia, of the confusion of forgetting.

The people I have initiated spent three days and three nights in a state of liminality. They didn't eat but they could drink water or herbal tea. Many chose to stay at our covenstead, because they also didn't speak. Easier than elsewhere. This allowed them plenty of contemplation on what they had decided to dedicate their lives to. Gave three days to change their minds, a thing most necessary if there is even the slightest doubt. They were always warned that something would happen. That their decision had nothing to do with me or them. Was like a Butterfly Effect and always culminated in something or someone's death.

I don't have a problem with the death by the way. When I occasionally mention this to the individual they will assume a sacrifice is made. No. That's an Abrahamic concept.

Simply something or someone dies. This could be about balance; something to do with the mystery of initiation being a pseudo-death. Could also be coincidence. Sara accidentally drove over her kitten on the way to her ritual initiation. She was gutted.

I have initiated so many people over the years that I don't even remember the first time a death happened. Seemed to creep in. Like my banishing of stray spirits or trapped emotions from people's houses. That started out fine back in the days with Julie, but something happened over the years and I ended up unintentionally nuking all personality from a place. I've stopped, by the way.

This night was the last in the lead up to Cuckoo's initiation. I received a phone call from Zenith, a marriage and death celebrant, founder and director of the Natural Death Centre. At around ten at night. She told me that four teenagers had died in a fire and one of them was Jessica Donnelly. Her mother Linda was asking for me. I dragged Cuckoo along. He didn't want to come but resigned himself. All the first responders, parents and relatives of the children, social workers, medical personnel, clergy and celebrants were at the community center when we arrived. I sent the Cuckoo to a corner so he could experience what went on around him while I went to Linda. She collapsed into my arms in utter devastation. Jesse wasn't her only child and her brothers and sisters were likewise held, until we all just crumpled onto the floor in a clutch. I had nothing to say. There was nothing.

She loved your book, said Linda.

I rocked her like a child in my arms.

She had so much respect for you.

I kept rocking.

She considered herself a witch, you know.

I know, I whispered.

Will you come to the funeral?

I will.

I stayed with her until her family took her home, and the following night the Cuckoo took initiation.

The funeral the next week was monumental. Tattoo Zak accompanied me but before he arrived I prepared a small bottle of red wine, my chalice and my athamé just in case they were needed. Because I had a feeling.

A processional funeral. Teenage boys on BMX bikes or skateboards lined the streets in homage. The procession was a serpent that snaked all along the main road and all along the back streets for easy three miles. To the cemetery. There would have been at least five hundred people.

A hole in the ground, fake grass covering the pile of dirt dug up, the coffin on the ground on the other side of the grave, white roses on the closed lid. A white marquee, with a large framed and wreathed photograph of Jesse, and a mike on a stand. Three strangers—preachers from the Salvation Army with bibles—said all sorts of religious bunkum about Jess going to a better place while Jess's blonde relative from the Gold Coast stood with them waiting to say her eulogy. Linda was prostrate beside the coffin.

Tattoo Zak and I stood towards the rear of the crowd, wondering what on earth was going on when the blonde tapped the microphone. She spoke for quite a while and I had all but zoned out until she began discussing Jess's appearance, her Goth makeup and clothing, her black lipstick and nail polish, her piercings, and that beneath all of that there had been a really pretty girl and that, had she lived, she would have grown out of it.

I don't know what she would have said had I not interrupted but I did, because Jesse had every right to express her identity however she chose, and what that woman said, funeral or no funeral, was insulting.

I never did, I called out.

Heads swiveled in my direction. Kids applauded and hooted. Linda turned towards me and held out her hand to me.

I walked to her and took her in my arms. When I pulled back I took my ritual things from my bag. I filled the chalice with red wine, consecrated silently with my athamé in front of the hushed crowd. Then Linda and I both held the goblet aloft. That's when everything that had been annoying about the coven of Phoenix paled into insignificance. I had learned that book of shadows off by heart so I could say what I said without feeling like a hypocrite.

I am the beauty of the green earth

And the white moon amongst the stars

> And the mystery of the waters
> And the desire in the heart
> Arise and come to me
> For I am the soul of nature.
> From me all things proceed
> And to me all things return
> So before my face, beloveds,
> Let your innermost selves
> Be unfolded in the rapture of the infinite.

Linda drank from the chalice first, then I did. It was passed around the crowd and unerringly returned to me. Even made big, badass Tattoo Zak cry.

I wrote on Facebook a while back about Jesse and what had happened. An old friend of the four that died, Nyree, was initially upset that I brought up a painful memory for her and who was I and why had I done this? And why only Jesse? I wrote that I was angry that no memorial had been put on the site of that fire. That the bulldozers couldn't wait to raze the burned out flats to the ground. That the site stood abandoned for a year, surrounded by cyclone fencing but was then sold and developers moved in. She said that if she had a million bucks she would buy the whole block and make a little Goth-punk garden and I agreed. For the record, and to quote Nyree, "Scott 22, Rosie 17, Jazz 16, li'l Jess 14."

Serenity, then fifteen years old, had planned to hang out with Jesse and the others that night as they were all friends. At the last minute something caused her to change her mind.

Shops were eventually built on the site of the fire with a café, just across the lane, called, eye-wateringly, St Elmo's Fire.

CHAPTER 18

In late 1980 I was managing a coven, reading tarot in my spare time, working with astral projection, putting others through the kristos experiment and creating my first extensive grimoire. Covered in green leather and handwritten in calligraphic script. Out went the brown, green and red ranking system of the Phoenix coven and in came your basic black. In came the rituals of dark moon and new moon. In came the requirement for each initiate to write their own book of shadows by hand and to learn every invocation by heart so that they would eventually play jazz with the magic instead of chopsticks. No one would be lazy enough to be reading any of our coven's rituals. How could one work properly while wondering how to pronounce *bagabi laca bachabe* or *imbolg* (it's imelich, by the way)?

I reworked all the rituals to attune them with the southern hemisphere as what part of sunwise didn't everybody get? Initially the others were horrified, thinking they were working widdershins and still deeply conditioned to consider such as sinister, in the same bigoted way the Roman catholic church did, whipping the hands of southpaws till they learned to write right handed.

Where words are concerned I can experience difficulties as I hear literally what another person says and often people throw their words away or are quoting alternative sources and pretending the words are their own. Or any of a vast number of uncomfortable variations, I see the words. And the coven members were, in the early days, brainwashed by outmoded terminology and theist-speak.

Training to think analytically and creatively, as I had with the first coven and the Independent Theatre, were the first conversations in a series of long, drawn-out, cup-of-tea weekend afternoons with those original wiccans. None were witches, witches are feral in the true sense of the word.

After almost a year I ditched the ankh for a pentagram, but I was still wearing the former one afternoon in a fabric shop in Chatswood. I was admiring a bolt of black raw silk when a woman walked up to me and indicated my talisman.

You know that's a symbol of the devil, don't you, she insinuated, smiling.

Really?

I've been well informed.

If you'll excuse me—

She grinned and pulled her own from beneath her T-shirt. Ornate and engraved with arcane symbols, some unknown to me.

I'm Fran. I work here. Can I help you?

I need this, I think, I said stroking the exotic silk.

For a new robe?

Exactly.

Spare no expense.

I lifted the bolt of cloth from the shelf.

Would you like to come to my place for a glass of red? My flat mates are also into magic.

Sure. Where?

And she wrote down her phone number and the address in Potts Point.

Tonight?

Friday night?

Friday night it is.

I rode to Potts Point and climbed the stairs to their second storey flat. Fran introduced me to Wayne-somebody and the Historian, a mix of a young John Cleese and something very Goth. Occult paraphernalia was everywhere, as were posters of Aleister Crowley and Iron Maiden.

We sat at a table by the window and talked. I stayed pretty sober but the wine and nibbles, conversation covering vast swathes of arcane lore and history, were consumed until well after midnight.

Wayne was by far the chattiest of the bunch as well as the heaviest drinker. Our discussion turned to debate as the hours continued and the debate became argument—at least, from his viewpoint. I annoyed the shit out of him by refusing to agree.

He stood. And swayed.

I do not concede defeat.

We all waited.

Fuck you all then. And goodnight.

Like a tree felled by loggers he pitched backwards onto the mattress behind him on the floor. Lights out.

As the weeks and months unfurled with the pale leaf bud of Sydney's European spring I came to know the Historian better. He was twenty four years old. At six feet tall he did not lean forward or drop his nose to speak to me, unapologetic of his height. Raven haired, severely blue eyes, pierced ears. He was beautiful, daunting and gay.

Since the age of seventeen the Historian had been a scholar of all things considered 'occult': Blavatsky's *Isis Unveiled*, Israel Regardie's material but particularly the O.T.O and the works of Aleister Crowley, books about *Chaos Magick* and Franz Bardon on hermetic mysticism. We practiced the exercises in the book *Initiation into Hermetics*, together in later years.

He asked thick, challenging questions about witchcraft because he was confused. Prior to meeting me he had considered the work low magic, worthy only of peasants and women in the suburbs but I explained the symbiosis with wildlings, relationships with forest, crag, cave and unseen things brought into this world by art or dreams, ecologically-centered, hair-raising. This rang true to him and he empathized with its non-religious, non-dogmatic, and especially, its non-hierarchical mysticism, its art, its weavings within the worlds of myth to manifest in some unpredictable future. I didn't gloss what wicca was presented as but that I did adhere to, and respect, the ritual and trappings. A person agreed that they could agree to the theater of wicca and still be witch. Similar to a horse learning the tricks of an equestrian event while still dreaming of galloping with her herd.

I'd taken one of the initiates of my inherited coven, Irene, through the ritual of high priesthood with the secret hope that she and her now partner/lover (the little ex-hari krisna Slug boy) would go away. They insisted on continuing as they'd been taught by

Copperhead and Blackadder and maintained relations with them. Her immediate action had been to initiate Slug to high priesthood and they formed their own coven. Wiccan covens in those days were rigid in their rule that a man must initiate a woman, a woman a man. Plus, a blatant homophobia at a time when that was becoming absurd. And whilst a high priestess outranked her consort within this tradition, the thinking was that on the whole a coven was better placed to have a couple, preferably a husband and wife, at the top of the hierarchy. It was all fetishist, but they presented as very straight and didn't believe in fucking around.

That tired banality was soon to be ousted by the myriad offshoot styles of wicca that erupted over the next decade, from Z Budapest's dianic wicca, from seax wicca and faerie wicca to the church of all worlds that was inspired by the 1961 Robert Heinlein book, Stanger in a Strange Land.

I had my time with Adam after work and on much of the weekend and twice a week I met up with Moses, enjoyed the shamanic work and the studies of Celtic and European history that included druid lore.

I knew what being witch is but I was decidedly dissatisfied with any of the authoritative definitions. They were too modern. Invented. There was no anthropology to them; nothing raven, nothing deep water or rustlings in the underbrush. There was no lore and no language written or spoken in the communication of meadow and stream. I was hunting a mammoth and to find such necessitated exploring myth despite anyone's opinion, despite any consensus of what was currently considered authoritative. Nothing I read or was told convinced me of authenticity. Too much sugar and too much fear. "Whatever you do comes back at you threefold." "Do as ye will so long as it harms none." This was morality catch phrased with a "ye" thrown in. There was no wit.

Living in the backwater of Australian spirituality I had not heard of the rising movement that was to become deep ecology; the rewilding movement. I was also unaware in those days that my ancestors had hunted badgers, salmon and bear. Oared the Baring Strait in boats of willow and seal hide. All I had was Lewis Spence's *The Magic Art in Celtic Britain, The History and Arts of Druidism* and James Frazer's *The Golden Bough*. Old works. Not Timothy Leary yet, or Carlos Castenada. Vast quantities of literature on the indigenes of other people, mainly the tribes of First Nation people in North America. Non-existent or non-newsworthy from Australia, or even New Zealand and the Pacific.

But ancestry and truth? I didn't know mine.

I was still socializing and performing ritual with Irene and the others, usually at Irene's house in Lane Cove but within weeks that coven introduced a new rule pertaining to neophytes and I was disgusted. A neophyte was a person thinking about initiating. With no obligation. Their time in relation to a coven was all about mutual liking. There was never a time-imposition, everything was meant to be very relaxed and very clear so that both the non-initiated and the initiated were sure they could work together, over several years if need be. The new law demanded that the neophyte take oaths of allegiance for an entire and exact year and a day. That's when I backed out.

I'm going solitary for a while, I announced, one Sunday afternoon.

Will you still work with us? asked the Lynden.

With you at your place studying tarot? Sure.

Why won't you do the rituals with us?

I glared at the Slug and I said outright that I didn't like where they were going with this. He just smiled and said this was a very important step towards the devotion of a student.

I said, what the fuck? Devotion is not a word that belongs anywhere in relation to witchcraft.

And I walked out.

The Historian was in the room. This was the first either of us had heard of this devotion demand. He phoned me that night. Upset because he'd been going to ask me to initiate him. That he couldn't really tolerate Irene and the Slug's parochial dogmatic stance.

Sorry. I'm jaded.

But I really want this.

I've spent way too long swimming in that shit.

Can I ask a favor?

Sure.

If I go ahead and take initiation with them can you and I work together in secret?

Sure. You going to stop pretending to be straight?

No. They won't take me.
Shit.
I know.
He went ahead with the neophyte oath-taking.

We still met several times a week to discuss natural magic and explore Bardon's work. Over the next couple of months, I watched his spirit sag after being told that everything he had learned was to be forgotten and that only what they told him was important.

Okay, I laughed, over coffee one night at the flat. I'll initiate you. This is getting silly.

He told Irene's coven he was out. And that he was gay.

The perfect storm.

I don't remember anything of the Historian's initiation except for the after-party. Blurry on red wine drunk in celebration after the event, he and I caught a cab to King's Cross all still robed in black cloaks with pentagrams and occult jewelry.

You lot going to a fancy dress party? asked the cabbie.

No, we're witches, I replied.

He said nothing and didn't even look sideways. The eighties were still cool.

We exited the cab on William Street and caused general mayhem amongst the crowd, particularly when straight men made snide, out of the corner of their mouths comments about the Historian's cloak. We made for the only occult shop in Sydney besides the Star Goddess. Run by a man named John, who called himself a warlock. Funny, retrospectively, that the word warlock went out of fashion for naming men practicing witchcraft. The word means oath-breaker and has been shunned, as a result, by the broader *pagan* community. No one asked an appropriate question, traitor to whom? The oaths these men are supposed to be breaking are to christianity. In a time when if you weren't christian you were in league with the devil. (Had the devil been invented when this word became popular?) According to an online etymological dictionary the word is Scottish circa 1560. Smack in the middle of the witch mania of Albion and Europe.

We explored the shop and bought ourselves gifts before launching back onto the street where the Historian, by now quite drunk, hailed a car and the driver, a man in his twenties, actually pulled over. Historian asked politely if the stranger might possibly drive us to Bondi Beach and he did.

Irene was as angry as could be and word spread throughout the community that I had betrayed them, stolen a neophyte and initiated a gay man. I had a phone call from Copperhead, she of the coven of Phoenix:

Ly, there has been a grand council of witches.

Really?

You have committed a taboo.

Really?

You have initiated a homosexual.

And?

This is not sanctioned by the grand council of witches.

What grand council of witches, Copperhead? And what right do you have to interfere in who I initiate?

You have been black-banned.

Go fuck yourself.

CHAPTER 19

Queen, Jethro Tull, Steeleye Span and Pink Floyd. The Wall album had recently been released and was influencing yet another generation. Bon Scott, lead singer and lyricist for the Australian band AC/DC, died in February 1980 from too much of whatever he had been drinking. Metallica formed. Clannad, the Chieftains, Dead Can Dance and Loreena McKennitt sang of Celtic lore and ancient wisdom. Alan Stivell was also reviving the strangled Breton muse. Music to trigger memories. Like bagpipes.

More animist—*pagan*—ethics and curiosity, the rise of modern druidry and neo-druidic cosmology, deep ecology and the gradual kindling of a Celtic identity now changing us and in truth, since the sixties, music was remembering and revitalizing our obscured culture. These were the new bards and revolutionaries. This was witchcraft. Knowledge of orality, ink, customs and tribal territories sustenance to the hungry. I studied Irish folklore, archaeology and the psychology of identity and stolen culture. That included knowing how to pronounce the language I read, even though I could only count from one to ten orally.

In early 1981 Bobby Sands, whose true name was Roibeárd Gearóid Ó Seachnasaigh, was imprisoned in Long Kesh, in the town of Maze not too far south of Belfast. Bobby and his fellow protestors made headlines across the world for their ongoing hunger strike. Bobby's story struck me because so much counter-opinion had been conveniently forgotten. Not many knew why he and the others did this. Impacted differently to when Mahatma Gandhi did the same. Starved.

Things change, sometimes imperceptibly, sometimes dramatically, but with the passing of generations and a transforming of cultural zeitgeists some things seem to disappear forever. This is called Shifting Baseline Syndrome. A seeming forgetting. But nothing truly goes away as long as someone remembers and passes the story along. Once upon a time in Ireland if a man did not pay another man what he had promised the swindled man would sit on the first man's step and stay there. This tradition is *troscadh*. Hospitality was of utmost importance so to have a person go hungry when you had plenty to eat, particularly when he had worked for you for an agreed payment and the deal reneged upon, was the depths of dishonor. The unpaid man would not eat or drink. He went on strike until the money or goods were acknowledged. They were always paid.

So Bobby took up the position of so many Irish of the past. He made a stand to shame the Thatcher administration and the English government, generally, that had robbed his ancestors and their children for six hundred years. Those men were deceitfully doomed because the English did not concede *troscadh*, or else had forgotten. Bobby and nine other men died of hunger but that deeply-rooted tradition, perhaps thought irrelevant, touched the hearts of the world and Ireland in particular, so much so that, decades later, Republican Ireland was to slip from the shackles of its tormentors to join the European Union as independent and liberated from domination by the English monarchy, its Sinn Féin government to sit in parliament alongside the misappropriation, by the English Crown, of Northern Ireland—specifically the Pale.

Still no government support for sole parents—and so I missed the majority of my son's trauma-inducing childhood years. I put out a spell for something to give and fate intervened not long after. I took three weeks off work that summer to immerse us in long days at the beach, to continue learning archery and to just switch off. I had asked that none of my friends or the coven disturb me.

At night on the weekends I invented stories with Moses and hung out till the early hours. He called me his Moonstone Lady and I sat with him when he had his vasectomy.

Two weeks into my holiday I received a desperate phone call from Lynden, her voice croaky, her nose blocked.

Hey, Ly.
Hi. What's up?
I ab so sick.
Poor thing.

I deed your help.
What?
Cad you fill id for me at Westfield?
What?
Tarot. I dod't wad't to lose by place. Please?
Westfield Plaza?
Please?
Okay. When do I have to be there? Only a for a few days, yes?

This was to be the first time I had ever read for strangers. Was I nervous? No, but I was in dread. I shoved my cards, in their ornate, hand-made velvet pouch, into my shoulder bag and rode to Westfield Plaza where a large sign on an easel on the ground floor announced FORTUNE FAIR! THIS WEEK ONLY! The psychics' photographs surrounded with stars and crescent moons, their skills outlined. Directing the punter to the first floor. There was my card table with Lynden's panné velvet cover in midnight blue. The others had already arrived and I introduced myself. I was the only one not dressed in some form of faux-gypsy outfit. At eight thirty in the morning I sat down, pulled out my cards and waited. We were to charge $10 for ten minutes. I had decided to do a spread known, then, as a *celtic cross*. And give the people a question.

By nine I was busy. Lynden must have made quite an impact on the locals. By nine thirty there was a queue. By ten I was sweating and swearing and not giving a shit what I said or even whether I could be understood as there were many people who spoke very little English. I might have even been rude.

I'm never going to see any of you again, I thought.

Your aunty is terminally ill with cancer.

I know, was the reply, but it's restful to confirm that there is nothing to be done.

I worked all day, non-stop till five thirty. No lunch. No tea break. I only left my table to go to the loo. I phoned Moses that night and begged him to pop along around lunchtime next day to drag me away. I explained about the river of encounters; need. He sympathized.

I phoned Lynden and had words.

Keep all the bunny, she spluttered. I'm so sorry. I should have warred you.

I'll get you for this, I assured her. She laughed.

What have you beed tellig theb?

I have no idea.

The following day they were waiting for me. A queue snaked from the escalator to my table and the first person—a widow in black—was already sitting. Some had brought interpreters. Strega, was whispered time and again. *Strega*, knowingly. Witch.

Moses, as promised, entered the queue around midday and actually pulled me bodily from one woman. At least I ate. And made quite a lot of money. After just a couple of days people were requesting longer readings; my phone number.

Will you be here next week? they asked.

No, I said. But the phone at our house rang and rang. I gave up the corporate work and began reading tarot at Fortune Fair in the city.

Moses and I had no time for each other and we slowly drifted apart. Not long after Fortune Fair we stopped seeing each other.

This was my first Saturn Return. I ceased to be a member of mainstream society completely that year and have never gone back. Tarot was to become my greatest teacher about human nature and the world as a whole. Tarot is not the cards. They are something other. I was privy to wisdom that I have never stopped attempting to fathom. How could something seemingly random and irrational foretell events with such precision? Tell of events that had not happened. In explicit detail?

How's my marriage in the future? asked one woman.

I threw out the answer spread.

Dead in the water.

There's nothing wrong with us, she assured me, very upset.

Don't shoot the messenger. How many times have I said that? I received word a few weeks later from her friend that the woman's husband drowned.

CHAPTER 20

I taught numerology classes and one of the students in this new batch was the Trickster, again, disguised in a mortal man about my own age with a Native American look to him. Straight dark hair loose down his back, dark eyes, hooked nose.

He was well read if not a little overly eclectic as so many New Agers are. He borrowed several books from my library. Within the first month he had decided that witchcraft was the path for him, and he became deeply engrossed in learning. We became lovers a few months later.

He was initiated into the coven.

Within a month I was pregnant. At thirty. Did I really want to raise another child? This time with a man around? One who didn't seem able to get a job? I didn't really want to tell him, more out of instinct than the obvious. But I did, stating that there was no obligation. He was delighted.

I had a choice, of course, but I wanted the baby and I wanted a home birth. I struck gold. I hooked up with Maggie Lecky-Thompson, of the Midwife's Guild of Australia.

I rented a house at the end of a road that backed onto a national park in the northern suburbs of Sydney. To do so I sold my car and downgraded to another and also sold my motorcycle because the Trickster had no money but assured me he would find work soon.

Adam was happy when Historian moved in.

The coven was invited to the inaugural Mount Franklin Pagan Gathering being held not far from Daylesford in Victoria's high country, for the spring equinox of 1981. Once we'd passed the sign warning Duck Creek we entered a green land of boulder communities. They resided on either side of the road leading south alongside massive eucalypts mottled with lichen and moss of startlingly diverse varieties of green, red and gold.

We finally arrived at Mount Franklin, the bowl of an extinct volcano, and set up camp, meeting organizers Linda and Michel Marold and settling around the fire. The park was a sap-risen profusion of every conceivable European tree, all in spring bud and early flower, filling the air with a snow of petals throughout the day. To the indigenous people, the Gunangara Gundidj of the Dja Wurrung nations the place is Lalgambook (smoking grounds). Ceremonial. Women's territory.

I cannot recollect much about that weekend. It was a bit of a Bacchanal and our coven did not participate in the public ritual as, in those early days, people still worked against the sun. The Order of Chaos and the O.T.O crew also had their beers and joints as was only fitting their ideology. Names from the dim past such as Simon Goodman, Tim Hartridge, Andrew Poliopolis all come to mind. Understanding permaculture from Rod. A maypole dance. Historian haunting the surrounding forest with music played on recorder as he wandered alone in communion with a somewhat north-of-the-snowline pine grove.

Z Budapest from that *dianic* wiccan coven in America sent a tape discussing the rights and wrongs of cursing the man who raped and glassed one of their initiates considering the catchphrase to "do as you will as long as you harm none". Debate had been healthy. I was all for the cursing.

The seed was sown at that gathering, though, for an eventual relocation to Victoria. Such a *pagan* community would be invigorating.

Back in Sydney, Nevill and I continued the shamanic-style drumming workshops and when I was eight weeks pregnant I was drummed down the roots of that mythic tree one travels to get to another 'reality'.

I landed in a galleried, stone hallway lined on either side with twelve foot high granite statues of hawks capped in red leather. I walked the length of the gallery and through a high arch into an almost empty but expansive room with a raised dais at one end; two closed doors on the wall behind a throne on which sat, laconically, some hunky-looking monarch. He was shirtless and wore jeans and his feet were bare. I walked up to him and he reached behind his throne and pulled out a three-legged stool, indicating I should sit.

Smug, I thought. What's your story?

He laughed as though he read my mind. Watch, he said.

He leaned towards me holding out his hand, palm-upwards. There was a movement, almost a trick of the eye, but that gleaning grew into a live young falcon, eyes covered by a leather hood, legs belled with bewits and leather jesses.

Teach her to fly and to hunt, he said.

I don't know how.

He smiled and looked down his nose at me.

In that liminal place one never knows how long one does anything, but I stared him down.

He was dauntless and I relented. He passed her to my arm, talons biting into my flesh.

Outside was night, the hilly landscape devoid of any visualization other than limitless grass. I hadn't a clue.

This is nuts, I thought, so I simply took the hood off, removed the jesses and flung the youngling into the air thinking, take your chances, kiddo. Everything went slow motion and my vision zoomed into an extreme close-up of her black, black eyes. She looked right back. Before I knew what had happened the falcon landed on my head, talons entangled in my hair.

In that most ridiculous state we re-entered the throne room and I sat on the stool. The king smiled as though something this strange was commonplace.

Well?

Well, what?

Did you teach her to live?

No.

What did you do?

Set her free.

He smiled with delight.

Well done, he said dismissively.

Then, Nevill's rapid-fire tapping of the tipper against the bodhràn brought me back to awareness of the room where I and the others then recounted our journeys.

That night I dreamed of a small girl about four years old. She ran with a dozen red balloons, across that barren landscape. She stopped and turned in my direction and, as with the vision, I was drawn into extreme close up with her eyes.

I'm Romany, I heard.

I woke up and told the Trickster my baby's name.

I was so pregnant that I needed to stop working. In those days the welfare cheque was still always in a man's name and if the couple were unmarried the woman had to agree to sign as an unpaid housekeeper. I was not going to sign. I raged until things became dire but in the end there was no recourse. I climbed down to my cave in mythworld, my pride in a small den for now. Once back in the shallow world I slipped on the mask of control; of suppressed fury. I was not about to let this bureaucratic insult ruin my otherwise well-being.

That weekend the newspaper headline was that a Romany queen named Ruby was in critical care in the Wollongong Hospital. Gypsies had come from all over Australia and had taken over the waiting rooms; were camped in the hospital grounds. I was nine months pregnant.

Well will you look at this? I turned the article over to Historian and the Trickster.

How often does the word Romany made the front page an Australian newspaper? Never. Most intriguing.

One night the following week I fell asleep early. I awoke knowing that the baby's name was not Romany but Rachael. The Trickster had been playing guitar quietly beside me. He leaned the instrument on a stand near the wall opposite our bed. He came back and sat beside me.

You know you're being fickle.

I paused, confused, just long enough for the pegs that held the guitar strings along the bridge, to start popping out, hitting him like small angry bees.

The follow-up story was again front page a week later. The

Romany queen was dead. Her photograph was on the front page. A big woman, likely in her sixties. She was bedecked in an elaborate gown and her family "took her measure" in red thread, a thing also a tradition in several forms of initiation. What about that, though. Her nickname was Ruby but her real name was Rachael. According to Romany legend the soul of the queen passes into the body of a newborn baby three days after her death. A day later I went into labor. When I was sure I was having contractions I phoned Maggie to let her know that they were still only twenty minutes apart.

At least we know the child isn't the Romany queen, I said to the Historian as I headed to the kitchen to make tea. Oh, and just in case, I've picked a boy's name.

Why?

A gnawing feeling.

Really?

Yes. Jarrod.

Julie came and made tea. She never had children and was staying for the birth. Jan turned up but was so uncomfortable at my near nakedness she talked of nothing but her financial woes until I had to ask her to leave. Adam and the Historian placed bets on the gender of the immanent child. They were both in attendance at the birth. I had a forty hour labor and Jarrod was born exactly three days after the death of the Romany queen. His eyes were dark, dark brown, just like the child in the dream, not quite as dark as that falcon. I was strong. I was up the following day doing washing and starting to pack. A week later the four of us were on the road to Victoria, to what we thought would be the loving embrace of a widespread alternative, *pagan* community, leaving the Historian behind in Sydney.

CHAPTER 21

We rented a four bedroom house in Guildford in autumn. The temperature plummeted that first month there. One room was kept locked. My room. I had the only key. In plain sight in that room were my ritual things: books, grimoires, sword, staff, athamé and other assorted objects where I could access them without having to take them from the trunk.

Lynden, her partner and her two daughters were visiting from Sydney when the cops raided us. Two of them. They said they were looking for stolen white goods. They had no warrant, but we weren't about to cause a fuss. Cop One searched everywhere including up under the roof, climbing a ladder and pushing back the manhole cover. Cop Two leaned casually against the hallway wall playing Donkey Kong. Cop One came into the lounge room, where we sat about in relative silence, and he opened a matchbox. I followed.

What's he looking for? Lynden's daughter asked.

Stolen fridges, Lynden replied.

She beamed at him when he scowled at her. I continued to follow him.

As we walked down the hallway towards the kitchen, he tried the knob on my locked room.

What's in here? Where's the key? he asked like an accusation.

You can't go in there.

Open the door.

No. He can come in, I said, indicating Cop Two, but you stay out.

Cop Two peeled himself off the wall and jostled Cop One aside.

He thought the whole thing most amusing. Cop One, unfazed, folded his arms across his chest and waited across the hall.

A few days before this a friend had brought a small, injured bird for me to heal. Its wing was damaged, and I knew that a few confined days would be enough, so I half filled the room with branches where the sparrow now flitted from one to another. I hurried Cop Two in and closed the door behind him.

He took all of thirty seconds, turned and opened the door carefully.

Just storage, he said to Cop One.

Why all the secrecy, then?

Embarrassed at the mess, I replied.

Cop Two said nothing. We didn't hear from them again.

Word spread, the following week, that the "arch demon queen of witchcraft has come to Castlemaine" and that her familiar is a raven that lives in a black room. Small towns. I was not used to them. I did not know about gossip and rural politics. I learned the hard way that a city woman could never, really, understand people born and educated in the country. Not in Australia, anyway.

I was pregnant again but within the first month I miscarried. I'd still been breastfeeding Jarrod and had to immediately stop because I was admitted to the Castlemaine hospital for a standard curette.

I went home with an infection in a small cut on the middle finger of my right hand. No idea how that happened. Over the next few days the pain worsened and hurt like nothing I'd ever experienced. I went back to the doctor and complained. He said go home and soak the wound in Dettol and warm water. No one took me seriously. Thought I was being silly. Inconsequential. I stopped complaining despite now being in an agony that no pain-killer would fix. That same day the Trickster and Adam went fishing.

Jarrod was asleep in his cot. I shivered uncontrollably, freezing. I got into a scalding bath, but the ice was on the inside and I scalded my skin. Jarrod was crying somewhere but the sound was as muted as though from behind thick stone walls. I couldn't have got to him anyway. I wore every piece of clothing that I owned and sat on the floor covered in two feather doonas with a bright red line going up my arm. I knew that this was septicemia and that I was close to death, but

I was too tired to do anything, and the shaking was uncontrollable. Then nothing.

Castlemaine hospital the following day, with drips and beeping. I had no idea what had happened. I pressed the buzzer and a nurse explained that I was being intravenously ministered the biggest, meanest antibiotic known to man. That had been flown in from Canberra at some stage in the night when tests had confirmed the infection was golden staph. Fred, a recently befriended lad from two houses down, had heard Jarrod crying for way too long. He told me later of the dread that had come over him. He had run as fast as he could to my house. He saved my life.

We only stayed until October 1982. The winter was freezing, and I missed Sydney life dreadfully. By December I was pregnant again and knew, without doubt, that I would give birth to a daughter. I wanted out of the relationship. The Trickster would not get a job.

He would rely on me or welfare for as long as I stayed because I was very certain by this time that he wasn't going anywhere. I again caged that thought in the deep. I could not raise three children alone. There was nothing I could do

Still trapped.

CHAPTER 22

We returned to Sydney and rented a two storey, hundred year old ex-bordello in Surry Hills. The Historian lived with us again. House of many ghosts. Young women in red dresses, their nipples rouged, their smiles never reaching their eyes. I sensed syphilis, absinthe; the sweet smoke of opium. Death at sixteen. I did a banishing on the place, but remnants tattered here and there, mainly at night. That house was alive. I could smell history. Historian and I spent the first week decking out the front downstairs bedroom for ritual. We were studying Sumerian lore and magic and he was deciphering cuneiform and writing a Sumerian-English dictionary.

Every day I crossed a little park with its scattering of used syringes. Flaccid beige condoms. McDonalds wrappers. A public bin, always overflowing. To the little shop across the road. For bread and milk and disposable nappies.

I was exhausted. To the point that, at around five months pregnant I thought I could just curl into a burrow somewhere and die.

Maggie was up for delivering this child also, so I drove to her house on the north shore. A huge, glass-walled central living area enclosing an enormous boulder. While I waited for my consultation I climbed up onto the rock and sat cross-legged on its mother-coolness. And the tiredness was drained from me. I sighed with understanding. That small park was cruelly used. Men solicited other men for drug money. Dealers sold baggies of white powder laced with bathroom cleanser or the ashes from their dead mother's funereal urn just to make an extra buck. Homeless with their stories and their lives dripping through the slats of benches. That neglected landscape wasn't what drove us to move from that house though. We'd pulled up the carpet in the upstairs hallway, as filthy and as ugly as racism. That action liberated a flea plague from the cracks between the floorboards. We got out before the fumigators.

I found us a cottage in Blackheath almost at the very top of the Blue Mountains. That's where my daughter would be born. We moved in June. Winter, sweet with rarefied air and mists in the morning, the muffled song of magpies through the pines and wood smoke, as intoxicating as oak moss oil. I developed a pregnancy craving. I had to bake cookies every day. I didn't want to eat them so I gave them away.

One night in the midst of winter the Trickster and I had a massive argument. Over money. An argument that was becoming repetitious. I didn't sleep. I was four months pregnant and I simply sat in a chair just inside the French doors looking out into the night. All night. With the predawn light came a fog so thick I could not see a thing. But I heard the first laugh of kookaburras, the call of ravens and magpies, countless other birds. Then the first sunlight like prisms rose from the lip of the cliff top at the end of our garden. I thought the word serenity because all enmity had drained from me. I decided that would be my daughter's name. I had a battle with the rat voice over that.

At twenty eight weeks pregnant I bled. I was miscarrying. I phoned Maggie.

Get down the mountain. Now, she said. Put the Trickster on the phone.

She told him to get me drunk because alcohol is a muscle relaxant. Then drive me to Sydney immediately if I was to have any chance of keeping the baby.

I phoned Jan and said we were on our way. She said no. I was stunned.

I'm having friends for dinner, she said. You can't come here. I don't want you in my life anymore.

The Trickster again called the midwife and she agreed to put a mattress in her garage. Then he drove to the nearest bottle shop and bought a bottle of single malt. I stayed drunk for two weeks and remained pregnant.

Back on the mountain Nevill came to visit. While I made us tea he leafed through the pile of notes on my desk.

What's all this?

For the outer circle students, I said. All the books are written for the northern hemisphere, so I'm fixing a problem.

You going to write up the sabbats and other rituals?

I can do that. Why?

Send me a copy when you've finished?

Sure.

And he neatened my unruly stack of handwritten pages.

Serenity was born in September after thirty five hours labor. Maggie arrived at the very start of the contractions and we made birthday cake. She and Adam and I wandered the cliffs a thousand feet above the Cox's Rapids. Adam was on school holidays and was with us for the birth. I buried Serenity's placenta at the base of a single tree that jutted above those vast canyons. When Adam went back to school and the teacher asked what every kid did in their holidays he explained he had a new sister and that he had cut her umbilical cord. He was proud but no one but the teacher would have known what he had done.

Within a month we returned to live in Victoria and I regained my driving license. Relocating so often was becoming exhausting, endless, a chaos of new schools for Adam. Impossible to avoid during these trapped years. Housing was plentiful in the times but not long term rentals. The Trickster continued to inhabit the same man, challenging me to go deeper, seek more courage. I didn't have that yet.

Linda Marold, Mt Franklin Pagan Festival organizer arranged for us to again stay in Guildford. This time in the double garage of Poppy and her stoner husband. They lived in their caravan on an otherwise clay-baked, potholed block of land with an area of mud brick wall in the process of being built. I mention stoner because he had home-builder approval for five years. He arose every morning, made a cup of tea and smoked a joint. The rest of the day was for reading the paper.

I bought a large tent, from which I intended to read tarot at the Daylesford Sunday craft market at the old railway grounds. I'd loaded the van with everything needed for the day and driven to town. I bedecked my tent with table and chairs, candles and Alexander palms. The local artists' co-op worked and exhibited on the actual station. Someone waved from there and headed in my direction when I'd put out my small sign.

I was busy from the very first but midway through the morning the bloke in charge of the markets strode over to me, sneering, his neck red and blotchy.

Pack up and get out, he said.
What?
You're a tool of the devil and what you're doing is evil so get

out now before I call the police.

Call the police. I don't care.

We were drawing a crowd and he worked hard to intimidate me.

I've been to every stall. They all want you gone. What you're doing is illegal. Under the Fraudulent Medium Act.

I'm not a fraud.

You've got fifteen minutes before I call the cops.

He stormed away. The big man in the stall beside me came over and said he'd heard everything and that he was on the Castlemaine council. He offered to help me get a petition together because that man hadn't spoken to anyone. So we did. The letter was simple and asked if what I did offended them, yes or no, their names and their telephone numbers. Of the hundred or so I asked only one, a guy who sold war memorabilia, wrote yes.

What I didn't then understand was that the people of the region, prior to the surge of the alternative movement, were all conservative and old fashioned. Farmers. Laborers. Men killing at the abattoir. Men drinking hard and hitting their wives. Men back from Vietnam with no one to tell of the horrors. Silenced by an all-christian community fifty years behind the times who believed in hiding emotion behind the fellowship of religion. To never admitting to hardship. Worked their potato farms or at the local mechanic shop, the hardware shop. Trusted football, beer and their various vicars and christian ministers. Distrusted the new council rules on mud brick self-building and resented the government grants available for them. Mistrusted multiple occupancy and permaculture. Felt invaded and outraged by the waves of city folk—including us—bringing unfamiliar ideologies, alternative therapies, music other than rock and roll and a kind of medieval revivalism they thought ridiculous. They were bound to hate me.

When the bloke in charge returned the council man and I confronted him and called him a liar. He assured us he was going to phone the cops and I'd be forcibly removed.

As soon as he'd gone several of the artists' co-op people came and offered me a place up on the platform. They helped me move everything. I read for the remainder of that day, ignoring the baneful looks sent my way by that bloke. The co-op was not under the market agenda so he could do nothing. The police never came. I was, however, approached by a woman who was about to start up the same kind of market in Kyneton.

You draw quite a crowd, she smiled.

Yeah, well.

Could I offer you a permanent and complimentary spot at my new gig?

Be glad to, I replied.

Poppy's husband Ray was given two weeks to evict us from his property or his building license would be revoked. Seems the other Castlemaine council members weren't all like that nice man at the markets. Haylock, the boss of the church of christ in Castlemaine had heard about me. This was the beginning of a campaign to drive us away.

What can I do? Ray pleaded.

Nothing to do, I said.

I searched for rentals, but the word had spread and we were knocked back either because of Haylock or because we didn't behave like we were supposed to; weren't from there.

I eventually acquired eleven acres of land on vendor finance at twenty-five percent interest on the loan. I knew it couldn't last but we had no option. Haylock had effectively impoverished us. People gave us tarps. I went to recycling centers, called tips in those days, where everything could be found from dead dogs to church pews and yes, one could build a house from what other people thought worthless.

The initial dwelling was a tin cottage between four living trees with a tarpaulin as a roof. I gathered enough carpet to make a snug home, a slow combustion stove, a bathtub on claw foot legs and other assorted furniture. Car batteries for lighting and running the television. A bench car seat squatted outside on the veranda and just down the hill was a stone-bottomed dam, the water pristine and drinkable.

Zero money so the few friends we had provided us with food until the first welfare cheque came through a week later. We loaded the children into the car and while the Trickster went to the bank to withdraw the money the children and I turned up at the rectory of the church of christ. I banged on the door and a woman answered. Turned pale. His wife.

I want to talk to Haylock.
I don't know anything.
About what?
Nothing.
Is he here?
No.

You tell him to come and visit. I want to talk to him. His behavior is threatening my children.

I'm sorry but I don't think—

You know exactly who I am. He'll come unless he's a coward.

She slammed the door in my face.

The following day was bright and sunny, crisp, and sweet with the scents of eucalypt, stone and wood smoke from the outdoor hearth. A long-wheel-base four wheel drive lumbered up our dirt entrance track and parked. Out came an ordinary-looking man with two large books under his arm, followed by a bruiser, well over six feet tall and built for chopping down forests. The preacher and his minder. I put my breast away and hefted my daughter to my shoulder, rubbing her back to release the wind. The Trickster went elsewhere.

Sit, I demanded, patting the car seat.

I can't stay, he said, high on his own self-righteousness.

He was with me for three hours as we debated religion and mysticism. He consistently misquoted biblical texts and I'd read enough to counter him. I have never ceased to wonder at how folk actually believe what they do, but they do. In many instances their clergy don't. I have spoken to several, christian and Jewish, all of whom have university educations, so they do know the text is all cobbled together from bits of this and bits of that, superimposing itself over an alternative heritage, from the Babylonian exile to the Diaspora in seventy C.E. when certain sects, arriving in Europe and facing a Mithraic culture, necessarily merged their beliefs with that of Rome. In order to flourish. A thing that did not happen to those who refused. They became candles, were used for sport or enslaved.

The problem, for whatever Jewish sect that evolved into christianity, was that they were monotheists. Romans expected them to also respect roman gods. So they were bait for the crumbling empire's entertainment.

Regarding Constantine's conversion? There are theories about whether or not his decision to declare christianity the state religion was spiritually motivated or an act of caving to a nagging wife as he lay dying. Or simply well-considered propaganda. The meek shall inherit the earth? Turn the other cheek? Forgive your enemies? Humility? A good way to control people is to instill these qualities into them as exemplary traits.

By the third century christian zealots had rooted out their gnostic sects and slaughtered them. They then mobilized themselves militarily. Come the end of the fourth century a feud in Alexandria that began between Jewish and christian factions culminated in a massacre of christians and banishment of the Jews responsible. The killing of a woman named Hypatia, Greek philosopher and head of the neo platonic school, the first recorded atrocity of christians against women. She was battered to death and, once dead, her bones were scraped with oyster shells to remove the flesh. The monks then burned the bones.

All this I knew while talking for those three hours with a person who believed himself to be better than me.

Utterly pointless and boring because, like jehovah's witnesses, he couldn't accept a word I said.

I asked him how long he'd been an initiate of his cult. He'd been offended so I reworded the sentence. He'd become a minister in 1972. The Trickster wandered from the forest with an armload of wood and entered the shed. I could hear him open of a can of cat food. Egypt, the black Siamese-cross we'd brought with us from Sydney had recently given birth to six black kittens.

Oh, I outrank you, I said.
What?
Yes, I was initiated four years before you.
But I don't acknowledge your ways.
And I concur.
I'm leaving, he pouted.
Do you want to see a black mass before you go?
What? Really?
Come on.

I ushered the excited, but baffled buffoon inside. Egypt and the kittens were all around a bowl. The black mass. I had him now. I could see him. The man was obsessed.

The last thing he said as he was leaving was, my congregation and I will be willing you to jesus or willing you dead for as long as you remain in my town, little lady.

I didn't hit him. I couldn't be bothered. Not for the death wish but for insulting my height.

I had been warned. He had a reputation around town. Kathryn Matthews, then a friend and witch, later to become an initiate of our coven and co- author of The Way of Merlyn, had been to his office with others, all under the ruse of joining the church. She explained his chair system. In front of his desk were three of them. The one furthest from the door was directly beside a glass-fronted cupboard that held assorted statuettes and objects of some alternative-to-christianity-type-significance. His evaluation as to whether an individual was open to salvation was decided by the chair they sat on. If they sat on the furthest chair they were already satan's.

He wasn't funny although I wanted to laugh. There was nothing benign about him; he was as dangerous as only a fanatic can be.

The very next day the bruiser who'd come as Haylock's bodyguard drove his four wheel drive up our dirt track with a long wheelbase trailer loaded with eight foot by eight pine Hino truck packing case sides. He proceeded to pull them off the trailer. We came and helped, momentarily confused.

Best conversation I've heard in years, he said gruffly. Don't care what you believe in.

We got the whole lot on the ground and he presented us with a huge bag of nuts and bolts, a battery-driven drill, a bag of batteries and a chainsaw.

I'll be back next week for the equipment. Think you can make a house?

I think so.

Me and the missus and the kids've got an eight bedroom one built outa these. Built around the caravan. Like to invite you up. You'll like the missus.

Adam was helping us, and the bloke said to him, Got lads your age, son. You should see the cubby! Then he drove off down the dirt track.

Jarrod followed Adam down to where he was building a sanctuary in the forest while I and several friends mattocked and shoveled the ground level, Serenity in a sling on my back. We laid three meter lengths of logs, every so often, as a foundation to keep the pallet floor off the clay. We hammered nine inch nails through the pallets and into the logs before raising the walls and bolting the whole thing together. Over the following weeks we acquired recycled everything: tin for the roof, cladding for the inside walls that also acted as support, carpet, a slow combustion heater, as many batteries as we could and the bulbs and wiring from old cars to string about and light the house. A volt converter transformed electrical equipment from two-forty to twelve volt. We were able to watch the news on a night of horrendous storms when the rest of the region was blacked out, on guard to evacuate if the flooding came.

One afternoon Adam came to get me, horrified.

Mum, the tree's screaming.

I followed him outside to where the Trickster had driven a nine inch nail into one of the big gums for whatever reason. Adam had me put my ear to the metal. The screaming was anguished, terrible. That sound changed me.

At the Kyneton market one Saturday two things happened. The first was a middle aged woman with her three daughters who all had readings one after the other. She went off to get her husband after the session. When he entered my tent a psychic bubble exploded in me and all the little hairs on my arms stood to attention. He had a ghost behind him. He was just an ordinary looking man, maybe fifty, balding, overweight and sad. A black lake under a dirty wind, waves breaking over me.

When I read his cards I didn't say much. He'd held a stranger in his arms till that person died. My client was responsible. He wept. When his daughters were very young he'd been a heavy drinker and went to the pub nightly. He was driving home drunk one night and hit a young motorcycle police officer who died before anyone came along that stretch of highway. He'd gone to prison for manslaughter. He'll never recover. I didn't tell him about the ghost. Would have been cruel. After that the word spread like wildfire and I was reading for everyone from sheep cockies to judges from as far away as the Mallee.

The other event was a young woman who came three weeks in a row. I asked her who she was spying for. She blushed and left. The following Saturday a Seer entered my tent, sat down and shuffled my cards as though they were diseased.

I laid out a spread of cards and said, oh, you're a tarot reader and you work from home, if I do you will you do me? Swapsies?

Where on earth do you see that, she asked.

We had very different ways of reading. but both delivered. She was snowed under with clients seven days a week and had been hunting another reader to help with the load.

I went to her place in Bendigo and we talked for hours. I asked how her psychic life had started. She'd been woken in the middle of the night some years back and seen the shape of a tall man in a top hat and overcoat filling the doorway. She'd switched on the bedside lamp and no one was there. I told her about my own episode. Same thing, when I'd been aged eleven.

I read her clients that weekend. And were they upset.

At first. To them I was an upstart, a newcomer, unproven and from the city. Then two things happened. First was a man who wasn't going to pay.

Oh, I must have left my wallet at home, he said, patting his pockets.

Did you drive here?

Yep.

If you're lying your car's buggered, I said.

I went to make tea between him and the next person.

The Seer answered the door to him.

Can I use your phone?

Sure. Problem?

My car won't start.

The roadside assist people came about half an hour later and charged his battery. He came in and paid me before he left. The second was a social worker in her late forties, married to a man she had come to despise, intimidating and nasty. She intended to leave him. I read her warning spread.

Can you wait a month?

Why?

Can you trust me on this?

Okay. Why?

Trust me.

I knew what I was seeing: three of swords, ace of swords, death card. He dropped dead of a massive coronary. She hadn't given him any reason to write her out of his will, so she was the sole beneficiary. And he was a very rich man.

Clients began coming to the cottage, but I also opened a bookstore in Kyneton. I taught meditation, visualization and astral projection after the shop shut. I had a small but dedicated group, but I never discussed witchcraft, magic, covens, initiation. I never discussed an alternative animism. That'd be proselytizing. No. Closed up the shop, drank a coffee, lit a candle and meditated before the class.

One night as I sat with my eyes closed I heard and saw, in a loud, neon-lit assault, *You. Deny. Me.* Shook me like a bloodhound with a guinea pig. Disseminate information to the class and stop being self-righteousness. So that night I spoke candidly about witchcraft and animism, and what it felt like to live in the grace of the mysteries. They were so very interested because this form of spirituality was unknown to most people and the group grew to the point that I had a second in Bendigo. I worked with people who were not witches but were innately open to alternatives to what they had been force-fed. They wanted to learn about ritual, and Celtic-European lore, herb craft and mythworld. I held weekend workshops out of an old church in Newbury, the irony not lost.

The bookshop closed down and my property came under the scrutiny of the local council. The packing case house was illegal. Within a week I was given orders to vacate. My student, an astrologer, invited me to rent one of his family's cottages across the road from Mount Kooroocheang.

While living with those eleven acres, in that house that was a potential tinderbox, I learned to use a chainsaw, overcome a fear of heights by tying tarps to a leaking roof while hanging upside down in a gale. To become comfortable with poverty, or the consumerist concept of such, gained a huge circle of fey friends, a deep, inner core of wisdom from the surrounding countryside and to experience intimacy with a woman.

Haylock, the pastor from Castlemaine, made two mistakes. The first he got away with, the second he did not. The phone rang. A client.

Young woman in her twenties with two small children whose husband had died months before in a motorcycle accident. His family were members of the church of christ and they blamed his death on her because she had an interest in buddhism. According to Haylock anything not christian was demonic.

While she was shopping her neighbors saw two carloads of men break into her place, then nothing for at least half an hour, then smoke coming from the back of the house. The men left.

The neighbors did nothing other than tell her what had happened. The men had rifled through her cupboards and drawers, making no attempt at subtlety. Her tarot session tape had been in her underwear drawer and she had several books on non-christian spirituality. She also had a pair of black slippers that she wore for tai chi. Everything had been burned in a fire in her backyard.

She wanted me to set up psychic protections. I told her to go to the police as everything about what had happened was unlawful. She should fight along those battle lines. I would do what I could to protect her. She did not. Because of her dead husband's parents. They threatened to take her to court over the children. They said she was a bad mother and that they knew she dabbled in witchcraft and they knew they would be granted custody. I heard no more from her.

Poppy gave up on her husband and left. She was staying in a friend's caravan till she found a better place. She was offered a room at Bruce Jacob's house. He was the Dingo Man and he had several in his care the day two carloads of Haylock's men turned up. The door was open and they walked in. Bruce had a plaster motif of a sun god on his wall. This was smashed by one disciple.

He said that if Poppy was allowed to move in they were both damned.

Bruce told them to get fucked.

Several days later the police turned up with a warrant to kill the dingoes. They shot all except one pregnant female. That's when the shit hit the fan because the story made the national media. Haylock was removed from Castlemaine.

CHAPTER 23

Word spread that a local battery farm was selling off chickens for a dollar each, rather than slaughtering them, because they were past their high yield date and were a) not laying to the farmer's expectations and b) too old for meat. I drove to the battery with a hessian sack. The hens were kept in a shed. Huge. Closed to daylight. Inside was an abomination of the cruelest kind. All those feathered women crammed six to a cage.

Pick 'em and bag 'em, said the farmer, directing us to a huddle in a larger cage against the back wall. Twenty of them. Featherless, their beaks clipped, their spirits fled. I bought them all. My body flooded with adrenalin. I wanted to savage that man and release every bird, but I did not. I shoved them, with as much kindness as possible, into my sack. The purchase of hens was predestined.

This was no random acquisition.

Backtrack several weeks and we had built a nesting shed surrounded with a huge free range area, fenced as well as possible against predators. The morning of their arrival we dumped all our kitchen food scraps into the middle of their yard before releasing them. The ladies initially dropped into cowering huddles of mostly puckered skin dappled here and there with drab, limp feathers, multi-hued in shades of white, brown and russet.

We waited. The kids were impatient. Twenty minutes passed before the first hen rose. She slowly circled the mound of leftovers in the center of her home. She didn't know what food was. She was so brave. Finally she took a peck and rumbled. The noise she made began low in her chest, brwwww. She pecked some more, flapped her winglets and yelled BRWWWARK! She continued to cheer her victory song, and strut, as the others slowly followed her example. We named her Bokety and she outlived five such gaggles of hens, the others eventually taken by foxes; some just old. Their feathers grew back, and they laid and laid, and laid.

After being threatened by predators they refused to come into their enclosure at night preferring instead to roost up in the eucalypts. Which is where the silly women laid their eggs every morning. I warned my friends to look up. We could not corral them until we moved to another home. Bokety became head chook and chose to live in our outside bathroom at Jubilee Lake, Daylesford, perched contentedly on the edge of the sink, pooing into the drain. She was a survivor. She was last seen by my neighbors, one christmas a couple of years later, leading all the other hens down the street. My wish is that she and the ladies became feral and their offspring pepper the surrounding bushland contentedly.

I learned about the Pecking Order from them. And dogs. And horses. And what an alpha female and an alpha male are. I learned that they were never savage, never cruel. Natural leaders. Compassionate and firm with the other members of the coop, the herd, the pack, and the people. Humans try to be alpha females or alpha males but they either are or are not. Like respect, power is not something anyone should just take or demand. Real personal power is inherent in the nature of a human. Just like any other animal. In many species the head of the pack—the alpha alpha—is the female. Sought after for her eggs by every male at breeding time. In our own species this natural trait has been suppressed. Why? In a heterosexual relationship that truly works the woman is head of the home and her mate acknowledges her as such. He has nothing to prove. He can relax and just love. Many relationships hit trouble because one or more of the participants is driven into a stereotypical paradigm. Resentment and bitterness the result.

I don't have all the answers. I don't know why our species mutilates their genitals. I have read that genital mutilation goes far into the hoary depths of time, to Egypt and Rome, performed on both boys and girls. I also know that female genital mutilation was done by physicians to cure masturbation and 'nymphomania' in England, parts of Europe and America into the nineteenth century of this, known as the common era. Isaac Baker Brown, president of the Medical Society of London in 1865, believed that the "unnatural irritation" of the clitoris caused epilepsy, hysteria, and mania, and would cut the woman or girl whenever he had the opportunity of doing so.

These and other practices are religious in the true meaning of the word for, as Émile Durkheim the French sociologist suggests, religion differs from private belief in "something eminently social." Who would think of cutting off their daughter's labia? And her clitoris? And putting a twig into her vagina to keep a small hole open for her to pee and menstruate through later, then binding her legs together for weeks? Until she is of marriageable age. According to the culture that perpetuates this mutilation the practice purifies a female. Makes her special. Gives her the grace to be a seemly wife. Like breast implants and designer vaginas.

Religion blinkers people and causes them to consider themselves apart from the unconditionally connected universe, a wound we cannot sustain. Religion permits unconscionably deviant behavior and doesn't relate to the suffering of other species experimented upon in vivisection laboratories. Doesn't see destruction in the burning of forests through unequivocal greed. Doesn't even seem to cotton on that we are quickly being poisoned with chemical and plastic ingestion through the promotion of cleanliness. A minimum of one fifth of the human genome has already been patented. Owned. Therefore, the future is open to slavery once again. Legally.

King James was the man responsible for the English translation of the bible into a language for all who could read. The children of christians are taught, from very young, the quote from the biblical chapter genesis: Let us make man in our image, after our likeness: and let them have dominion over the fish of the sea, and over the fowl of the air, and over the cattle, and over all the earth, and over every creeping thing that creepeth upon the earth.

The "our..." refers to elohim, the pluralizing of an earlier Canaanite concept represented in many instances by bulls. Very phallic. Whether religious, atheist or nothing at all, we've all been indoctrinated into this fascist ideology in some way or other. As much the cause of our soaring architectural wonders as our capacity to water-board or lobotomize dissidents. People raised amongst religious communities are brainwashed into believing they are better. Than what? Than whom? There is no love in this. There is also no logic.

I worked to weed out the religiosity from both my language and behavior. I have been called a cultural pedant because christmas, easter and halloween are nothing. For not participating in the con. I just can't. I hear all the reasons why I should, but why?

The difficulty in knowing something is that one can't unlearn. In Joseph Campbell's Occidental Mythology, he speaks of the three creation myths in genesis that were somehow missed in the editing process. I've pondered the culture of the Pazyryk people and their elaborate burial of a sorceress or queen, or both, two and a half thousand years ago, exotic, powerful and heavy with tattoos, beneath her four horses. And the mystical journey experienced by psychiatrist Olga Kharitidi in the ways of the Siberian shaman. She wrote Entering the Circle to describe her quite ecstatic experience.

I know that woman in the Altai Mountains. She's somewhere in my bones. Somewhere in all our bones is the lore we no longer speak and voices of spirits that howl across the barrens of the tundra from before, when it was a forest.

Everyone will be forgotten and that really is not a problem.

Immortality, despite any theory or ideology, is real. Cannot be otherwise. Because of compost. The *I* ceases to be, but matter becomes ash or food for other species. Grandeur. To know I feed the descendants of eagles a thousand generations after I am Ly. To be those who eat the beast that grazes the grass that grows from my remains gives me deep satisfaction. Awareness of love. Everything I eat or wear or touch or look upon is a relative.

Once upon a time, in my life, I wore silver and bronze, carnelian, turquoise and garnet. Talismans and amulets, many of my own making. While I lived in Kooroocheang I learned the art of the silver smith from Russell, a master of metal, who had a reputation in his younger years of seducing the wife of every man in the Ballarat football team. We lived just up the road from him and an entire alternative community. My astrologer friend wore an amulet of solid silver that he'd made with Russell's help, using a carved cuttlefish as a crucible. I decided I'd like to learn, and I asked Russell if he would teach me.

Sure. What do you want to make?

I don't know yet; can I get back to you?

You teach me a bit of tarot in exchange?

Sure.

At home I designed a talisman of ridiculous intricacy for someone with zero understanding of the discipline. The base was the flat circle of a crescent moon, onto which would go an equal-armed cross lazily representing the four Greek elements of earth, air, fire and water. On top of that was to be another, small crescent moon. I arranged to spend the day with Russell, and I showed him the drawing. He grunted. He handed me a one millimeter thick sheet of silver, showed me how to place the double-zero blade within the saw, taught me to use the Archimedes drill and the vice, and explained the fine polishing papers and rouges. He demonstrated soldering and then left me.

Several hours and many broken blades later I had my flat crescent moon. Polished and taken to him for comment.

Not perfect, he said.

Where?

Everywhere. There are imperfections everywhere. You want coffee?

I went back to the bench and my work. What could he see that I couldn't? A sweet shot of espresso later and I could see, because I was determined to, smaller and smaller imperfections.

A couple of hours passed and he came over to the bench. He studied my drawing.

He made a small scoffing sound in his throat and said, you won't do it.

Fuck off, Russell.

By evening the amulet was made and Russell sauntered over. You ever going home, he asked.

When's my next lesson.

Don't need one.

What?

Perfection and challenge. Feel free to come and play anytime.

I gifted or sold every piece I ever made except two. One was a small silver dagger, its hilt bound with black linen thread, dressed with ochre-stained oak moss oil and wrapped around that tiny handle. The pommel, a crescent moon. Halfway down the double edged blade a serpent coiled around a delicate silver staff. The other was an interwoven pentagram.

I eventually even gave them both away.

CHAPTER 24

1986, the year of the Chernobyl nuclear meltdown and European acid rain, I finally had the time to finish the outer circle notes that I'd began in Blackheath. I mailed them to Nevill Drury.

Several weeks later I received a contract with a note that said, bet you didn't think getting published was this easy. Unity/Prism in England was to be my first publisher. I didn't even give the work the title. Nevill did. This was a decade of *ways*: The Way of the Peaceful Warrior, The Way of the Shaman, all eighties books, so in 1987 my first book was called The Way of the Goddess. A very wiccanly flavoured textbook because by then I had forgotten my own language. Written primarily as a training manual for those of us living in the southern hemisphere, most of whom were practicing wiccan ritual but according to practitioner and writers of the northern hemisphere. Later that year I received two pre-release copies of my own book and partied hard. Got exceedingly drunk on Dom Benedictine with Tamara Dmytryszyn, bestie with whom I later learned about wonder through the forest medicine psilocybin.

We moved from Kooroocheang to a house near Jubilee Lake where peacocks raided the veggie patch and I salvaged the withies of a rowan tree that a farmer in the field next door had cut down. I made a wand of them. I braided them, tied them with red thread, sealed the ends with sealing wax, tied bells on red ribbons and hung several raven feathers from the same ribbons.

We relocated from there to a house surrounded by dozens of elder elms. One night, in a wild thunderstorm, lightning struck one of the trees, severing a six foot long, slim branch that became my staff. Powerful magic when a storm creates art and mystery.

Why did we move around so much? The Trickster had picked me a man who had as addictive a personality as one could get and he was a collector and hoarder of things he might one day fix and use.

An initially lovely cottage would, within months, be a junkyard of parts for anything from sewing machines and pushbikes to fridges and copper wiring. I couldn't afford to renew my driver's license for a few years when the younger children were small so while I'd be reading cards the Trickster, wondering how best to piss me off this time, would go to a tip somewhere and scrounge for treasure. When sufficient treasure had built up and not been fixed and not been used we would move on because I would be too embarrassed to invite either coven or client.

The last house we occupied in Victoria was just down the road from Kattemingga Lodge, a bespoke horse riding retreat at Blackwood on a vast spread of native bush. Nola and I had met over her reading. What turned her from client to friend was the prediction that a mystic mountain on the land would go back in time and make her a bucket-load of money.

    How did you know? She asked after the reading.
    What?
    That I have a little tourist attraction down the road called Mystic Mountain. Come and have coffee with me. I'd love to show you.
    We drove there in her clanger of a Mercedes Benz. She pulled off the road at the klutzy Mystic Mountain sign. We accessed the park past a little café and kiosk. A walk-through fenced bush with native wildlife for families.
    Wrong mountain, I said.
    What?
    The mountain I saw was bare.
    Oh. Then I have no idea what you're talking about.
    I think she was disappointed. A few years on The Man from Snowy River television series took over a bare mountain on her property and built a nineteenth century village there.
    She, my kids and I rode through the high country on her great, tall, rough haired horses rugged up against the cold or near naked when the temperature soared to forty five degrees.

CHAPTER 25

Exxon-Valdez befouled the world in 1989 with the tragedy of that oil spill, considered one of the most devastating human-caused environmental disasters in known history, the largest oil spill to have occurred so far. There had been many. The first in 1967: the S.S. Torrey Canyon's dump off the coast of Cornwall.

I wrote The Way of Merlyn and I taught the first tarot collective. And I overheard a Radio National interview with a husband and wife couple who were scientists. Travelling the world exploring different forms of divination.

Tarot defies the Laws of Probability, the woman explained.

What's that? I thought, my ears pricked as up as possible. Some unknown knowledge.

So I embarked on a rudimentary study of quantum physics: the philosophies of Gary Zukav in The Dancing Wu Li Masters, Fritjof Capra's The Tao of Physics and others. When I taught, I taught about eternity. That nothing is either good or bad, that life just is, that destiny is both written and unwritten, that light is both particle and wave and that one would never know if an event was destiny unless predicted. That reading tarot for oneself, friends, family and loved ones, is dangerous or impossible because no one can have objectivity with someone well known to them. I read for people only while they remained relative strangers.

Those were the days when correspondences seemed to be the way of magic. One had to follow rules. Friday was the day of Venus; the corresponding color was pink. Cast the enchantment to summon love. A waste of space in memory's mansion. I learned to do what was needed whenever necessary. The same lesson as that of the ouija board. Time and again anarchy blew down straw houses, liberated wolf from under the man-made mantle of monster.

On occasion we held large public gatherings or weekend workshops. To hand make incense, experience ritual, teach seasonal ceremony. At one of these I met Sara McQ destined for initiation.

Now everybody, tense your fingers, I said softly, walking carefully between their floor-bound bodies. All twenty people clenched their fists except Sara. Her fingers splayed wide. Later that day, as we talked, I looked into her eyes and saw witch, like pack or tribe. She went on to initiate. Now there were eleven in the Victoria coven, including Sara, later to be joined by the ice-blue eyed Glenys and English woman Virginia, our destinies forming a tapestry of prophesy and magic. The others of the coven, irrelevant here.

That year's spring equinox gathering was held at Kattemingga. Guest reservations had been cancelled, with the exception of an old couple that couldn't be shaken off. We wanted to celebrate the dawn and subsequent tree-planting, feasting and abandon without unwanted attention.

Kattemingga is eucalypt country and Nola had requested that the coven and all our visitors bring European tree seedlings so that a traditional grove could be planted in a clearing, especially prepared. The Olympic-sized, indoor swimming pool had been boarded over for the winter and we held the ritual there. With all walls made of glass the night, the candles and an outside storm of white, took us all to Europe.

The local men had built a pyre of seasoned, crisscrossed logs with a chimney in the center. Ten foot up. To be lit at the turning of winter to spring at dawn. High on a ridge overlooking miles of forest extending to the eastern horizon.

The ground was thick with snow as, huddled together and filling the air with breath-frost, our forty or so friends and our families readied for the spectacle. Four big blokes thrust burning brands into the base and the flame took within seconds, the chimney of air in its center a funnel of roaring flame, the blaze towering twenty feet into the twilight of sky just as the sun limned the distant horizon with an intensity that hurt the eye.

A collective deep-throated roar rose from the pack until slowly, hungry, we made our way into the lodge with its huge open hearths and a feast that lasted all day. The children played in the snow and Jarrod built the perfect ant.

Later we carried what we needed into the forest to the clearing. To plant. We hadn't known we'd been watched.

Each spring, just after the equinox, the coven and our families packed cars and trailers and headed north to a place called Araganoon Bay near Tathra on the south coast of New South Wales. Through the grapevine we'd made contact with local Bega witches Bill and Naomi Lewis who put out a quarterly magazine. We met Bill on our first reconnaissance to the region and he showed us a secret track to a deserted beach.

Once camped, set up, fires alight, we swam naked and ate our fill of fresh local produce, glorying in the end of the cold.

That holiday was different for me. I thought I had a really bad case of the flu. I found out later that it was bronchial asthma.

We returned to the headline The Devil Rides Down to Daylesford splashed across the front page of the local paper, the Advocate. People wanting to remain anonymous had reported to their local pastor that they had witnessed dozens of black-robed and hooded figures carrying a dead horse's head into the forest, in an ominous, candle-lit procession in the middle of the night. He had notified the newspaper and had been given three pages to carry on about the dangers of witchcraft and satanism.

One of our friends who worked for a real estate agency was fired because she was also an astrologer, another tool of the devil. A single woman with two small children. Were we pissed off or what? Another preacher. Again.

I requested equal space with the paper. They agreed if I'd write my own copy. I'd had public interviews and debates before. One with John Singleton (Singo) on his radio show. He set out to bake me. Laughing that witchcraft as a thing for weirdoes. Futile goading. His big Rhodesian Ridgeback was under the desk, though, trying to get to the packed lunch I had in my bag on the floor between my legs. Most of the interview was one sided with Singo asking questions and me responding to his dog's attempted thrusts between my closed knees. Fred Nile on radio in the studio for a talk-back about witchcraft. When all of us witches phoned in that night we pretty much worked out that no one can debate a brainwashed person.

    The Advocate allocated three pages and the local radio station 3 CCC suggested a public debate. I was ready. The preacher, however, had gone to ground. 3 CCC played The Burning Times song by Charlie Murphy, every hour for three weeks, trying to drag him from his bolt hole with no luck. I'd had just about enough of that place and these priests and the people who believed them. The following full moon I gathered enough wide, flat stones for my purpose. I took myself into the fields—this time alone—and created a stone guardian as a gift to the earth, to guide us to somewhere more home. That was destiny, but not yet.

Adam lived in Daylesford, in a house all on his own. The Trickster was his enemy and I couldn't leave. There was nowhere to go.

    Tamara found a fledgling hawk on the road on her way to work. Alive but fallen from some unseen nest, unhurt. She swaddled the raptor and drove to the vet. She then called me, and I phoned Adam. He went straight there and claimed her. The vet had agreed.

Adam taught her to fly.

CHAPTER 26

In 1990 the Berlin Wall came down and later the same year Pink Floyd was to sing the iconic The Wall to a united Germany. Nelson Mandela was released from prison after twenty seven years and South Africa and the African Congress began the talks that would liberate its people from the condescension of apartheid. Nothing Compares to You, by Prince and sung by Sinead O'Connor was my favorite song. Victoria, Australia made riding a pushbike without a helmet illegal.

Early in that year what was left of the coven, however, prepared for a series of rituals that began in August. What inspired them was yet another overwhelmingly vivid dream. I stood amongst a crowd of thousands in a grey square surrounded by massive, grey stone constructions. High up at the rampart of the hand-built fortress was a woman, a silhouette, her hair the color of shadow, a pennant in the dawn wind. The throng shouted asherah, asherah. I woke still hearing the chant. I didn't know what the word meant but I intended to find out.

These were the days when we kept vast libraries of reference books on all aspects of magic, mysticism, myth and lore. I called the coven and suggested they rock on over and have tea. When I spoke about the dream word they were in my library for the remainder of the day, searching through as many books as were pertinent. The first reference we found was in Barbara G Walker's Women's Encyclopedia of Myths and Secrets. She explains that an asherah is a grove in which a certain sect, also called the asherah, used to gather. The word was considered both a tree and an anthropomorphic female deity with an upper case A.

Other texts write of Star of the Sea, Queen of Heaven, Stellar Maris. Canaanite but with references to lion, cow, serpent and tree. The second discovery was in a second-hand, 1967 edition of Raphael Patai's The Hebrew Goddess and the next, the classic Merlin Stone's When God was a Woman. The asherah is a *tree of life* and has reflections in druidry, a language of trees called ogham, a magical system of writing, the only one used by the Celts. Ogham (pronounced och-am, or, in Irish, *og-úaim*) uses twenty letters, each relating to a plant or tree. The Hebrew alphabet utilizes twenty two letters. How the series of rituals unfolded from the original dream to the last rite is a whirlwind because everything happened so fast.

Through divination we understood that human-related harm to earth was moving towards some sociological and environmental tipping point. That, no matter how small, our input was still important again, in the way of the Butterfly Effect.

When the coven learned what had to be digested in just a few weeks most bolted. Four of us remained: Virginia, Sara, Glenys and me. We planned the first of the rituals—six nights a week for ten weeks—for imbolg (pronounced imelick) on August 2nd. In the lead-up to that date we learned the letters by rote, made a rose cross and carved the letters' positions as the diagram showed.

We studied every aspect of every sephirah, the four worlds, their numerical significance, the esoteric and exoteric meaning of each letter, the branches linking sephiroth on the glyph of the Tree and the associations of all branches and tributaries. Sigil magic. Grimoires were hand-made and leather bound for the purpose of these rituals. Each of us was to work the rite on her own for five of the six nights and we'd come together on Fridays and work the sixth together before discussing how we'd gone during the week. One aspect of this kind of magic is the use of harmonics as well as image. I was spooked when whispering the sigil for kether, metatron (of briah), a word represented by the letters mīm, tēt, tēt, rēš, nūn. As I breathed each letter aloud there was an echo to tēt, tēt. I heard death, death.

Afterwards I ate a meal to ground myself. I made a cup of tea and turned on the television to the late night news. Saddam Hussein's Iraqi army had just invaded Kuwait.

Finding the ritual in the first place had been a sleuth-like adventure. Buried in three separate sections of Israel Regardie's book, The Golden Dawn. We removed all the sexist, dogmatic, religious connotations and it was then able to breathe in a vigorous, old-growth, organic way.

Strange things happened. My family and I lived in a bluestone house and the walls were eight to ten inches thick. My nemeton was a small room off the sitting room, the stone painted white. The four of us were together for the Friday ritual. When we were done and the candles extinguished, I switched on the lamp for us to disrobe. The back wall had cracked across all the stones in a zigzag from floor to ceiling. There had been no sound.

We had no expectations so when visions and communications began from the first night, as though a window had opened to other places and times outside of time each of us filled our grimoires with the words spoken from intelligences—perhaps considered spirits or djinn—of that tree. Lucid and present, intelligent and poetic, cutting and dangerous. The war in Iraq was over the night the rituals ended and we had received wisdom and prophesy over those ten weeks that continue to inspire and unfold decades later. But I was ill. Too many people and too much to juggle. I suffered violent fits of coughing, the breathlessness of a deep sea diver only relieved when I could get into a room alone.

I was thirty nine. A bone-deep certainty filled me with dread. If nothing changed I would die very soon.

PART TWO

On the dirt track, miles from home. Sleet. My big old army greatcoat dragging in the mud. I must have looked like a mad woman. But at the base of an elm just up ahead seven raven feathers lay in a row, glossy, pristine, like a talisman. I just stood and stared for a very long time. Oblivious to the bite of the day. My mind wandering myth world in search of meaning.

This was the premier of the journey into another life. Initiation is just that. A moment. Terror, amusement, curiosity and awe. I was leaving this life. I had no idea what lay ahead.

WILDING THE BITCH, WITH MORE PUPPIES OF HER OWN

CHAPTER 27

1991. A Saturday morning. I opened the newspaper to the full page advertisement for Terminator Two. Linda Hamilton in black top and jeans, sunnies, fully automatic rifle on her hip and arms of serpentine muscle. I thought I want to look like that. I didn't. I was overweight. I smoked dope at night and ate my way through the house until I fell asleep. To avoid intimacy. But the deep world was thrumming with mystery and pulling me like a curious puppy nosing the musk of a bear.

Just after the midwinter solstice I began to wake from dreams of communication with one entity or another. I'd look at the clock and the digital display was giving a show, mirroring digits such as 2:42 or 1:21. This would necessitate me getting up, going to the kitchen, making coffee, lighting a ciggie and writing furiously. Everything that had been in the dream. Usually I went to sleep again but the longer this went on the stranger the feelings of waking from a deep sleep bathed me. I was in shadow. In mist. In a relationship I had no idea how to escape from. Living the lie that everything was okay. Wolf jumping through hoops in a traveling circus, despite deep friendships, despite the magic. How could I dare tell that I was tired and weak when I had a reputation as a mask? When things must be done? Be powerful. Raise my puppies?

Another life initiation began. Again, I was clueless.

That merciless forest. Impossible maze. Actively seeking the deep green and grey of winter's heart. Outside, bulky with warm wool and sturdy boots, my face invisible. To be walking away from expectation within the days and nights of that tiny cottage became an imperative. Weather bleak and bitter cold, with teeth that tore at exposed skin. The sky just above my head as dense as steel-wool. I walked the dirt track that began beside my garden and wound and meandered and disappeared into and through the darkness and perpetual twilight of the forest of ghost gums and paperbarks and thigh high fern dripping with pearls of moisture. The path threaded ten kilometers to the back door of a friend's house. We had coffee. I didn't need to talk. I walked home again. I lived on salad and soup because everything else was just too heavy and I didn't know other ways of cooking yet.

You're going to Byron Bay. The statement woke me from a deep sleep at 4:24 on an August morning.

When are you going? Virginia asked when I phoned her the next day.

October. After this tarot group.

I'll ride shotgun, she said.

The following Saturday I told my students about relocating, assuring them that I'd complete their training first.

Do you know where Byron Bay is, the Guide to the Return asked.

No idea.

An hour south of the Queensland border.

Oh. Okay. Interesting.

You don't do you?

Know what? I dreamed the name.

Byron Bay is the alternative spiritual heart of the country, he said. I've got land there.

Really?

There's a camper van. You got a place to land?

I hadn't thought that far ahead.

Stay as long as you want. I'll be surfing the Great Ocean Road all the way into next year.

Money was a problem though. Think, Ly.

The Trickster took the children to and from school while I worked. He came to the door with his hand out after the last client of the day. The kids stayed with me and he'd go shopping. By now shopping also included alcohol and marijuana.

My tarot parlor was the front room of the house. I had a densely woven, green antique velvet cloth on my round table. Every day, from when I knew I was leaving, I hid most of the money under the cloth, spread out so carefully as to be unnoticed. The Trickster would come in and I'd cough up twenty bucks.

Where's the rest?

People are having a hard time. Doing a lot of freebies. He knew I was lying.

Adam was nineteen and in a relationship. He remained in Victoria. He'd come when and if he wanted to. The day we left Virginia and I, the two younger children, a dog and two cats (one with newborn kittens), our clothes, treasures and toys, took off in my old, blue Holden station wagon with a goat trailer towed behind in which were stacked all my trunks and books. I thanked the stone guardian. We were going home. The Trickster was stunned and confused when told I was leaving.

We arrived in Byron Bay on the seventeenth of October 1991. To paradise. We set up camp, the kids and I in the caravan, Virginia in the huge four-person tent on the other side of the moat, a dam built in a circle surrounding the site. The weather was balmy, the ocean ridiculously perfect and the people we passed in the street all smiled.

The first week there I enrolled Jarrod and Serenity in the local state school, and Virginia and I explored.

We discovered Triado's coffee shop (I'd never been to a coffee shop). We had come to a part of the country where people were environmentally conscious, aware of the impact they made and determined to be better.

I unpacked my ritual things and there, forgotten in the bottom of the box was the velvet necklace I had sewn the snakeskin into all those years ago. So often, I know with the gift of hindsight, something precious or profound must be discarded or given back to the world. Now was that time for the snakeskin talisman. I unpicked the threads and unrolled the material. Long black seeds.

Virginia looked over my shoulder.

Can I touch?

Sure.

She rolled them between her fingers. What are you going to do?

Come on, I said, wrapping a sarong firmly around me, pulling on shoes against the snakes, her doing the same. We climbed the gravel driveway, crossed the road and entered the forest on the other side. And we scattered them. A mystery forever unsolved because we never went back to discover what, if anything, grew. Hadn't occurred to either of us. Strange when I reflect. Like a veil across the event.

We swam naked in the sea at Kings Beach, wandered the shops, ate fish caught off the rocks at Suicide, enjoyed the ambiance of the cafes and the hippies, the travellers with backpacks from America, Japan and Norway. We danced to the music of buskers and discovered Pendragon's books and magical supply shop. Decorated in dark grey. Doesn't sound like much but the experience was earthy. Walking into the cool of a cave.

A copy of The Way of the Goddess was on the bookshelf. I ruffled the pages at the man behind the desk.

I wrote this, I said.

His eyes widened. Are you that Ly?

Yes.

I can quote your book from cover to cover, he smiled. Will you be running workshops? Will you be initiating people? Will you read my tarot?

He thought himself a metaphysician, but he was actually the Gatekeeper of my own initiatory Return. He wanted me to teach him. He could arrange everything. He would spread the word that I had come.

I've just arrived, I said. I don't know what I'm doing yet.

The woman who has the crystal shop behind Triado's café has a big spare room, he said, grinning like a fool. I'm sure between us we can afford the rent. I can help.

Thanks, that'd be lovely.

Another lifetime, in a wild wood and a warm new burrow.

But then the Trickster arrived. The Guide had been a drug dealer and had sold him pot. He had told him where we were.

He had nowhere to stay and Serenity and Jarrod begged me to take him in. I didn't know what else to do. I often had trouble saying no. I relented. Big mistake. He was from the last life and had no place in this one.

The crystal shop owner said yes, and the word was spread. Within two weeks I had an occasional clientele and ten students for the tarot collective.

Sara McQ arrived, and she and Virginia took off north, like nomads.

The Hapkido studio at the end of town. I'd learned about this style of martial art in the Paddington days. Guys down the back lane were practitioners. I asked the kids if they wanted to have a go at learning self-defence; at knowing how to fight. They did. I took them on the first evening and sat on the bench at the back of the room. And watched. The bubble of excitement got bigger and bigger as the class, children and adults under the supervision of three black belts, went through their warm-up, katas and training. I desperately wanted to do this.

You're too old, said the rat voice.

What is the rat voice? It reminds me of a parasite contagious with cultural criticism, the backyard barbeque or family dinner sarcasm that's supposed to be funny but is subtly cruel.

Seeking symbiosis it suggests I sympathize with mediocrity. Tells me to behave like some version of lady that I cannot comprehend. I am simply not modest. Do not cut my hair just because I am old. Choose study over knitting even though I enjoy knitting on my own terms. I tell Irish legends to Irish catholics and am politically incorrect. Too many people shut up and say nothing in the face of disintegrating rights. I embarrass the rat voice. Always present, I at least have sufficient sense of humor to cause the snide creature to cringe.

Thirty nine isn't old, I countered. And I was healthy and lean by then. I'd shed kilos of body fat on the long winter walks down the back roads in sleet and killer winds and, to my children's despair, I no longer cooked macaroni with triple cheese, or lasagna.

You are, you know.
What?
Too old.
Shut up.

At the close of class I spoke to one of the teachers. I asked if I might try out.

Of course, said Aruptananda.

What do you think, I asked the kids? They both agreed that mummy also training would be loads of fun.

You're too old, said the voice, more a whisper than anything. Defeated.

Two nights later I attended my first class and I had never known such pain and breathlessness. And that was just from the warm-up. I carried on, however, and got through that first session alive. The following day I was so sore I could hardly move. I was back again two nights later.

Michelle trained with me at the first tarot collective and we'd go for coffee most days. I confided to her that I had to move out with the kids. She had an apartment right at the beach front, with a double garage converted into a studio. The kids could have the other bedroom.

The Trickster had been up all night drinking and filling my ears with verbal venom. Waving a knife about threatening to kill me, or else do himself in.

When he fell into a comatose sleep just after dawn I packed everything I could into the car. I walked the kids up the hill to the bus stop and kissed them goodbye, said I'd pick them up after school, walked back down the hill, got into my car and drove away.

Once at Michelle's apartment I phoned a local doctor and suggested a man at a particular address might be either destructive or suicidal. The doctor rang me later. He had temporarily admitted him to a psychiatric facility.

After school that day I drove the children to Michelle's and explained the separation. The change took a lot for them to come to comprehend because they had not witnessed the misbehavior. I explained that he was sick and was working on getting better. I agreed to them visiting him when that happened.

When he was released from the institution he returned to the property living with the cats. Over the months I was able to retrieve some of my possessions including a kitten that had been a newborn when we had left Victoria. The others were dead.

I named her Pyewacket. The year was 1992.

Master Kim, the teacher who introduced Hapkido to Australia in 1979, double-graded me from a white belt straight through to yellow. He had little English and was a happy, soft, round man. Looks can be deceiving. I knew that and still he took me by surprise. Through an interpreter he asked for a volunteer from amongst the black belts and

Dans to demonstrate ki and the way of circular movement. All except Aruptananda took a step back. He went a sickly shade of pale. Kim proceeded to hurl him across the dojo with the mere bend of a knee and hint of a movement, a guileless smile lighting his soft brown eyes as he demonstrated for another ten minutes until he decided that we juniors understood.

CHAPTER 28

The first fingernail crescent of moon rising in a pale turquoise sky takes my breath away. Always a surprise. Like something voyeuristic but delicate, only seen in the early part of the night. The first glimpse represents so many things but not one that is forlorn or done. This is the new moon, the crescent a sign as old as humanity, of renewal. Of a cycle within a cycle. Trusted. My first tattoo was a crescent moon, inked into my pectoral by hand by one of my initiates while I lived in the shadow of Mount Kooroocheang. The needling took three nights, and hurt, but the experience changed me. Deep within my DNA I felt the ancestral people of the woman that birthed me. And because I felt thus, so would the roots of trees, horses and owls, bat clouds and the mountains in Connemara. The Pennines of the northern tribes of the Britons. That tattoo has long since been covered by more ink because body stories can trap a person, too, if we're not careful.

    I was inked after many years of studying the known cultural practices of my possibly-Celtic ancestors. Priteni. The painted people. They ink-, soot- or ash-filled themselves with tattooing just as is done from Scandinavia to Samoa to Alaska to Aotearoa, to Japan, with the art of culture, status or clan. Just like that woman buried within the tundra in the Altai Mountains. But the practice was outlawed. The Romans banned their soldiers from the procedure. The custom became a rarity due to the subsequent invasions of Celtic, Irish and European territories. Tattooing was non-Roman. Deemed barbaric (foreign).

    There is an order to things however random they might seem: the moss and lichen covered rocks amongst the behemoth rowan trees just off the road in South Wales; the movement of the rivulet between one bank of blackberries and another. These movements are the earth mother's art. She sucks up her center, sometimes, and spews out ash plumes from volcanoes, higher than the mushroom cloud over

Maralinga or Hiroshima, and we watch, thinking ourselves observers and commentators on a film set. But we are amongst her, we are her. And everything. Knowing this is the way of witch. I can send my secrets through tree roots and know the message will reach a destination. Unlike people who can be blind and lonely and caught within themselves, tree roots reach out and are connected. I could send a soft sense to a nightingale in China and is the touch received, or am I delusional?

Through word of mouth the children and I were invited to live in the Pink House in Shirley Lane, Byron Bay. This communal house had been held onto by the alternative movement for years. The owners—an artist-writer couple—lived in Sydney. A studio-style garage and an indoor bedroom had become available. I transformed a former into a cottage and my nemeton (safe-place) and Jarrod and Serenity shared the pink and pumpkin bedroom along the hall inside. Rats lived in both the ceilings and the walls, so I hefted Pyewacket through the manhole into the space between the ceiling and the roof, with a bowl of fresh water and a blanket. A few days and a lot of noise later she came down, her tail a pennant of pride, to immediately search the neighborhood for a worthy mate. We had to clean out the carcasses because she only ate bits.

Adam, his girlfriend and a dog named Crow moved to the shire and hired a caravan at another bay just up the coast. Having all my offspring close brought me great happiness. Being with the Trickster did not. He was now dragging the man whose body he possessed down the rabbit hole. He hid the addictions well from the younger children, only indulging at night. But his mind was sick. One of us had to leave and it was me.

Why do we stay when we know the relationship is rotten? We really ought to forgive ourselves in the light of the confusion of consciousness. Chemistry? Getting used to having someone around? Fear of ending up alone? All of the above? We all join when the dysfunction exposes itself. We all become complicit. Many of us hide what we know in cupboards and down drains. No, he's really okay. He's got other qualities. He's very helpful around the house and with the children. Oh, really?

Take a chance. Get out. We can't lie to ourselves, only pretend. Cultural suicide. But also more than that because these thoughts are predictable. They swell from the place of city streets and suburban graveyards.

Deepen. Summon courage. Cat-cunning. Men can't surely all be this weak and lazy? Into the ownership of motherhood and women? With very few exceptions, however, this was my experience of them.

Then came the eureka moment. I was being haunted by the Trickster from within the world of myth. I saw him in every situation. Knew him with every bone in my body. That Penny spun again.

I had been sliding down a mountain of words made of other people's decisions of how I should behave and why I should do anything, since I can remember. This landed me in a valley of amber, sap from the trees of a million years ago and I smelled the beauty. What am I to do now?

Six months into this season of happiness I was tested in Hapkido a second time. I passed and was again double-graded but Aruptananda suggested that, although I had excellent form I was too petite to cause any damage should I need to defend anyone. He suggested I pump iron.

I began working with free weights at the old gym downstairs from the dojo, owned by a woman named Fairlie who went on to study tarot with me in later years.

I was the only woman doing free weights.

Not since the chainsaw days before Kooroocheang had I been this physically active. After the children had gone to school I trained. Five days a week. My workout included half an hour of intense cardio, then an hour of resistance training and two nights a week Hapkido. Then twenty four year old Lisa Engeman, once a client and a wild young seeker of something, became a friend. She joined me. She was later to do all the artwork for The Feast of Flesh and Spirit, to suffer a life-threatening brain tumour, become partially blind, live on an island as an artist and become involved with this book. But for now she lived across the road with Virginia in a caravan in her back garden. We trained every morning, drank coffee together, laughed about anything and discussed magic.

Next to join us at the gym was Tattoo Zak. A round, bald, heavily inked man. I'd acquired their Byron Bay Creative Tattoo shop for him and the people he worked with after Pendragon's closed down and we became friends.

I'd been sitting on the ground outside the fish and chip shop waiting for an order when he had seen me and burst into tears. I patted the ground beside me. His wife had left him for another man and he was devastated.

But... I began.
What?
Zak, you're a fricken butterball.
You think that's maybe why?
Tell you what—
What?
Come to the gym with me. I swear on my life I can give you biceps and triceps in twelve weeks.
Not gunna happen.

But he came. And I did. And I talked him into joining the mainly female cardio group. At first he again said no way. I just looked at him, telepathing all that female flesh into his awareness. He joined the group. Before he went the other way, downhill, he had the body he'd only ever dreamed of and was in love with several women. So began my relationship with ink. Each glyph a story, each coloring a meaning into my skin. After many years and much thought I decided to get tattooed on my face.

When I first asked Tattoo Zak he went green around the mouth.
Ah, darlin', I'd be breaking the law.
What? Why?
Under British Commonwealth law to tattoo the face or hands is illegal. It's considered an offence to deface the property of the crown.

My expression caused him to laugh. He never disagreed, but he took a long time to consider me. Me, not him. What I was about to do. That I would cross a line and do what, culturally, was a taboo thing. I didn't, then, know the word was really *tapu*, and was an altogether necessary reason not to go to the river at certain times of the year. Everyone thought taboo meant evil or bad.

I explained about the killings of our ancestors and the demise of the cultural practice of body art by us Celts. I explained that no, I didn't have to do this and that I was under no illusion that I could possibly be culturally outcast. But some things are just appropriate.

He had me kneel between his knees. He placed his hands on my head in a strange biker benediction. He even wept a little and quietly. And with the lightest touch of a single-needle gun he tattooed the delicate crescent, three ravens and a movement of wind in their sky, and finished with triple dots beneath the moon to represent the trefoil of earth and wind and water. As I lay under the gun, entranced, I saw all my mothers in a Fibonacci spiral into deep time. All would have been punished or killed for this, their cultural right. It's gone now. Lasered off when others began copying it. Getting rid of it wasn't hard. I learned more about my indigene in later years. It's been surpassed by other work.

The tattooing ended in a geis (pronounced *gesh*). An Irish word. Not a curse exactly, but strange. A geis can even be a gift and is definitely a reckoning. Can be known immediately, as in the Irish annals, or can creep up on one as did mine. The more tattoos I acquired the less jewelry I felt able to wear until I was down to just one earring. I only became aware of what was happening around 2009 or thereabouts, and at first I thought, don't be ridiculous. But when I attempted to thwart this presumed geis, and wear rings or talismans, the metaphorical shit would hit the fan and anything that could go wrong did. I challenged, pointlessly. From the first moment, in the morning, of popping that pentagram around my neck, chaos, and a maelstrom of discord, would rise towards some silent crescendo. Once I removed the offending token or jewel everything becalmed.

I tried time after time to thwart this with always the same result. From arguments for no reason, to someone I loved getting hurt. Patterns can be beautiful. Random. Places like the forest in South Wales that continues to flourish. By being left alone. Not interfered with. I came to understand that beauty is a thing that needs no garnish. That witch needs nothing to show for being witch. Nothing predictable like the dangle of a pentagram or the amber and jet in a so-called traditional witch's necklace. Friends and family don't even think about my tattoos. The designs have blended with my personality and are seen as nothing different from lips or fingers. Strangers sometimes want to know what they mean. I usually ask if they would inquire the same of a Samoan. They wouldn't.

Same thing, they ask.

Ask them, I reply.

Most say *ahh* in an understanding they don't feel the need to rationalize.

It wasn't until I relocated to Melbourne that I comprehended the reason for the geis. Once I knew it was associated with a person who had moved in with my family in 2007 I threw caution to the wind and ornamented up. They were eventually 'sectioned' for alcoholic dementia, but not before the madness. I slept with a hammer beside my bed, despite other weapons.

In 1993 I began a second tarot collective, all women. A disjointed mix of rebirthers, sannyasins, druids and Margaret, Celtic enthusiast and radio host. The only all-woman class I've ever taught. Not the most exciting group as they were all deeply entrenched in their own dogmas. What percolated, though, was the idea of a festival for women. Nothing against men, just a chance to talk about things that many were too embarrassed to discuss with men present. I came up with the name Wild and Wise Women's Festival. To be held over a long weekend in two months. Involved were Ayla, Noni, Jacinta, me and a few others. We used some of the tarot sessions to explore the outcome to our venture. One of the women asked what we should charge while she shuffled the cards. The only thing that stands out in my mind was the devil card.

We don't charge, I said.

We have to.

Why?

We'll have to hire equipment and feed the facilitators, not to mention advertising.

We can ask for donations.

No. I think around a hundred and twenty or thirty bucks for a full weekend isn't asking too much.

The devil card, huh? Corruption is one of its meanings. Poison another. Fear another. Addiction and sickness another, hate-based religions and cults in general.

I couldn't afford to pay that, I said. No single parent I know could. You'd be closing the doors to people in need.

What you're suggesting could get us into debt.

Been reading tarot a long time, I said.

The festival went ahead by donation only. We erected tents for massage, rebirth, discussions on contraception, birth and menopause. Two tepees, one topped with rainbow pennants in which children were told stories, had their faces painted, dressed up and generally played, and plenty of cooking fires and food to share. One enormous tepee dominated. Everyone gathered within every afternoon for discussion: topics from experiences of violence and rape, from loneliness to orgasm and first sexual encounters. We had a hundred and thirty participants not including the facilitators.

First we paid respects to the traditional custodians, the Bunjalung of the Arakwal Nations. Then everyone set up camps and made themselves a home.

The first night was full moon and we worked a ritual to merge ourselves with the spirits of earth. The women put their arms around each other's shoulders and stomped to their right. They made a deep noise in their throats as they did so. I had my broadsword and danced in the center. The experience was immensely powerful and tactile. Each woman was covered in sweat and each woman reported goose bumps and tingles. One almost fainted and had to be supported. The ghostly image of grandmother Snake formed above the circle.

The weekend was outrageously successful, and we made a profit. The women who couldn't afford anything provided help cooking, cleaning and child minding. They also did most of the bump out at the end. Other women—wealthy women—gave large donations. Everything hired was paid for, as were all the facilitators.

The week after, on the way to Triado's to gather with the wolf pack for coffee, I was confronted by guys whose partners had attended the festival. Each of them either hugged me or shook my hand. Most had spent the weekend with their friends playing music. To quote one man, "I don't know what you did but I really don't care. She came home so happy and relaxed... I was seduced for goodness sake!" They'd been together four years and had a one year old daughter. He asked if this was going to be an annual event, I said I didn't know.

Ayla phoned me a year later to invite me to participate in their second Wise and Wild Women's Festival.

Same setup as last year? I asked.

No, we're not prepared to take that risk again.

Really?

Yes, we've already had a meeting and decided to charge.

Really?

Yes, and we've invited a well-known American witch to facilitate and open the event.

My, my.

Well, will you run a workshop?

When?

We open Friday night, thirteenth of August and go over the weekend.

That's a dark moon.

More interesting, don't you agree?

You think?

Are you in?

Sure. We'll come on the Sunday night. Do a dark moon rite, maybe, in the big tepee.

Not outside?

My gut says no.

Three initiates, Serenity and I rolled up in the afternoon. Rain had muddied the entire weekend and we were accosted on arrival by a posse of angry women demanding to know if I was one of the organizers. Half the facilitators hadn't shown up, no child-minding tepee and no undercover cooking camp. They wanted their money back. I said I'd see what could be done. Turns out the American witch, whose name I forget, and who no one had heard of, had opened the festival on Friday night by invoking Kali Ma, a female hindu deity. On a dark moon night. In Bunjalung country.

We carried my box of ritual things into the large tepee, stowed them out of the way and sat towards the back. Women crowded in for the afternoon's open discussion. In the center, like a ringmaster at the circus, was the American woman. She held a large stick decorated with bands of color and hung about with eagle feathers. A *talking stick*. She shouted that to be allowed to discuss anything the woman had first to request the talking stick.

Fuck your talking stick, I said.

You're not allowed to speak.

Fuck you and fuck your talking stick.

Who are you?

These women are angry.

You can't talk without the talking stick, by now yelling at me.

You want to stand up and have a say, I asked the women.

One by one they stood until over thirty women, many with children either on the breast or by their sides, glared in the direction of the administrators.

We want our money back.

A debate erupted without the talking stick. The American left at some stage and was never seen again. Eventually the organizers agreed to refund the money.

I explained we were holding a dark moon rite and that everyone was welcome. A rite of silence. I rummaged through my box and pulled out red twine and a pair of scissors.

We lit a fire in the center of the tepee, robed and adorned ourselves and waited. They came just after dark. All hundred or so (with the exception of the organizers who by this time quite likely despised me). They sat in three rows, the children playing where they wanted, the fire guarded by initiates.

I bound the red thread around the wrists of everyone; bound them all together. They knew instinctively what I was doing. Understanding is inherent in certain circumstances. At the end the tension was palpable, and the children had gone quiet. I then handed the scissors to Serenity. She understood. Walking sunwise she cut their bonds. Many wept openly. We packed and departed without saying a thing.

Within weeks Noni, one of the women in the tarot class, also one of those rebirthers left the region to travel the world. She returned with cancer everywhere and very little time to live. She phoned me three weeks before her death and asked if I'd come to her house in Mullumbimby and read her tarot. This was the first time ever that I was to read for someone on the threshold of death. When I arrived she was being assisted from the bath to her bedroom by the palliative care nurse and, although weak and without a hair on her body, she was radiant in the face of the inevitable.

Where are your cards? I asked.

In the garage somewhere.

In one of the cardboard boxes I found what remained of a pack of tarot, some thirty-odd cards. Didn't really matter how many. I asked her to shuffle, saying I only wanted her to pull three cards. I laid them out on the counterpane: ace of wands, ace of pentacles, the strength card.

New matter, I said.

New matter? What an unusual, unexpected answer. All three of us were confounded and, of course the answer was inscrutable. We turned our attention to Noni's imminent death.

Right, she said, matter-of-factly, we have to come up with a plan.

She turned to the nurse and asked her to take notes. We waited till she sat on the floor beside the bed, ready.

We need a symbol, Noni announced. Something that you wouldn't see every day.

What's happening, asked the nurse.

Noni's going to contact me after her body's died, I replied.

Oh.

So what?

We went through thing after thing, for most of the afternoon, dismissing each as plausibly reasonable.

A flower on fire, Noni finally decided. When you see a flower on fire, it'll be me.

She was dead a week later and the sannyasins held a large gathering in ceremony for her in Mullumbimby.

Damini, lead singer of the Celtic group Tané, sang a lament at Noni's funeral. Our stories were yet to cross paths.

Damini started going out with one of the tarot students, an ex-priest, and was at my house the night we went to see the movie Powder at the Pighouse Flicks. We had a row in the kitchen, her saying life was maya—illusion—me disgusted at that and arguing that life is magnificent.

Eventually Steve came and asked if we were going to yell at each other all night or could we please go see the film?

Midway through the movie she hugged my arm and whispered, I get it.

Just a few weeks later she took another person's place in a light plane ride. The plane clipped the trees at Tyagarah on elevation and exploded in a ball of fire. It was a witness described the catastrophe as looking for all the world like a chrysanthemum on fire.

CHAPTER 29

1994 I performed at a gig called Still Ain't Satisfied, based on songs from the sixties. To be performed in the main hall of the ex-whaling, ex- cattle abattoir complex called the Epicentre, just across the road from the beach. Through new friend and artist Danyelle James, just up from Sydney and camped in my backyard, I met a young virtuoso rock musician named John, who had once been lead guitar in the band Def Fx. When the director/producer of the show suggested I sing I asked John to accompany me on guitar.

What's the tune?
Simon and Garfunkel's, The Sounds of Silence.
Um.
Just make up what fits the song for you.
Oh, okay.

I sang, and John wrote this wailing, powerful, heavy metal creation that gave a dark and haunting air to a tune already dark and haunting.

I knew a music producer in Melbourne. I phoned him and asked if he could compile about a minute's worth of footage.

Like what?
Oh, I don't know, helicopters over Pnong Penh, men marching, lots of sirens going off, people screaming, you know, general pandemonium.
I can do better.
How?
I can get you live archival footage.

Our performance was just before interval. A blacked out theatre. Then the sound compilation screaming from all four corners of the vast room, ending on a siren. John took up that sound on his guitar and played the introduction that he'd composed before I sang. My voice is very gravelly but I can hold a tune. When John played his last chord the room was silent.

Oh my, that went down like a concreted criminal thrown into the Thames, I thought, glancing at John who shrugged.

The applause was then deafening.

That first night Serenity, aged eleven, sang a Supremes' number with two older women and later, Jarrod, and three other thirteen year old boys in caps, t-shirts and baggy pants down low as was the fashion, brought the house down with Heartbreak Hotel because they had all the Elvis moves.

Yantra de Vilder was the sole pianist and even though I'd only met her that first night we became friends before the following dawn. There were way too many acts and during the dress rehearsals we concluded that many were mediocre, Yantra and I sat up all night working out who we would cut despite how unhappy we were to cause offence. The following night was as successful as the first but a more restful one.

The Pink House occupants received notice that the owners were relocating from Sydney. That triggered one of the biggest and near-best spells I have ever done because I put out for something I'd never had. I worked a spell to find a free-standing house with a garden, separate bedrooms for me and the children, a kitchen that was not open-plan, a place I could afford all by myself, for just my family. Oh, and with a fireplace.

Then I found the lumps in both breasts. I had a mammogram and other tests and my doctor sent me to an oncologist in Lismore who examined me.

Hmm, he said, they could be cysts but unfortunately I'll be away for two weeks and ah... If you have cancer they are very large lumps, so you had better prepare your family for the worst.

Adam was in the caravan in the back yard and I told him, but I did not tell the younger children. Instead I sent them on the train to Ballarat where the people from Kattemingga picked them up and took them riding.

That same day the man in the house, with whom I'd been lovers but who was doing more and more methamphetamine who had asked me, a week before, if I'd drive him to Lismore for whatever. He didn't have a license or a car. I'd been flabbergasted at his lack of empathy and said no. He broke my chest bone with a palm strike. I had to get away. Again.

I began a journey inward, preparing to die. Yet another Threshold. This time I was afraid.

Darryl Reanney wrote a book on quantum theory, The Death of Forever, and I was profoundly altered when I read it. I'd picked it off the shelves at the library three times previously and hadn't been able to read past the introduction. This was my fourth attempt and I could not put it down. Darryl weaves a tapestry of physics, poetry, spirituality, anthropology and cosmology and even though I'd come close to death many times they had been quick, thoughtless. Now I had a few weeks to dwell on possibilities.

How poignant and idiotic the illusion of separation is. An impossibility. To understand that to define intelligence by standards of us as a species is inspirational and humiliating simultaneously. Everything is relative. When I suggest that a book attempted to gain my attention on four separate occasions like a raven sitting on my shoulder, gack-gacking in my ear, I don't mean to suggest metaphor. Darryl wrote that book for anyone. And that book was as much a messenger as the eighteen-wheeler that overtook me on the highway with a sign on the back saying CHILL when I was driving home in a mighty and impatient mood. As much a messenger as Viggo Mortensen reading, I never saw a wild thing feel sorry for itself, from a volume of D. H. Lawrence's poetry, in the movie G.I. Jane.

Everything talks to us if we listen. There is something to be learned every time we look out from ourselves and our own circumstances. Even in the experience of grief and sadness because at least we're feeling, not living under the plastic illusion of segregation to which consumerism and religion would have us on our knees.

I began a series of deep trance meditations. I chose consciously to drag the skulking beast, that was this fear, from my shoulder to my face, and stare.

Being stolen from my mother at birth meant there were some things I hadn't fixed. What was occurring was an initiation and the only way I could explore, pay the ferryman and have coin enough to return was to understand the myth at play. I chose the Greek legends because so much literature, in the nineties, abounded with these female archetypes.

I summoned the two with whom I empathized the most: one, Artemis the huntress, the other, Aphrodite the seductress.

The summoning was rather amusing. At first. My visualization of the images of Artemis and Aphrodite could have come straight out of a book so I knew my psyche created them. But why were they standing so close together?

What are you hiding?

Nothing.

Then move apart.

They attempted stubbornness, jutting chin from Artemis, a turn of the hips from Aphrodite, just not enough.

What's behind you? What are you hiding?

From my position as observer in the vision I became a participant, striding to the two women and heaving them aside. What was behind them was a four foot square hole in the ground with a solid iron grille. I looked in. Twenty feet below me, seated on a concrete floor, was a woman in her own underworld. Still mindful of the pantheon, I called her Persephone. Naked and painfully malnourished, she had her knees pulled up to her chest, her arms around them. Her face was to mine, and her mouth was open. Like a raptor she continually screamed, Why?

I was appalled.

Let her out.

We can't, they said. You put her there.

Let her free, I demanded.

I came to from that trance in a sweat. I knew who she was, and I knew she wasn't just me, even though I'd experienced her. She was every woman not able to comprehend why she was being punished. For anything. For being a woman. But she was me.

That's when that bright copper penny spun once more. I thought I now knew what the Trickster was all along. He was Hades, or any other name. Kept abducting me. Well, fuck you Hades. I deny you.

I didn't go into that vision again, but I knew she was released. I felt her rather than saw her. I sensed her as part of me although, other than the legend, I didn't know what part her liberation would play in my/our life yet or that she was, in the way of indigenous practitioners of healing, a little piece of my 'ness' that had been taken from me. The piece of myself that could cope with anything. How long had I denied that? Since I was born? My teenage years of both insanity and wonder? Since I was twenty eight? Was I so deeply influenced by the cultural zeitgeist of the role of woman?

I wanted to be brave. If I hadn't put myself in that hole, there who had? So many questions. I had to weed out the falsehoods and dig deep into the compacted earth to rewild myself. I had to absorb that stolen, howling woman back into me and let her find the house we were to move to next. For the first time in my adult life, without considering anyone other than my kids. I could be ready to die if I achieved all this.

I finished reading Reanney's book but there was one more thing I needed to do. Freefall to the bottom of the mythic pit. I'd been there before. Usually pushed or forced or dragged. From the rejection and misappropriation at birth, through my teen years, drugged and embarrassed or defiant and rebellious, for daring to be different and say what I chose, to not behaving the way a culturally acceptable woman should, to becoming muscular. Who was I? I had pretended to be the daughter of strangers. I had pretended that my last name was my own and not that of some man or other back into the depths of time. I could pretend I was doing life without grief. I'd hung on to the edges of an unseen cliff to stop myself falling, time and time again and I knew so many others—friends, family, students, clients—who hung there, often for their whole lives.

Now I wanted to be brave enough to willingly die. So I did.

Darkness. Then the voice of some disembodied entity.
What's the one thing you fear more than anything else?
I don't know, I said. Can I come back?
No answer.
What's the one thing you fear more than anything else? The question didn't leave me. What's the one thing you fear—
I climbed a mountain of countless options, but the final part of the request had me stumped. What's the one thing you fear more than anything else? Because all the things that I thought frightened me weren't that one thing.
Then I knew and I dove back down into the pit.

What's the one thing you fear more than anything else? He said, right up close to my ear, almost sensually.

To live my life with no tenderness.

The Trickster didn't say anything at first.

I didn't expect that, he said eventually. What if that's destiny?

I know what you are.

Yeah, well, you kept failing.

A shard of glass formed in the pit of my groin.

I can't avoid destiny, but I will challenge you.

I paused, conscious of soft breath at my ear.

I was never your problem, he sighed. Write me a poem. Be my love.

You're always a liar, I said, and he shrugged one shoulder, as liars do.

I opened my eyes.

Another Trickster attempting to reduce my cool to ashes.

That afternoon the oncologist's receptionist called, asking me to come the next day and to fast from midnight. I awoke from the surgery with my torso in bandages. I had no idea whether I had breasts or not. The doctor came soon after, smiling. Fibroadenomas. Benign lumps, several of which were deep within the breasts themselves. He had excised them all and a small amount of breast tissue. I would be fine. I was allowed to leave hospital several hours later. I slept for three days.

The week after the doctor removed the bandages I began hunting for our next home. I went to every real estate agent and followed up on every ad in the local newspaper. Nothing. I hunted for several weeks. I was running out of time.

I was constantly alert to the Persephone-archetype. That she was me. I did not pretend to anyone that this was easy. Then the magic kicked in.

A woman from around the corner came to see you while you were out, said my housemate.

About?

Her place. She's moving to Thailand and she heard you were looking. Note's on the bench in the kitchen.

The note said 76 Shirley Street and a phone number. Signed Debbie.

CHAPTER 30

March 1995 and I was forty four years old. Adam moved to another share-lodgings and Serenity and Jarrod had several friends living in our lane. Therefore, I had to find a house, or have a house find me, close enough so the band of ratbags was not disbanded.

Other than my own training and one-on-one with Tattoo Zak and Lisa I was now running free-weight and nutritional seminars for small groups of women. My body was like Linda Hamilton's, from her part in the movie Terminator Two by then, and others wanted to know how.

One morning I trained with six of them. I was bent over, about to pick up a barbell to demonstrate biceps curls, when a large, overweight, shaven-headed man in his late forties barged between us and grabbed two heavy dumbbells from the rack. I came up and cracked my head on one. I swore at him for being such a sleazebag. The least he could have done was say excuse me. I then asked him to kindly pop on off and join the ladies doing cardio. I'll explain later why I mention this seeming-trivia.

I went to the back door of 76 Shirley Street, literally around the corner, and Debbie invited me in. She was a heroin addict and the three guys that shared with her were potheads and alcoholics who didn't much care for keeping a place clean. She apologized for the state of things. The floors were covered in linoleum. Walls that hadn't been repainted for decades were the colors of pus: yellow and green. Large blooms of mold covered most of the house. A garage was full of dead white goods. A lawn with one or two straggly trees.

Hello Home, I thought. Three bedrooms and a closed-in front veranda, a separate lounge room and kitchen. And a fireplace.

Home. And I knew what I could do with her but I didn't say.

So, Debbie, what's the plan? I asked, sitting at her kitchen table drinking instant coffee and smoking rollies.

I'm going to Thailand to live. In a few weeks.

Great. So I can take over the house? What about the guys? Because I just want to live with my kids.

They'll go when I go.

Who do I see about the rent and the bond?

No, don't do that. Easier if you pay me and I pay the owners. That way you won't have to worry.

Can't do that, Debbie. I want the house in my name.

Okay, I'll sort something out and get back to you.

Two days later a note was left for me again. Debbie had changed her mind and was staying.

Growling, I returned to checking the papers and the estate agents. I'd been so sure.

The May moving date was imminent and I was quietly desperate and silently pleading to whatever earthy grace was listening.

Debbie came again and said she was definitely leaving and to come the next day and she'd give me the owner's details.

I went and she said sorry, I've changed my plans again.

I've got kids, I yelled. I need a home. I need one soon. Just make up your mind. Yes or no, I don't want to play this game.

No then.

Fine.

I went home, did a number on my punching bag and got on with my day.

She phoned later in the day. Said, sorry, please come around, yes I am definitely leaving.

I did.

The owners were a married couple who also managed a little service station one house down from 76 Shirley Street. Debbie warned me they'd been trying to get a development application passed through the council for four years, for a massive all-night truck stop. Blocked by neighbors.

Have you given notice? I asked.

Not yet.

I'll get my references ready, so that no one gets in before me. Two weeks enough time?

Yes.

That would be three days after the deadline. I phoned Sydney and the Pink House person said that was fine. I then introduced myself to Carol, the woman in the servo, handing her my references.

Is Debbie leaving? She was confused.

She hasn't told you?

No, I'll go see her. You know the house is up for demolition? You can only have a month's lease.

Sure. I understand.

She phoned me the following day.

My, my, she said, that was hard work.

Pardon?

My husband knows you.

I'm confused.

You told him off at the gym one day not long ago in front of several women. He didn't want you to have the house.

Oh.

But I said to him, read the references. He still said no. I said read the references. He said I don't care. I said, read the references, so he eventually said okay. But he's not happy.

So I can have the house?

Yes.

Really?

Come sign the lease. Debbie is moving out this weekend.

That was Monday. I was packed by Friday and on Saturday was due to move around the corner. In the morning I went through the back yard of 76 Shirley Street and a truck was being loaded.

Can I help?

No. And by the way...

Debbie stood up straight atop all her possessions.

Why am I moving?

Because you want to, I said.

We were in by nightfall and the kids were horrified.

Mum, ah, it's ugly.

Mum, this is embarrassing. We can't have friends here. It's filthy.

Trust me.

That night I took the front veranda as my bedroom, but I couldn't sleep because of the mold. At three in the morning I began washing. First the ceiling, then the add-on walls before tackling what would have been the original weatherboard frontage of the house. And I felt a shudder. A sigh. The house awoke from wherever she had hidden. Through neglect and lack of love. She felt me. If she'd been a dog her ears would have pricked. The sense I had from her was one of hope.

Yes, I said honestly. I am going to love you.

The Aboriginal people right across Australia began having victories in the courts, regaining land rights. In Byron Bay the year before, Arakwal Elders Lorna Kelly, Linda Vidler and Yvonne Graham made the first Native Title Application for the recognition of the Arakwal people and they were going to win.

The coven and I washed 76 Shirley Street from floor to ceiling. We painted her the color of vanilla ice cream. We pulled up three layers of crumbling linoleum and exposed cedar floorboards that just needed polishing. Slowly but surely all the junk piled under the house was dragged out and taken to the tip.

In the very pit of me was the knowledge that the development application would not be passed for ages. Within the same depths of me was the knowledge that the day would come, but as I'd said at the bottom of the pit. Not today.

Oh, about that pit. I never climbed out. I planted roots there and I grew towards the sun. I understood that I could only be truly strong like that. I would not cling to any edges again.

I hired a trailer and friends helped me clear out all the dead white goods from the garage. We transformed a rusting tin shed into a den for an ever-expanding group of teenagers. The boys set up benches and trapeze-type things from which to swing from the rafters. Computers came next, the big tape decks of the era. The back of a wardrobe was removed and discarded, and the wardrobe became the doorway.

Everything was most amusing for a while. The problem was that all these kids were taking food from my fridge and using the landline and having showers. I was footing the bills and slowly drowning. All the boys. All Jarrod's friends. I spoke to him time and time again. He could not refuse them. Eventually, fearing abject poverty, I gave him three months to stop them.

He agreed but that's not what happened. I begged them. They'd be adamantly agreeable one day and empty the refrigerator the next. At the end of the three months Jarrod moved out.

He went to the caravan park where his father now lived, several miles away and with a girlfriend as heavily into drugs as he was. Jarrod came home often, and I would feed him and take him shopping, shore up his pantry and give him money. Then off he'd go again, insisting he was fine and everything about his dad was cool. I had no idea that the shell of a man that the Trickster had left behind was dealing drugs to the kids and turning my son onto smoking heroin.

By now some people would be thinking I was leaving out copious amounts of personal information and they'd be right. I have not forgotten but some of the information affects others moreso. Their stories will be their stories. And yes, Serenity and hers, and Jarrod's friends, travelled to the caravan park to visit him and no. Not good.

CHAPTER 31

Jarrod came home. Was coming home. He had paid off an old caravan for the back yard. Of course I said yes, and then proceeded to pay exorbitantly for the trailer hire. I didn't care. All was right with the world again. Adam had fallen in love with a woman I admired as much as a personal friend as his partner. They moved into a place of their own in Lennox Head.

The cops came and arrested Jarrod for dealing pot when he'd been at the caravan park. He had to go to court. I slammed on the brakes and got legal representation because I knew what this was about.

The lawyer got the story out of him. When the bust went down Jarrod's father had talked his own son into take the rap.

No longer under the wily influence of the Trickster the man made the mistake of coming to the courthouse. The case against Jarrod was dropped and his father charged with possession, instead. He was fined a whopping sum of money or a prison term. He could never pay, and he would not go to jail. Instead he disappeared from our lives.

Sometime during the first year in Shirley Street, Fiona Horne, lead singer of the band Def FX asked if she could come and interview me for her book Witch. She'd read The Way of the Goddess many years before and as a result had self-initiated. Her photographer for the book was Milo, wild, raven-haired child of magic and style. She and I remain friends and decades later she and her partner trained with me in a Melbourne tarot collective. I was housed with them when I began reading tarot in Melbourne.

The double garage that had been the clubhouse for the Shirley Lane gang was now empty. Virginia and Sara returned to Byron Bay before Sara went home to Victoria. Virginia and I turned the space into a sort of studio. The walls needed paint but all I had was a large can of red roofing enamel. So I painted the inner walls with that, chain-sawed a hole in the wall and made French doors from four old windows. I added a solid door to another chain-sawed hole. I laid carpet from wall to wall and hung a few drapes. Virginia moved in for several weeks before deciding she disliked living there. When she found other accommodation I took over, moving into yet a third transformed double garage.

I turned the space into three compact rooms, dividing them with dyed muslin, Moroccan tapestries and copious quantities of mosquito netting. I now had a temple/parlor, a veiled-off bedroom and a tarot room.

The carpet went the following year after a flood, replaced by terracotta paint and a large, encircled pentagram that I hid from the non-initiated with a huge black bullock hide. That was the year of Boar, an occasional lover. I also pounded away on my electric typewriter with an early draft of a novel called Genesis | The Future that had, as its inspiration, one of the visual experiences of the ritual workings in 1990. That book incomplete for years. I learned to write more proficiently before that could happen. I was still quite lousy. Good at lists, though.

Jarrod had his caravan down the bottom of the garden, Serenity had her private room and now the Historian moved to Byron Bay from Sydney. He completed a degree in philosophy and won honors to study at Oxford University, England, but decided not to go. He took what had been my room, taught astrology and did the occasional chart; worked on genealogy, the art of Celtic knot work and the vegetable garden.

The tarot collective of 1995 included Irish woman Paddy O'Reilly, Steve, that ex-priest and Margaret, scholar the Celtic and radio host. Halfway through the course Steve moved into the spare bedroom to continue to learn from me. With a problem dealing with confrontation and conflict he was living in the house to explore the art of debating instead. Steve was now as far from christianity as he could get, focusing on mysticism and permaculture.

Halfway through the course Paddy announced that the *saint patrick's* day of the coming year fell on a Sunday. After the Irish rebellion of 1798 the British occupying forces made wearing the color green seditious. We decided to hold a celebration of diverse community on the seventeenth of March. A mere couple of months away. The Wearing of the Green Pageant.

The Byron Shire, like so many, was divided into an anthropologist's dream of sects and exclusionists, surfers, hippies, farmers, ravers, indigenous folk and travellers from all around the world, originally drawn by the now famous Blues and Roots Festival, then by the drug culture and the alternative lifestyle of a tropical paradise. But a place divided. Diversity is healthy but divisionism and elitism, not so. By the time my youngest children were teenagers there was battle on the streets between rival gangs and the council refused to provide anywhere worthwhile. Byron Bay was becoming a town of development and money laundering. Pillaged by anyone who factored building infringement fines into the costing.

Our festival was to be a nobody-pays-nobody-profits event.

People would come together around the village green (without which a community ceases to be a community) to celebrate all things Celtic and the two thousand year erasure of our own indigenous heritage.

Naysayers said our festival wouldn't happen. One can't create a day like this with no money and almost no advertising. No one will come. We handed out photocopied leaflets. We decided we'd hold a wildness parade, and included rocked-up Celtic bands, story tellers, master harpists, fire dancers, swordplay and an archery competition in the local park. Crazy witches. We had to get council permission to conduct a street parade, so we applied. The shire Council said we had to have approval from the police, so I went to the police station and the copper on the counter said I had to speak to the sergeant.

I first came to metaphorical blows with this man when Jarrod and his friend, both only fourteen, were strip-searched by two of his underlings in an arcade in the center of town in front of a crowd of tourists because their baggy jeans exposed the tops of their underpants. Gangsta fashion. Without parental supervision what the police did was illegal.

I received an apology. I said to the cops at the Byron station, say sorry to my son and his friend, not me. That didn't happen.

I was walking to the market grounds where we had set up targets for long distance archery practice way down the back. I had my compound bow and a quiver of arrows over my shoulder. The sergeant came storming down the stairs, one hand a clenched fist, the index finger of the other hand puncturing the air like a weapon, his jaw thrust towards me.

You're carrying an illegal weapon.

No I'm not.

Yes. You are.

I sashayed up the stairs into the station. Inside on the wall was a poster of illegal weapons I had noticed last time I'd been there. He thought my thundercloud grey compound bow was a cross-bow.

Cover the thing, Ly. You'll scare people.

You'll arrest me for carrying a concealed weapon.

Now I needed his permission for a street parade. We had to plan a strategy. I typed up the proposal of the event, walked to the station and to the counter. The sergeant was talking with other cops in the background when he saw me.

What's that?

The logistics of the *saint patrick's* day festival. Council sent me to you.

I'm busy. Come back in the morning.

Patricia Hooper was visiting. She managed Spiral Books in the day. Patricia is a lesbian and wore suits. She could pass as media or a lawyer. She was perfect for the plan. I also needed a male presence because the sergeant was sure to be setting me up. Steve and I sat in the kitchen with Patricia and I said, he'll have no chairs, you'll see. He'll expect me to stand like a good little woman and then he'll knock me back. So Steve? When we get there you shake his hand and be pleasant. Introduce yourself as a member of the team. I'll shake his hand and say hi and Pat, you shake his hand but don't say who you are.

The following day we were ushered into the sergeant's office. The only chair was his.

Um, officer could you bring chairs for these people. Sorry, Ly, I forgot you were coming.

That's okay, I said sweetly, shaking his hand. Sergeant, this is Steve Williams, part of the team.

Nice to meet you mate, Steve smiled, shaking hands vigorously.

The cops brought the chairs. I sat on one end, Steve on the other and Patricia, in her suit, sat in the middle. She took out a notebook and pen from her satchel and wrote something.

And you are? The sergeant reached out his hand and she shook it.

A friend from Melbourne.

So, what do you want from me?

Did you read the proposal?

I haven't had time, Ly.

That's okay. We've spoken to the council and they've agreed to a development application for the street parade, we just need you to sign.

Do the police have to do anything?

No, mate.

I suppose so then.

He had an officer find the necessary permission form, signed it and shooed us out. We took the form to the council who signed their permission form because the cops had.

Willie McElroy and his rocked-up Irish band Wild Zinnias cancelled a Brisbane gig to play with us. Damini's band Tané was also in. A storyteller named Robin was in and a Celtic harpist was flown from Canberra. We rehearsed sword dancing; the fire wyvern whispered their incantations and those of us with bows practiced on targets. The community center gave us the keys, so we could use their building. The Beach Hotel sponsored us their sound equipment.

On the Thursday night prior to the event Margaret phoned me. She'd been at the Rails Hotel and was approached by a very angry Aboriginal man.

You're one of that mob thinking we'd be alright about you having another whitey takeover day. Well, we're going to blockade your fucking event, lady. You can expect trouble.

Should we call the police? she asked me.

Ah, no.

The local radio station invited me to talk about the Priteni; the Celtic diaspora. I rattled off the names of the territories from before the first of many invasions, from the Coritan to the Silures, I chatted about the Fomorians and the Firbolg, the Dumnonach in the south to the Cruitne and Picts in the north and loss of identity and language; a culture almost extinguished from history.

The following night I drove our sound technician to pick up the equipment. I crossed the road to the rocks above the high water line and looked out over the black and white of the breakers. Lupa approached me, hands in the pocket of his jeans, dreads loose around his shoulders. Lupa was a Cleverman but he never told me what country his people were from. The drink had him but not his magic. We'd known each other since I first moved to town and he'd always say, Hi Sis, and walk on.

He sat on a rock and patted the one beside him.

What's the story?

So I told him.

Figured something like that, you being you. There'll be no blockade.

Thanks Lupa.

On the Sunday morning Steve, Margaret and I opened the community center doors at nine and put the urns on to heat. People wandered in excited as birds, piling food onto the benches, lighting ovens to cook and making tea and coffee. Lupa popped his head around the rear doors and crooked a finger at me. We wandered out back where three First Nation people—two men and a woman—sat on the grass. We shook hands but they didn't say their names.

Lupa already told us, one man smiled. We've arranged dij-making and a few other things, if that's okay.

I was surprised. I forgot I could be surprised.

Another thing.

Sure.

Can we walk up front of your parade with you?

They did. And so did three and a half thousand other people, dancing and drumming. The local fire truck was festooned in green bunting. The chamber of commerce had complained all along that we should not be allowed to go ahead. Potentially financially devastating to the community because no one would attend the cafes and businesses would lose money over our stupid idea. They had to pull their heads in. People came from Brisbane, Sydney and Melbourne and all the cafes were packed. At eleven that night Damini, lead singer of the band Tané, sang a haunting Gaelic lament a Capella. Then everyone went home.

We sat on the steps of the locked community center marveling that there was no litter anywhere.

CHAPTER 32

On my birthday in 1998 my sons gave me my first computer, a DOS Windows 3.1. I was puzzled but curious.
 Why?
 Better than your typewriter.
 What can a computer do that my typewriter can't?
 Cut and paste.
 What's that?
 I'll show you.
 Okay, where's the on switch?
 I began writing Witchcraft Theory and Practice that year and I also contacted the post adoption agency again. I didn't want to burst the unknowing bubble and learn of anything terrible, like the offspring of rape, but I needed the truth of my identity. I was issued a caseworker.

I had to change my last name, desperate to be free from something I could not, then, enunciate. I was known only by men's names. Like I was cattle. Sometimes becoming oneself is like challenging this impossible-to-navigate maze made up of cultural pretentions, so high and so deep that to get to the center seems impossible. Foolhardy. Before that name I had the last name of the man who bought me, the one who referred to my bastardry while he beat his wife. I would not be his. What about her name? Maiden name? Her father's name. I was named for a man, as was she and her mother and her mother back into the mists. Even if biological parents were found? The same would be true.

 I was buried in something like metaphorical ash. I couldn't even begin to consider using some man's name for my next book. I had even given these names to my offspring, perpetuating the cycle of disempowerment. The personal and territorial occupation of individuality.
 More than any love except for that of my children, was my

experience in the company of the entities that communicated with us at the kabalistic rituals in 1990. So-called angels and archangels. Greek words for messengers. Nothing fluff-winged about them. I'm one—a messenger—through my work. Start again. Fresh. Even a little bit fancy. I prepared a dinner and invited my children and told them. There was much thinking and consideration. My sons decided not to join me, but my daughter did. We legally became de Angeles.

For weeks after the official paperwork had arrived and I had updated everything from my bank account to my passport I felt weird. Like I didn't fit what I'd done. As though even the air had to adjust. Was this another Butterfly Affect? Then elation. I had broken a chain. One link was enough. Sheer and clean. A mountain lake. Fresh fallen snow on cedars.

Jungle, a Doberman rescue dog, came to live with us. He was two years old. The family he'd been with couldn't cope with his bigness. And he was big. His playfulness knocked the woman's sons off the back veranda. He seemed threatening to his people. So he was given away. I know how that feels in the marrow of me but I didn't understand consciously. I had to learn his language. Because of Bodie. Then Shadow, thanks to Mother-of-Dogs, I knew a little of the language. So when I sat on the couch on the first night and Jungle came face to face with me, his brown eyes shining with green I knew he was about to attack. I put my nose in the air and turn away as though he was beneath me. He lolled then, tongue hanging out, farting with happiness.

Next day I walked him to the beach. and he was exultant. Gulls! Waves! Smells! I let him off the leash and he barreled up and down the shore until his legs gave way. Then we wandered back towards the road and home. I called him to come onto the leash—no road sense, not then, not ever—and he refused. I chased him. He ran. I would never catch him. He stayed twenty feet away. I yelled at him. Now that was beyond stupid. In dog language this is the height of aggression. I was defeated. Instead I became engrossed in the lines on the palm of my hand. Took him a while, but eventually he couldn't stand not knowing what so fascinated me.

I learned so much. To slow down. To be quiet. To have nothing to prove. To be an honest guardian of potentially savage things. That they had no reason to harm me but I needed to learn from them and not the other way around. Different to the language of people. Many in the culture in which I live use aggression, snide, elitist criticism, looks without softness, the violence of denial and injustice. An incorrect language. Even the word love has been misappropriated to sometimes mean self-gratification. Because of the demands, the grip, the expectations, the hierarchy. We should rightly be able to join the pack, the flock, the pod or the litter that has no demands except for food, shelter and community because real conversations are wordless.

We are not chained.

CHAPTER 33

Not a night went by when at least half a dozen of Jarrod and Serenity's friends weren't somewhere on the property, either coming or going or seeing to their business in Jarrod's crowded caravan. By now, though, instead of driving me to the brink of financial ruin they had come full circle to where 76 Shirley Street was their safe haven and I could leave money on the kitchen table for a week.

One evening we all gathered spontaneously around the back steps. I listened to the sad stories of those who'd dropped out of school and could not get work, that there was nothing to do except take drugs and get into trouble.

I don't want to be a dole bludger for the rest of my life, Ly, said Andrew, my unofficially fostered son I had renamed Andy Pandy Puddin' n Pie. The cheekiest puppy in the pack.

Where did that expression come from?

Everybody.

Well, everybody isn't thinking. You only ever get the one cheque.

No I don't. I get paid every fortnight.

Same cheque.

How do you figure that?

What do you do with the money?

Buy stuff.

Any left over?

Nope.

Why don't you save some?

You kidding?

Exactly. Everything you buy is taxed so the shopkeeper gets your money but so does the government. On top of that the shopkeeper pays tax. Same happens with everything you spend.

So the government makes a profit from my cheque?

See the logic?

Bastards.

Be happy. They're paying you to do nothing.

Not nothing. I have to apply for six jobs a week and we still have to do Work for the Dole or job skills training and that's usually how to hold a broom.

What's Work for the Dole?

Slave labor.

Hmm.

Mummy?

Yes, Serenity.

Can we put on Macbeth and charge people at the door? Would that count as Work for the Dole?

You guys want to do Macbeth?

You'd be training for a job.

What's Macbeth?

Serenity huffed and leered with scorn and went to get the Complete Works of William Shakespeare from the bookshelf and opened to the Scottish play.

She began reading.

I don't understand, said Andy Pandy.

Okay, I said. Serenity, you read, and I'll translate.

That went on every night, with more or less fifteen kids sitting and smoking and working very hard to comprehend. This was what they wanted, however. Then Serenity slammed the book shut.

Mummy— (My daughter uses this term of endearment when something is certain to bother me. I pretended that I didn't know.)

Yes?

I want to do Rocky Horror.

I couldn't get the rights, even if I wanted to.

Mummy!

We all crowded into the lounge room and watched the 1975 Rocky Horror Picture Show with Tim Curry and Susan Sarandon. By the end of that week every kid knew every song and gesture.

After discovering which of them could hold a tune we were given rehearsal space at the community center. We went hunting for corsets and stockings. Initially they were horrified at the idea of exposing their bodies to each other, distressing the sixties child in me, but over the following months they went from a gang to a troupe. The character of Brad Majors' mother sewed him a gold lamé g-string and one of the girls waxed his bum.

I became Riff-Raff and Serenity and Jarrod played Magenta and Eddy. They learned lighting and stage management, makeup and costuming, sound and ticketing. All in six months.

For promotion they all wandered Woolworths in costume. A store representative asked them to please leave, but Mechonan who played Frankenfurter, over six foot tall, in a corset and six inch red heels, frowned and pouted as he loomed over her.

It's not easy having a good time. Even smiling makes my face ache, he quoted, his diction perfect Curry.

She left them alone.

We planned a two weekend run using the high school stage and played to a packed out audience for the first weekend. Then I had a call from the Rocky administration in Sydney. Lovely woman.

Hi, Ly?

Hi, yes.

I'm phoning from The Rocky Horror Picture Show.

Hi, I said cheerily, sweat trickling from my armpits.

Someone has dobbed you in, I'm afraid.

Oh dear.

Yes. We checked up on you first, though, before making this call.

Ah.

And you've done everything else right, haven't you? We contacted the education department, the local school, Social Security. You had rather a few drop-out teenagers that you managed to get on Work for the Dole. We checked with Youth Services. We're not going to sue you.

I think I must have made a strange, relieved gurgling noise about then.

We heard you put on a really, really good show.

Thank you.

But we're just about to tour so I'm afraid you won't be able to do next week.

Oh, that's okay, I said, smiling down the phone, this was about the kids getting paid the door money.

I know. And you sold out so they should be quite proud of

themselves.

So am I. And thank you again.

You're welcome.

Each of the cast members got a wad of cash and a new perspective on life. Years later, in a documentary I created after the first of Mechonan's brothers killed himself, he said that the arts were one of the things that had saved him the same fate.

Jan was eighty two. When I did phone her the conversations were always about the sister-person and her family. Nothing new and often the same information repeated. This time I phoned and said I was coming to visit.

Bring shoes this time.

Can I bring my dog?

I suppose so.

Before the days of flight, the only option for travel was either the train, which took three days to get to Sydney, or to drive, so Steve agreed to share the navigation. He wanted to hang out with his own family anyway.

I dropped my boots onto her porch where they stayed until I left. After I knocked she took ages to unlock the front door.

She was strange. Unnerved. She'd had security installed everywhere possible. I couldn't go into the garden for a cigarette without her locking me out and me having to knock to get back in. Deadlocks on every window and door. Still a telly on in every room and she hated being interrupted when watching her shows. When she spoke she repeated herself going round and round the same litany about that faux sister and its family. But for the first time she said I think I should sell up and live with you.

Yes then. That's what I'll do.

When I again broached the subject of her relocating to, or even visiting, Byron Bay me she said, oh no, I couldn't just up and leave. Your sister depends on me.

Dementia.

As the days and nights passed I became more and more anxious. To not be allowed a key. To ask permission to go outside. To be locked in at night. For Jungle to be stuck in her backyard.

On day four I woke with chest pain. Earth compacted under

asphalt and concrete. And her. I could not take a deep breath. I was sure I was suffering anxiety, but I felt like I was having a heart attack. I knew I would die if I stayed.

I phoned Steve and said goodbye to Jan. Last thing, in her mind, was that she was going to live with the sister-person.

The pain was gone an hour into the drive. I knew she would not come.

The sister-person had her placed in a nursing home a year later and sold her house. That trip was the last time I saw the woman, who had pretended to be my mother, alive.

CHAPTER 34

1998 was the year Bill Clinton signed Resolution 71, urging the U.S. president to "take all necessary and appropriate actions to respond to the threat posed by Iraq's refusal to end its weapons of mass destruction programs". A few of us had intense discussions along the lines of: Do you reckon there's going to be another war? Because other sources wrote that Iraq had no such thing. By now the word terrorism was the current cliché being thrashed by the media, just like communism used to be, like A.I. will be in the not-too-distant future. Al Qaeda claimed responsibility for bombing U.S. embassies across several countries and the war happened in Kosovo—a humanitarian crisis that just keeps repeating itself like a plague. Spread by men instead of rats.

In Australia we had the first ever National Sorry Day for the theft of all those children, by governments and church, from the First Nation people that came to be known as the Stolen Generation and, with the help of the far right wing One Nation Party, John Howard was re-elected prime minister of this country. How stupid do voters have to be? This is the man who said in 1993 that the goods and services tax would never be part of the coalition policy. He was elected for a second term spewing forth that this was a mandate by the people to introduce that vile tax. Luxury tax on tampons with an added 10%. He lied about refugees and he was to back that deception-filled war that claimed weapons of mass destruction but was really about oil.

I learned to use a computer. Everyone at the local café said the internet was a fad and not much better than a glorified calculator and typewriter. Everyone I spoke to about it said it wouldn't last.

Every Saturday, after teaching tarot, I'd turn on ABC and watch a documentary called The People's Century. New Year's Eve, when the clock ticked over to 1900 Edison and his friends lit up a house

with electricity. Everyone then, also said it won't last.
    Then Byron Bay opened an internet café.

I finalized Witchcraft Theory and Practice and mailed the manuscript to Llewellyn in the U.S.
    In 1999 I signed a contract with them, and the book was released the following year.

Published under my own name. Ownership, in theory, erased. A book that's effect and immediate popularity changed my life. I was legally Ly de Angeles.

CHAPTER 35

Just before 2000 came the Y2K frenzy. When the clock ticked over from the last calendared century everything was supposed to go crash. The internet would collapse, electricity would cease, and there would be no more running water, no more petrol. People bought up supplies that would last them for years. They built bunkers, stored weapons, trained to defend from the Mad Maxian marauders.

Jan died.

Adam drove the two of us to Sydney, Jarrod and Serenity stayed home. They hardly knew her. The pretend sibling and its husband had arranged a hotel room for us in Chatswood and had seemingly kindly agreed to pay. A Novotel box. We drove from there to the funeral parlor. An open coffin. I watched Jan's stone cold face and remembered everything. I whispered, are you still here? As ever, there was no reply.

We drove to the sister-person's house the day of the cremation, the experience unnerving. A museum decorated with every piece of Jan's furniture. Acquisitioned was every photograph, including framed portraits of her and me as three and four year olds. Theft with a selection of finger food. We were introduced to their children, but we were strangers.

Then a religious service. Christian. Maudlin. Utterly and intentionally gloomy. I walked out, in grief and rage at a life of deception. Wanting the mother that this pretender had never been. Adam followed and we drove all the way home the same day. I did not, then, know there was no body in the coffin; the earlier viewing was just for show before her corpse was sent to some hospital freezer for spare parts.

Jan left me some money in her will, and I intended to travel. She'd always maintained the other acquired person and I would get equal shares of what was left after she died. That's not what happened. That was the final lie.

Around the same time the post adoption agency emailed. They had found the hospital records and a whole lot more. Did I want to proceed towards a possible reunion?

I said, no. That first time.

The book launch of Witchcraft Theory and Practice was to take place at the Abraxis Bookshop in Byron Bay. A few weeks beforehand I was contacted by a producer of the ABC television program Compass. They were doing a show about spiritualties that are alternative to the mainstream and Nevill Drury had put them onto me. I agreed to the interview but not to a public ritual.

They needed something visual so I contacted Danyelle and her partner who owned a property in the hills in the hinterland out back of Byron Bay and asked their permission to use their paddock. I suggested to the ABC producer that we hold a revel and invited him and his crew along if they agreed to switch off the cameras and go away if their presence became a discomfort to my friends. They interviewed me that day, attended the launch in the early evening and then followed us out of town. People had already set up a huge bonfire and by the time we parked, unpacked and joined them the blaze was raging. Fire-dancers lit their brands and opened the revel in honor to the four winds.

Then several of us, our friends and family, whispered over silver goblets of wine before sharing them with everyone else. The Compass people left not long after.

At one point when the program aired the presenter suggested that I was anti-feminist and not all that bothered about what was happening to earth. I wondered at her motive.

CHAPTER 36

Tattoo Dany's partnership dissolved and she moved into a room in a little pale brick house near the beach at Suffolk Park. I was there to help. When we arrived the owner showed us into the double garage. She said Danyelle could store things if she wanted. Inside was a selection of potted plants, one of which was barely alive. A ficus. Strangler fig. Almost four foot of spindly branches and half a dozen leaves. Given up on daylight and water.

Who's this? I asked.

A pot plant.

And very sick.

What are you on?

What?

Its owner is overseas. I'm minding her plants.

Oh? How long is she gone?

Seven months. Why?

Just wondering.

Look I got stuff to do.

Um... I've got a big back yard.

No.

We waited until she left Danyelle and me alone. We loaded the pot into Dany's ute, closed the garage door and drove to my place. A serious case of fuck the consequences. Danyelle would explain that she had no idea what had happened and lie that no, we didn't steal anything.

I brewed a coffee and sat out in the yard, not yet a garden. That would happen over time. I smoked a cigarette, sipped the coffee and considered the ficus. I'm a plant whisperer. A curse. Can't go into a shop selling potted plants and walk out without the root-bound one. They breathe shallowly. If they'd had eyes they would be big and dark and moist asking, is this the way of things? How did this happen?

There was not one plant in that small pot but two. Oh, the cruelty. I put the rest of the day away from me and pulled the pot from the roots. No soil. They had devoured every grain. Just root. Tangled into such extreme knots that I could barely imagine their lives as they tried to nourish themselves. No one from the world of air would know about this. To understand one had to get down into the dirt. The Underworld. This was what happens when love dies, and people try to stay together. Soul-destroying.

I'm sorry, I said. I'm going to hurt you.

I began unknotting them. They were in a world of agony and anxiety; one I knew well. Not everyone comprehends the tangle, let alone what to do. Psychologists and counsellors can help, but distance heals the best. Get away. Far away. Be someone else. Be who you are not what you delude yourself into believing that relationship has made you.

I took three slow hours, every sense attuned to what could break, to which root could not take the damage. Almost holding my breath.

I prepared the earth in two places. I planted them thirty feet apart. I whispered to them that they might not live here forever because I only rent. I suggested a quality life was preferable to a quantity one with no freedom, no choice to either love or not. I nestled one close to the path near the back door, the other beside the way into the studio. So that if they chose they could meet. If such was against their nature they still had space to explore the deep soil and the vastness of the tropic sky.

The tree close to the studio thrived. I asked if I could name him Bran for my own reference, not because tree people require names. Naming is a human anomaly.

The other tree died. I named her Flidias anyway. Over the coming days her leaves withered and dropped. By the third week her branches were barren. Still I watered them both. And planted anything else pot-bound that turned up. I just wandered around with the person in the pot and thought, Where? Until I heard: here.

I was turning a fresh barrow of humus and compost when Steve Williams came bouncing down the stairs, hands in his pockets, ever-present Gardener smile.

You might as well pull that one, he said of Flidias.
What?
Unless you dig 'em up with lots of soil and hibernate them over winter they die. It's dead.

Fuck off, Steve.

Fair enough, he shrugged and went surfing.

The fourth or fifth week I came down the back steps with a pre-breakfast coffee and Flidias was covered in pink leaf buds.

What happened is monumental, healing and teaching of the deepest nature. Within a year both trees were twenty foot tall and spreading. They were as different as a hen from a hound. The roots of Bran, the big male near the studio, rose up above the ground in curving walls in which small creatures, several species of spider, moss, lichen, flowers (some so small I needed my glasses to see them) found sanctuary. Flidias' roots also rose above ground but were like basket weavings, close to her trunk, reaching deep underground. Over the years she lifted the concrete flagstones that formed the path to the Hills Hoist.

Bran was happy but Flidias was outright hilarious. She grew a branch straight out from her trunk that crossed the path to the clothesline at exactly my head height. Anyone taller was forced to bow. A branch that got no higher as she grew taller. I got her sense of humor and much more than that.

I had built a martial arts training platform beside the neighbor's fence and I trained there almost every day. Several times a day one or the other of us would either go to Jarrod's caravan beyond the strangler figs, at the bottom of the garden, or walk to town via the back gate. When Flidias was tall enough to droop her branches like a willow, she left two portals, like arches. One to my training platform, the other to the back yard. A very gracious tree.

Both she and Bran decided to like each other again and their branches interwove to form a canopy overhead through which only dapple could eventually penetrate.

During the wet season I trained in the empty section of the new gym usually reserved for cardio. A good two sweaty hours practicing jo and bo katas because I was now training in Aikido.

The afternoon of the most recent training there and Jamie phoned me to say he had been working out with an Iaido teacher in the weights room—Iaido is a Japanese sword martial art. They had watched me. The teacher asked if Jamie knew me and Jamie had filled him in on our mixed martial arts practice. He asked Jamie to invite me to train with them while he was in town.

When? I asked over the phone, a puppy with her whole body wagging.

We're over the road from you at the dance studio in the Epicentre. From seven tonight.

Karla, lean, long brown hair, young daughter, raising her alone, brave, had been initiated into the northern coven quite a while back. All of us were very much a storytelling of ravens and tended to share most activities, spent hours together drinking coffee or tea, supporting each other's families through dramas. The coven had refurbished the Youth Activity Centre, put on productions, studied, practiced martial arts and wove magic together. I phoned her that afternoon and she came as well. During his time in the shire the sensei taught us ten katas.

Over the coming several years I established the Byron dojo. Karla and I trained thirty six people. I graded to third Dan before the entire school was destroyed by our original teacher's boss. The reason? Misogyny and greed.

CHAPTER 37

Suzy, who had worked with us on the Rocky Horror Show, studied with me for a year before initiating into the northern coven.

1999 and she and I met for coffee across the road from the courthouse. She had a part in a local production of Jesus Christ Superstar and their current director had been sacked for thinking the thirty thousand dollar budget show should develop organically. Would I please consider directing?

What's entailed?

Oh, about a hundred cast and crew and a thirty two piece orchestra. I see.

Come on, Ly.

What's the pay?

Nothing, I think.

Oh. Jesus Christ Superstar?

Come to a rehearsal then decide.

What was I doing? I couldn't direct anything that promoted religion. What could the vision be? I was writing and researching the book Magdalene. I was roughly inspired by the dream in the past that had triggered the kabalistic rituals, by the asherah temples in the Levant before the Diaspora, its women. Could I give this show a non-religious perspective? Was
I up for the challenge?

Mary Magdalene, was based on the woman or title known as Miriam Magdal-eder, *she of the high tower*. She represented the figurehead of an ancient unknown. If I was to direct this show I determined to portray Mary as the above. I would also mess around with the apostles and have them be what they would have been: warriors of a resistance to occupation as well as friends, families and lovers.

At the rehearsal I attempted to be diminutive. Hunched in a

corner amidst a group of abandoned plastic chairs. I sat up straight when the lead sang Cup of Poison and even straighter, laughing, when Shannon, playing Pilate, sang "I wash my hands of your demolition, die if you want to you innocent Muppet." They were remarkable. Down the far end of the rehearsal space, however, Mandi, the Magdalene, was attempting to teach four part harmonies to the twenty or so people that made up the chorus. Many of them chatted amongst themselves or were distracted. I listened to the babble and the confusion for a good five minutes before standing on my chair.

Shut the fuck up, I yelled at the top of my lungs.

The three band members applauded, the remainder of the room went quiet and the producer, asked who I was.

She's our new director. Suzy explained, at the confusion on their faces.

Over the coming months we created a very unchristian Superstar with martial arts fight scenes and weaponry. Serenity was in the dance troupe, Jarrod a guard for Pilate and Adam got to whip Jesus thirty nine times every night for the three week season. Instead of a crucifix we had a blasted, metal tower erected and brought in a very modern twist with Pilate dressed as though he'd walked off the set of Matrix. The show was imbued with a kind of magic that was tactile and visceral, and after every rehearsal we had to bring many of the performers back from the trance of actually being the characters they portrayed.

We sold out every show of the three week run. Instead of a religious-style rock musical, the story presented the destruction of an ideal in the face of public betrayal. There wasn't a dry eye amongst the audience on any night that we killed that man.

One of the dancers was Josh Rushton. He taught at a local school, is a country fire fighter and a deep thinking man. We became friends. When we met he'd been training at free weights with another person working a Russian style. His neck went to his shoulders.

Come train with me, I'd suggested.
Why?
That's not a good look, Josh.
You can fix me?
Yes.
He was hilarious to train. He'd howl pulling off that last rep.

We'd laugh. He brought a group of teenage boys from the school for me to instruct.

Josh is the Woodsman in mythworld. If I didn't summon him into this story I could be accused of hating men. I don't. Well I do hate some. Men are men when they've nothing to prove. When they accept full responsibility. Could the same be said for women? Of course. But this is not about them. Carl Weschcke, of Llewellyn, hand-serving me lobster at the restaurant at the head of the Mississippi, Konrad continuing in deep debate with me despite how ornery or prickly the subject. Ari, covered in tattoos, silks performer, a calm man. Byron Boo, permaculturalist, musician and seeker of his purpose in the world, discovering his manhood through terror, lore, music and ceremony.

There are an awful lot of pretenders and bullies. Politicians, CEOs, right-wing louts, brutes, control freaks. Men who like to hurt other men. To brutalize women. To rape or proselytize children. To be on top. But then there are the few. And one cannot help but love them because how does someone stand against that mob and remain unique. Most make a name for themselves like Martin Luther King, like Chris Crass, social justice activist and writer. Others that make names for themselves through deeds of infamy. Others are Tricksters, Cuckoos, Vampires, the Devil. Mythworld needs its Woodsmen and Hunters, Heroes and Warriors, Seers and Scholars, Gate Keepers, Gardeners, Lovers, Chefs, Poet, Bards and Minstrels. What we do not need, anymore, are Kings.

The Iaido club's main headquarters—*honbu*—was in Adelaide. I flew there to ascertain those of us in the shire had the correct form for those katas a few months after the sensei had gone. Other than Karla and Jamie seven others joined us, including Helen, a future initiate. Within four years we had a dojo at the Arts Factory and had grown to be one of the biggest schools in the southern hemisphere. The only school with equal numbers of men and women by the time I left for a second trip to Ireland.

We had to represent the kami (spirits of many things) with a shrine called a torii. Jarrod and I went on a mission to the cave at the end of White's Beach and found three smooth, slate-grey chubby, flattish circular stones from large, to larger, to largest. They sat one atop the other on a white antique damask cloth at the end of the dojo. We registered our club as a not-for-profit organization and maintained full autonomy under the New South Wales government. We were graded by the head *honbu's* qualified teachers for a couple of years. I ordered all the equipment, the uniforms, the weapons and the identifications as well as handling the role of administrator. Private students began on the training platform in the garden if they were too shy to come to the dojo at first.

CHAPTER 38

The ritual of drinking coffee in a downtown café. Reading Charles de Lint's Someplace to be Flying. I looked up from sipping a cappuccino. A tall, dark-skinned man with long hair in neat dreadlocks, across the car park. I thought how very exotic, like someone out of a legend, before dissolving back to the story of the Crow Girls in the alleys of Newford.

Next thing two glasses of coffee slid across the table and in a soft voice that belied his size he said, I'm David and I can see the magic in you, can I sit?

He was a Featherfoot. Somewhere in his thirties. He had family in three parts of New South Wales between Sydney, the mid north coast and Nimbin, and he walked from country to country. To know what his mother, aunties and uncles taught. To earn the respect of the land, his ancestors and the spirits of place. The knowledge of this stone or this kangaroo track or that tree where the ibis nest only once a year or that dry riverbed with water several inches down. The colors of the days and the times of rain and fire. He'd been in the military in his early twenties. S.A.S. His mother was a First Nation elder but his father, a Scotsman. A brutal man. David was offended by his father.

Are you an archer? he asked out of the blue.

Yes.

Thought so. I've got a compound bow, but I leave it in the Sydney house. Cops are always hassling me because I'm black.

That's not a reason.

Is for them. I'm heading to Nimbin. Got mob there. I have to walk between them... or at least, ride the trains. I talk to the spiritworld, so I keep having to hide from strangers who want me committed. Or hassled by the coppers for being too big.

They can't do that.
You live in a dream, woman.
We talked for hours.
I really have to go home now, I said finally.
Can I come?
Yes, will I cook dinner?
Yes please.
And later that evening, Can I stay the night?
The house is full.
I've got a swag. I can sleep anywhere.
Alright.
On your floor?
Alright.
He rolled his swag out, curled up and seemed to settle. I went to bed behind the mozzie net.
    Ly?
    What?
    Can I?
    What?
    Can I lie with you?
    No.
    Silence.
    Ly?
    What?
    Please?
    I slid over and he joined me. We had such a sweaty wrestle that night, all night, we broke the wooden bed base.
    He loved our house and our family. In between conversations he'd say, excuse me, and have an unspoken, hand-gesturing communication with someone I could not see. Spirits of the land and sea and life.
    Anyone like tea? Serenity offered on her way to the kitchen.
    Yes please, I said.
    David held up a hand, nodded to the air and turned to her.
    Me too. Thanks, Serenity.
    His smile never lit his eyes.
    Will you tell me something?
    In the wet season and we were housebound as flood waters

tickled ominously at the back steps so that he was trapped in restless stillness until he could sleep dry on the beach or deep in the forest or under the tarp of a ute of anyone game enough or with sufficient vision to give a man like David a ride.

Depends, I said.

No one's ever taught me anything about your people's magic. Can you?

Yours too.

Yeah, well—

Sure.

I explained as much as I could, drew him diagrams and explained when he didn't get words like *geis* and *anam cara*. That the magic of lochs and heather, peat fires, oaks and birch. Of Avalon and Finn McCool and Cú Chulain. Mist and every color grey he could ever envisage. The ghosts of ancestors in the skeletons of winter trees. A symbiosis of truffle and boar. Then he cried. Because knowledge can gift a form of freedom.

Why are you ashamed of being a bit Scottish?

Most white people just think I'm nuts.

I'm pale. White isn't a racial trait, David.

Explain?

We've been led to believe white represents innocence and cleanliness. Children's books depict angels with white fluffy wings. White is good, black is what? Like saying light is good and darkness is bad which is stupid. Heard of a chieftain named Calgacus?

What? No.

A Scotsman. Well, a Caledonian. Or was he a Pict? You fought the Romans at the Battle of Mons Graupius nearly two thousand years ago.

Did I win?

Of course not. About ten thousand of you died defending your lands. Forty years later the Roman emperor Hadrian had a bloody-great wall built from coast to coast to keep you out of the lowlands.

I didn't know that.

Calgacus said of the Romans: they make a wasteland and call it peace.

He recovered after several minutes. He just stared off into space.

That night I led him down to Jarrod's caravan because my son was away camping with his friends up at Rummery Park and he liked David. Had offered before.

You can stay here, I said.

I want to be with you.

That's not going to happen anymore.

Have I done something wrong?

Magic does to this to me. Things become complicated.

He kissed me, turned his back and went into the caravan. He had that kind of respect.

Every time he came through he stayed, we ate and drank tea (he never touched alcohol) and we talked for days. The second last time I saw him he was emaciated, and his dreads had been cut off.

What happened?

Gaol.

Why?

I was sleeping on a bench at Central Station. The cops woke me and told me to move on. I said leave me alone I just want to sleep. They tried to drag me off the bench and I wouldn't let them, so they arrested me. I was inside for two months.

Bastards.

It gets worse.

What else?

I can't see or hear the spirits anymore. Every time they put me away for something I get less and less connected. They put me on meds. Now I can't live without 'em.

What happened in prison, David?

Silence.

One season he stopped coming. We never heard from him again. Serenity, Jarrod and I all thought he was either dead or institutionalized.

CHAPTER 39

I dreamt I was in the room above a party. I was a man. I sat on the floor opposite another man who was so angry at me he spat as he yelled. He pulled a stub of chalk from his pocket and drew a *deosil* (east to west) circle around himself. Oh, oh, I thought. Looks like war. Better do the same. And I did.

I can never understand the raised voices of angry people so nothing he said made sense, but I fell into his head. Inside was like a pristine underground car park with pillars as far as the eye could see. Endless silky buttery twilight, the light not discernible from any one source. What drew my attention was a slim, rose-gold pillar set in a circular base encrusted with rubies and garnets. Four thin serpents wound around that pillar from the base to the top, their narrow heads reaching towards an unseen sky in rapture. The whole turned slowly catching light, glinting, the jewels a-glitter. The sight took my breath away. Then I fell out of his head back into the room. He was still screaming. I just saw you, I said softly. A little more yelling then he registered what I had said.

What?

I said, I just saw you.

I went downtown for coffee and as I walked back through my gate I felt a tickle of words on the inside of my head. Something about the snow. I took the ever-haunting, hopeful notebook from my bedside table, and a pen, and I sat in the wicker chair within the grove outside the studio door and wrote. I sat from nine in the morning until sometime just after three in the afternoon. Seventeen pages about a young guy in a city somewhere in the middle of a deadly winter, meeting a forest god that hung out with a ragtag troupe that were actually sídhe Travellers. Fáidh. Faerie. Immortals journeying the country in a clapped-out old double-decker bus picking up the Lost, with a rocked-up Irish band and a habit of getting into all sorts of strife. They holed up through the winter days and nights in an underground service bay of the metro in New Rathmore.

New writing style, but for what? Two days later I had the same tickle and wrote another story. One set in a dead-dry, rain-desperate spring. That was followed by two more. When I See the Wild God was conjured around those four stories. The characters did look and behave uncannily like a lot of people in my life. Llewellyn agreed to its publication. I was assigned an editor named Natalie Harter. She and I become close. An entire book based around the people in the stories was her idea.

In the early months of 2001 Serenity and I co-directed Romeo and Juliet, a contemporary Shakespearean production in which she also starred as Juliet. During the lead up to opening night Bay FM, the local radio, had a fundraiser in Railway Park. They invited us to perform. We staged one of the choreographed fight scenes without alerting anyone to the stunt. Jarrod was just one of the show's many hoodlums involved in that brawl. A man, a total stranger, charged towards us from the other side of the street looking to get in on the rammy (Scots for a fight).

Raced our cars through the streets with fake guns and were not caught by the police.

We were very proud. The success of the show began slowly but by the third week we had bums on every seat.

A couple of lads bailed from another production company putting on a pantomime. They preferred the gang routines. And the fights. I didn't find out for decades that the person running that production company was my mother. She lived in Byron Bay the whole time I was there. Her name was Shirley and we lived in Shirley Street. The irony, eventually, not lost on me.

Right on the tail of that show came another season of Superstar due to public persistence. We auditioned and auditioned but no one applying for the part of Judas that year could hit the necessary notes. But I could. Could I do this?

You're too old, said the rat voice, and you're sort of a woman, despite the muscles.

We can have a female Judas, I replied. Fuck you, rat voice.

Nah.

Yes.

No!

Yes!

Then I remembered the night Jan and I sat through Jesus Christ Superstar sometime back in nineteen seventy three, in Sydney. John English played Judas and I'd thought I would like to be cast in that role one day. Some spells take longer than others.

Yeah, me, I said to the producers. I'll play Judas.

Much of the cast were indignant. How can she? She's a woman. She's—what—fifty? How can she both direct and play a major lead at the same time? A guy should have the chance. Someone find a guy. But we didn't.

Auditions were over with, every part filled. But then two young men turned up desperate to apply.

Sorry guys, we're done.

P…please give, ah, g…give us a go? William stuttered. The producers and I glanced at each other.

Why not, said the producer.

William sang Sarah McLachlan's, In the Arms of the Angels. We gave him one of Judas' songs, but I did play Judas. This time Jarrod got to whip the Jesus character and Serenity played a Pharisee. We sold out again and William became a friend for a few years.

In December that year Adam and his partner were pregnant, the child due in June 2002. Then the lawyers released Jan's money. I booked a trip for the August after my grandson was born, a pilgrimage from Cornwall, through Wales, to Ireland and across to France, before flying to America to meet the people at Llewellyn Worldwide in Minnesota USA. The Historian and Serenity would look after the cats and Jungle while I was away.

I booked Smugglers Cottage at Trebarwith Strand, Cornwall. Down the road from Tintagel. I wrote to my publisher that I was coming to meet them and I hooked up with the Artist, then living in Europe, to see if he could take the time out to travel with me. He agreed to meet me in London.

Adam had attended many births in his life, so he delivered their first child. When he was two years old I took a special photo of him. On the dragon throne with my twin katanas on a stand beside him, a crystal ball between his striped onesie'd legs looking like the child in

Labyrinth, the movie that starred David Bowie. That chair, made of resin, exploded a month before my trip. The heat of summer had activated an air bubble. The refund paid for most of the holiday.

I had formed a martial arts clan called Fíanna. A freckled redheaded Celt named Jess trained with a crew in Mullumbimby called The Enemies of Rome. Dark Age fighting. She taught me a broadsword kata that utilized every part of the weapon to its best advantage. The strokes and thrusts yelled numerically in Gaelic.

Karla and I trained with her. I studied up on Fionn mac Cumhaill and the nameless warriors with whom he rode. They were independent of any chieftain. Landless and free. To become a member of the Fíanna one had to run through the forest at night, barefoot, chased by the others, leaving not a mark of passing, stand in a deep trench deflecting the spears of the Fennian warriors, up to twenty at a time, creating and reciting an epic poem. I liked that. The mix.

We sourced a blacksmith who sold us planks of differing degrees of carbon steel and then I bought a few power tools and other necessary things. Anvil. Forge. Heavy hammers. We made broadswords in my backyard. I'd been shown how by Wayland the Smith. He's the man who made and sold me that dragon-headed athamé all those years ago. He'd moved to Mudgee and day by day calcium spikes threatened to sever his spine. He passed much of his equipment on to me when we all visited him for the last time.

We made swords of beauty and strength. Mine has the pommel of an ancient African ebony walking stick. The blades were not so sharp as to cut but sharp enough for wariness. Sharp only to the middle of the blade where they were sleeved so that one could thrust to the groin or the belly or bring the sword tip down through the front of the face in close combat.

Staves were essential to that training as was the learning by rote, not of epic poetry but of the book of shadows so that one could vary the rituals by knowing them intimately. Above my left eye, dissecting my eyebrow is a small scar, the result of a slash from a staff during one fighting session. Karla clocked me right in the face. Blood poured from the wound and she stopped, horrified, but with a near-perfect fight I yelled, don't stop now! That was only a few days before my first trip to Ireland in 2003. I had a black eye and a butterfly bandage over the cut. I smiled at the people who stared.

By the time I boarded the flight to England I was working on The Quickening and I was emailing chapters to Llewellyn editor Natalie Harter, as they were written. I was so deeply involved in the story—a novel in the style of magical realism—that no trip was going to delay the words. I was in a groove and a horse to a rider.

I'd booked a hotel room for one night, but the Artist planned to stay an extra day in London. The following morning I collected a rental car and navigated my way south. Only to encounter a problem. The road signs were all numbered. No GPS back then. The maps could have been in Martian for all I could read them. I ended up lost in Reading. I wasn't given a sensible direction for over an hour as most of the people to whom I spoke hadn't ever been to Cornwall and what was I doing crossing the country in one day, was I mad? I'm Australian, I said to the officer at the cop shop. She nodded in sage comprehension.

Think. Okay, the sun moves in the opposite direction in this hemisphere. Get your bearings, Ly, you're going south-west, so follow the sun. And that's what got me there just after dusk around ten at night. I picked up the keys and was given directions (that I never would have worked out myself) to our cottage. I unlocked the front door, dumped my bags, explored the house, chose my bedroom, poured a glass of wine and let my mind wander into the mists of myth. Tintagel. Legend is written that Merlin magically transformed Uther into the image of Grainne's husband Gorlois and they conceived a child during a night of wild lovemaking. Arthur is a bastard just like me. It was technically rape.

Smuggler's Cottage was home while I lived in Cornwall. Built under a cliff, opposite a car park with a spring-fed well, spoken of locally as magical. I spent my first night happily alone. I was up to the section in The Quickening where Michael Blacker's men, in an impulsive act of stupidly, abduct the forest god's son, a four year old half-mortal. He is imprisoned in the facility beneath the Church of the Penitents of the True Faith, the hate-based christian fundamentalist sect determined to drive the magic from the world.

The child is very scared and even as Brighid and the forest god soar between the worlds searching for him the little boy quickens, his heritage as the child of a forest god aging him and drawing from him a mumbled song, the lyrics in a tongue unknown to the world of today.

The song is an attempt at self-comfort, but it blacks out the entire city of New Rathmore. All the phones go down. The beginning of an emergency crisis requiring the intervention of the military.

Natalie had not long finished reading that chapter when the whole of New York State, then Ontario Canada, blacked out along with the phone lines. For three days.

Magic is a peculiar thing, so often like the riddle of the chicken and the egg. When I wrote the four stories for Wild God the one for summer saw the Travellers, and the humans they picked up along the way, in the north for meán samhraidh, a gathering to be held at the field maintained by the remainder of the O'Neill lineage for just this. The clans arrived to tragedy. The daughter of the O'Neill's, and her two children, died when their two storey weatherboard house burned down. They'd been trapped inside. The police were involved, and the case was considered suspicious because her partner (not the father of the children) was nowhere to be found. He was either away somewhere unknown, had been incinerated in the intense blaze or had set the thing himself.

The day after I'd written that the 6 o'clock news announced that just over the border in Queensland this exact thing had happened last night.

What was interesting, retrospectively, about that trip? I walked the streets and countryside, exactly, of my ancestors. Also retrospectively, as I write this, I am aware that nothing is really hidden but that sometimes we need to see ourselves reflected in a face or place to fully understand how whacky life can be.

The Artist and I drove along the coast road into south Wales and stopped at a roadside toilet block and barbecue shelter. I walked behind the brick structure. A rowan tree, its girth wider than much of my house, had its vast canopy buried deep within the white of the sky. Rivulets burrowed under every grounded branch and every log was covered in moss the green of hallucination. Forest quiet. Nothing but the mere susurration of the feathery leafscape. Now I felt home. Not London, not even Cornwall. This.

Our travels were without incident until Tara Beach, north of

Dublin. Crows warred with gulls, scavenging amongst the tourists that first day. Come sunset, however, they lined up by the hundreds like ducks in a shooting gallery, on the roof and gables of the bed and breakfast where we were staying. Disturbing the owner into a superstitious meltdown. We said nothing.

The Artist and I drove randomly across Ireland, trusting the magic more than ever. I followed the M6 all the way to just outside Galway and I was repelled. The emanation from the outskirts of the city was that of a dirty, industrial wasteland. I realized, retrospectively, that this was illogical, crazy and downright wrong but that's what happened.

I can't go in.

Why?

No idea. A psychic wall.

What do we do?

I don't have... Hang on, Willy McElroy told me he used to spend his summers by the sea at a place called Clifden.

Who?

The lead singer of the Wild Zinnias. You remember. You came to a gig with me once. Irish bloke.

Cute one with the curls. Yeah, I remember.

You're incorrigible.

Of course.

We followed the coast and stopped for water in Spiddal, a small tourist town offering boat trips out to Inis Mór. I parked down a tiny back road just up from a closed pub. Fat tourists sweated along the street. The gutters were festooned with fast food wrappers, empty soft drink cans, cigarette butts. Must have been thirty five degrees and I was really, really despairing and fed up. So much for the green land and finding a craic. Everything was hazy with dust and grime, the grass withered to straw.

Walking back around the corner towards our car I stopped to look at a poster for a music festival. Held a week ago. Sledgehammer of a mood.

Was I trusting the magic? No I was not.

As we crossed the street a tall, thin man made eye contact.

He was leaning against a silver BMW, his arms crossed across his chest. He smiled, indicating the hotel with a tilt of his head.

Best pub in Ireland, dat.
Hmph.
Are you lookin for the music?
The festival's over.
Dat was not my question.

I did a quick recalibration. Yes, I said, we're looking for the music.

This time he tilted his head along the noodle of a road on which we had parked. Then nodded along the narrow exit to where?

And I don't mind at all.
Really? Sorry. Thank you.

Beside where we had parked was a six foot high stone wall and beyond that a wood of many trees. We climbed up and jumped down into a soft, gentle shade on the other side, pervaded with a silence that again denied the traffic and tourists mere yards away. We drank water and I smoked a cigarette and we both sighed our distress into the dapple of oak and rowan and birch and beech and the thin silver of a try-hard stream at the base of our momentary knolled sanctuary.

We climbed back over the wall. The man and the silver BMW were gone but I followed his instructions and drove up the slight rise and onto the flat land away from town. Ugliness. A moonscape of rock and barrenness. Then we blew a tire that, on inspection, was down to the wire on the inside.

If we'd been doing a hundred on a main road? I shuddered.

With the little European temp attached we limped back to Spiddal and asked for the nearest service station. We were given directions out of town and when the mechanic looked under the car he informed us that the other was just as bad.

Better get onto the hire car people in Galway and replace yer whole thing, he said. The alignment's fooked. Lucky you weren't doing a hundred on a main road or you'd be dead. The hairs rose up on my arms at the echo of my own thought. We stayed overnight in Spiddal and were finally back on the road just after lunch the following day.

Where to?
Same road.
You kidding?
No.

The land was a moonscape for mile after futile mile but then we crested a rise and were struck by the vastness of a series of naked mountains called the Twelve Bens. Waterfalls. Rivulets, brooks, burns. Lakes with islands in the middle like something out of legend. And green. We followed the winding, meander of that road as though led. All the way to the coast and a small bay. A place named Roundstone. I wondered what the word was in Gaeilge and along the narrow road towards the village we passed a yellow, two storey house with a sign: Cloch naRon, Place of the Seal. Galway hookers were anchored in the walled bay, traditional fishing boats with black sails or else the color of dried blood. Currachs, once made of leather stretched over wooden bones are now of tarred canvas. In the distance, a little way across the bay, the island of Inishlacken, sea-misted and shimmering in the heat. Seals, like curious puppies exposing their heads just above the water near the shore. A horse, grey but with patches that hinted of rusty lichen. A deserted place haunted by stories of the long dead, its low stone cottages abandoned, occupied only once a year by artists-in-residence.

We asked at every pub and hotel, but the answer was, No rooms. Anywhere. Arts month. High summer. Should have booked. Six o'clock in the endless pale of twilight and we were desolate. Stranded in a car park at the end of town.

Like a marionette I crossed the street to the doily shop and asked the woman inside if she knew anywhere we could get a room.

Mad feller's house up road, she said all smiles.

Oh? I asked, thinking she could be playing me. Which one is that?

Big yellow place.

She never dropped her eyes from mine as if daring me to move my rook.

Is that the two storey house with the sign in Irish out front?

But I was no one so, to her, I no longer existed.

I thanked her for her kindness. She ignored me, her lips a line, and went back to her book. My tattoos perhaps?

I knocked. A tall dark man, head down and glowering from beneath fierce eyebrows, loped towards us from the rear of the nineteen seventies-style grand interior.

But when he looked up his eyes twinkled with humor.

You rock stars?

Like butter wouldn't melt in his mouth.

Witches.

Even better! You here about a room?

Please.

He led us through to a smoky, peaty, frying-fat, tailor-made-cigarette-smelling kitchen where his younger Down syndrome brother sat in silent seriousness. He made us cups of thick instant coffee, discussed the rent and where we were from. Chain smoked and talked. An hour later he dropped the cost of the room by half because he liked us.

As we walked up the stairs I sensed a hand on the banister.

Your mother. She's dead isn't she? I can feel her. Dazzling.

He stopped on the step above me. I almost ran into him.

She liked a party. Specially after she got rid of our waste of a father.

We took a few more steps.

Four years ago, he said. We only just opened again this week.

Took a lot of guts, I said.

He was on pharmaceutical meds for a bipolar disorder and depression and we drank a lot of that disgusting coffee with him during our stay. And listened when he opened up about his mind.

Grey here. For ten months of a year. I don't cope.

I know, I replied.

The Artist had run out of black paint so after breakfast the next morning we meandered up the only street in town, lined with little shop windows hinting more at homes than businesses, each looking westward over the bay. I stopped at random and knocked. The woman who opened the door was covered in paint and we could see a work in progress on an easel.

Know where we can buy black paint? I asked.

From me, she smiled. Come in. I'm Rosie McGurran.

Ly! I heard from the back of the room where a wild, shaggy-haired young woman sat on the sofa in front of the stove. She introduced herself as Sheena Keane, director of Bluegrace Music.

I brought the band Lunasa to Byron Bay a few years ago.

I was at that gig. They were fabulous. Do I know you?

Yes. You read tarot for me. Did you bring 'em?

Bugger me, I thought, bewildered. Ah... I'm on holiday though.

You did!

Yes.

Can I have a reading, so? I'll pay ya.

Don't want to.

A quicky? I'll cook dinner.

How could I refuse?

Seriously quick one, though, I threatened.

Several cups of tea later and we were introduced to everyone in the village and at seven the Artist and I went to Sheena's house, down on the beach beside the graveyard. We were introduced to her husband Keith and their five year old daughter Grace.

I asked if her house was haunted because I was picking up like mad. Too many voices to count.

Yer in Ireland, Sheena laughed. I understood. The west coast moans with the regret of rebels, outcast, the starved and the drowned.

I sat on the floor opposite her and handed her my cards.

Shuffle.

She did and I laid out three cards.

Car trouble.

Nothing wrong with my car.

I shrugged and put the cards away. Despite her mild disappointment and confusion, we had dinner and a lovely evening.

Next day Sheena intended to drive to Belfast to catch a plane to Manchester for the football game but that morning two men had their heads under the bonnet, hunting for the glitch, as we wandered up the hill into town. Sheena gave me a look that should have sliced my face open.

Don't shoot the messenger, I said, ducking into Rosie's gallery.

Between the seafood chowder and the Guinness, writing, warm friendships forged, naked swimming in the sea at Dog's Bay, icy and silken despite the heatwave and to furious glances by over-clad seasonal visitors. The Tour de Bog. I became a life member of the Roundstone library and said I'd be back.

I stayed several days in Paris afterwards, on the Left Bank in the Hotel Victoria just up the road from the Seine. I wandered the streets, drank coffee, soaked up the smells and feel and allowed myself the sensation of disgust, while wandering the Louvre, at the decadence of the church and the comprehension of just how vast were the riches used to fund their humility. I was homesick for this city. I could feel my bones humming. I found out years later that an ancestor, Aubrée (ne de Rumenel) de Jarpenville, was Sergeant of the Hawk there in 1207. And that the man who sired me was French.

    I flew from Ireland to France to Los Angeles. I spent several hours at the cordoned gates at LAX, security at an all-time high, before finally catching a connecting flight to Minnesota. I met Carl Weschcke for the first time and dined on seafood at the mouth of the Mississippi. Joined my editor, Natalie, in her office that was lined wall to wall with rejected manuscripts and drove with her and Lisa Novak, my other editor, to a Medieval town that was only open once a year.

    I concluded my trip in South Carolina with witches from my Wildwood Gate forum and when I finally arrived home after a month on the road Jungle refused to speak to me for at least a half an hour, he was so distraught that I had abandoned him.

CHAPTER 40

We finally procured the small spindly ficus that had been used in the Front of House for live shows since I don't know when. She had called to me on several occasions. I'd apologized because of the woman who'd refused to let the forlorn tree come home with me. Another sad, forlorn person. We planted her right up close to the fence on the other side of my training platform. Within weeks Flidias lifted her branches and joined not only the newbie but also the old eucalypt next door that overhung our yard. The branches on the other side were dead. Doug, our neighbor there, had a mug of tea in one hand and stood with the other on his hip.

What the fuck's this about do you reckon?

I explained about Flidias and that her purpose seemed to be a super-tree. That her capacity for kindness was boundless. By now the pot-bound menagerie had shaped itself, through whatever form of communication plant people use, into a semi-circle facing my studio. A grove. A haven in which I sat to muse in the wicker armchair. I was sitting thus one autumn afternoon, quite a breezy day, when Serenity swanned down the back steps.

Burned you this, she said, handing me a CD. Filippa Giordano. Vocal sorcery. I opened the studio doors, remembering Lyall Watson's Supernature, and turned up the volume. Every leaf stopped moving. Each plant ceased to quiver in case quivering was too loud. So eerie, such elation. I played that and
Alanis Morissette's Prayer Cycle to them all regularly.

The grove was becoming a small forest with Bran and Flidias canopying at least twenty five feet above the ground. Two more pot-bound trees were added. Lilli Pillis. Steve gave them to me. They were mournful and sparse youngsters, a little like starving children and he doubted they would survive but he gestured towards the giant, adolescent ficus and shrugged. The Lilli Pillis were planted at the rear of my studio. He was wrong again. They took off in the fruit rot soil like punks with spray cans, already gnarly by six months.

I moved into a bedroom in the house because William was having difficulties at his current home and was really quite shattered. He'd moved into the studio to heal and to learn. I only asked that he keep the rooms beautiful as she was as much a mother as the big house. He agreed. He got the only job there was, at the local chicken abattoir. Over the coming months he developed a cough. He got sicker and sicker. At times the fits would leave him almost dry heaving. I begged him to see a doctor as I feared he might die. He had to work, he said. He was sure the killing place was responsible.

Maybe, I thought.

He wasn't home the day I noticed a shin-high branch from Bran's trunk, about the thickness of an arm, extending across the path and pressing dangerously against a glass pane of one of the French doors to his room.

What's this you do? I whispered.

I stepped over the threat and opened the main door. To a disaster. Clothes dumped in dirty lad-piles. Mold on every wall. Empty take-away food containers, food-encrusted plates. Bong. Brown-stained coffee cups.

Oh, William. The room wants to kill you and so does Bran.

Arrow, Adam's staffy-bully cross had come to live with us a while back. He still had his balls but was so well trained he was kind. Gentle. But his job was to announce the arrival of anyone at the gate with a Gatling-gunning, savage bay. He announced William's arrival around six.

Hey, I called from the kitchen window, you got a minute?

Sure.

I put the kettle on for tea and we sat.

William, you're going to die. I asked him about the branch. Said I had looked into the room and wondered how on earth had he not tripped and fallen?

Well, I just kinda step across it all the time. (Cough. Cough some more.) And, oops, sorry about the mess.

You still don't understand, do you?

What?

I took his hand, the tea forgotten, took cloths, buckets and disposable garbage bags, stepped over Bran's deadly weapon and entered the murk, switching on the light.

Well?

Ly, I have no idea where to even begin.

Hang dog. Lazy man.

I picked up all his clothing and mildewed towels; his dirty sundries and threw them onto the bed.

Washing machine. Now.

Then we piled all the plates, cups, glasses, packets, old tissues and the bong into the garbage bags.

You start washing the walls, I'll go get the vacuum. You're not sleeping till we're done.

The following day the washing machine ploughed through the loads. I went to town and bought undercoat and white paint. The reddish brown womb of a room was about to become daylight pale. I walked back through the gate and Bran's branch was off the window and had turned towards the rear of the property on the soil. I walked the path to the studio unimpeded.

We now had internet to the house. I checked emails every day while letters still poured in regularly, mainly from Witchcraft Theory and Practice readers. There was my online forum to respond to each morning. My world—the-world—becoming smaller and smaller, more reliable. Tarot, writing to be done, coffee with friends, training and paperwork with Iaido, Jungle to walk, a lush, talkative garden in which to think. Nice house, nice town. Everything was alright? Somehow the September 11 destruction of the Twin Towers in New York, said to be the child of Al-Qaida in 2001 became the War on Terror, beginning with George W Bush's State of the Union address in January 2002 that involved ousting Saddam Hussein, declaring an Axis of Evil and striking Baghdad with the infamous shock and awe bombing campaign. America, Australia and England tried to convince the world that this was a just war; that they were the good guys, and this was us against them. A tangled web. The honest reasons why may come to light in a hundred years. Despite whistleblowers such as Julian Assange and Edward Norton. Torture became acceptable, Guantanamo Bay incarcerated possible threats. New and more ominous laws were introduced, including the reintroduction of the crime of sedition in Australia. News distribution was bought. Free speech terrified of itself.

Behind the brash tabloid displays an army of countless millions sat at computers around the world uploading documents and opinions, true and false. Because who knows which is which anymore? People still played war games on computer, killing with impunity. Had fun. Switched off from a hard day at the office. And all the while Mark Zuckerberg and his friends were in college inventing what was to become the new god, social networking.

The lies are getting worse. Politicians and consumerism. The other new god, insurance. Police in blue uniforms becoming militarized. Faces masked in black, black shields, black helmets, stun guns, loaded guns, more power in all the wrong ways.

I had to keep up to scratch. Tarot was, and still is, predicting world events but the desensitization of entire populations had just begun. In 2001 Wikipedia was named and within a mere two years over a hundred thousand articles were uploaded. Are all those articles true? A vast network of hackers and dark web infiltrators sprung up. New programming, new and deadly digital viruses. An entirely new economy. The job I had back in the late seventies, early eighties put people out of work. Where did they go? The system has become a monster. Or is it the very dawn of our eventual evolution?

Should the power go off or a super-virus take down computer technology? Who, on what's called the dark web, isn't trying?

Now I figure there are two worlds. There's the shallow world where all the above belong, including every news broadcast and cooking show. The commonality and acceptability of cancer. Nuclear proliferation. Micro plastics, now thirty percent of every living creature. Labiaplasty and seventeen different kinds of milk. Porn so aggressive that stockholders backing pharmaceutical industries are laughing as anxiety and body modification and dysphoria rises. Drugs for depression have become the new black. Well, prescription meds in general. Advertising on a billboard on my way home from Melbourne airport recently suggested that if I am "obsessed" with my hair color I absolutely must buy their product. The shallow land wherein an Australian prime minister considers a seventy-five-thousand-dollar car that of the average man.

Mass graves. Refugee tragedy. Genetically modified food. Irradiation of everything in a supermarket. Obesity off the charts.

Extremely fat children with type 2 diabetes.

What then, is the deep world? Stories with friends and family. Bonfires. Reclamation of language almost lost to colonialism. The seasons of the garden. The cacophonous forest. Rewilding. Giving birth. Challenging, laughing, loving. Study and seeking knowledge beyond what the textbook and the history book demands we accept. Quiet. Making. Poetry. Death. Art. Or is it something as yet unrealized? Nano-chipping? Selective breeding? Virtual reality with legs becoming superfluous appendages, removed at birth? Becoming unrecognizably mutant through the use of plastic surgery or gene interference?

The wonder of mobile phones that do everything except hold a conversation and wash the dishes. The *my* society that is the consume-without-consciousness zeitgeist while West Papua weeps and more and more habitats are destroyed, more and more species become extinct.

We need to hear the language of earth. To speak of her and for her seas and air, ice and islands. I too am a mother. Is this Joseph Campbell's savage forest on a vast scale? If so, what is next?

CHAPTER 41

The return trip to Ireland was two years later, for the pre-release of The Quickening. Sheena arranged everything. She pre-booked dozens of tarot sessions in Roundstone and set me up for readings from The Quickening both there and in Galway and Cork. The year before this the Artist had lived a season as artist-in-residence on Inishlacken and was commissioned to paint the festival poster and to exhibit his newest collection at the Staric Gallery.

Sheena had also asked that I bring my weapons with me to perform katas on stage at the close of the Galway Arts Season. I had both my bo and jo staves in their black-on-black ornamental linen bags and my training sword in its leather case. On arriving at the Shannon airport I declared my weapons.

The customs officer laughed and said, Ah, good girl yerself. G'on now and have a grand stay. He smiled as I exited towards the bus terminal.

I caught the train to Galway then the bus to Roundstone. The Artist and I settled into an old stone house and I smelled the sea—the barnacles and kelp—of the west coast of Ireland and mused about how much I love this place and how much it was influencing my newest work, The Shining Isle.

I was to read tarot at the very back of the ground floor of the Staric Gallery that was made as welcoming as possible with some discarded paintings hiding the old iron bars that supported parts of the stone walls, others disguising exposed water pipes. Behind my chair was a door. I opened it, the bottom dragging along the concrete floor. A windowless room. A malevolence that seemed to hide under abandoned benches. Not even cobwebs, just a mantle of ancient dust. No one knew the room's purpose. No one went in, ever. Made all the little hairs stand up on my arms and a bead of fear slip down my spine. It was a cell. Smelled of locked-up madness.

This is a land of paradox. Of Yeats and Wilde and the Book of

Kells on the one hand, on the other a brutal catholic regime that invented the Magdalene Laundries where girls and women were locked away and abused, often for life, sometimes for simply being pretty because that could inspire lust. That's what the room behind me felt like. Thin lipped jealousy turning the key and pocketing release. Someone being imprisoned and left to die. The sewers of Tuam.

Next day I climbed the stairs of the Staric to Sheena's office on the top floor. She was on the phone with a look on her face I could not fathom. Keith stood close by, devastated. His brother was deep in the jungle somewhere in Cambodia and he was drowning in fluid trapped in his lungs, an untreatable virus. Sheena spoke to a doctor at the hospital who could give her no clear answers. The thing killing Keith's brother was immune to any treatment medical staff administered. He was dying. This was not the time to discuss book launches or anything at all, so I crept downstairs and across the road to where the artists hung out and were fed: the community center.

Then the Voice said, This is not his time to die but—
What's the but?
Silence.
Should I tell them?
Tell him.
The rat voice, alarmed, said, Fuck, what if you're wrong?
I knew I wasn't.

I went back upstairs and gestured for Keith to follow me into the adjoining room where I sat us both on the floor. I told him what I had heard. He nodded slowly, the lines between his eyebrows two deep slashes.

Ly?
Keith?
What's de boot?

Two days later on Tuesday his brother was still at death's portal. Sheena confronted me on the street, angry, scared, because I had given Keith hope.

When, Ly?
Thursday, I said without thinking. She strode past me towards her house.

Thursday morning, I had my coffee at the internet café. I read an email from home. An unseasonal, unprecedented flood had devastated much of Byron Bay overnight and a man had died across the road from our house. Seems he was riding home on his pushbike. He'd come off and his backpack had caught on a fence. He'd drowned in the street.

Sheena intercepted me as I walked towards the community center.

He recovered! Just like that, the medicine took. He's going to be okay, like you said.

That's excellent news.

I didn't tell her. I waited. The next day was the book launch and the Artist helped me decorate the top floor of the gallery with dozens of tea candles and several vases of the little white roses that grew in abundance around the church up the granite stone stairs beside our building.

Guests began arriving around seven and I could sense their discomfort. Sheena whispered to perhaps get rid of the roses because people associate candles and white flowers with funerals.

They stay, I said.

I opened the launch with a dedication to the man who drowned back home in Byron Bay and I explained what had happened. I looked across at Keith who mouthed, *dat was de boot*.

That night I dreamt that four old women walked around an open-cut abandoned quarry full of uncanny turquoise water. They were on their way to take tea at an outdoor table on the other side. Three of the women wore black but the fourth was dressed in red and shaded beneath a red lace parasol. She had forgotten something and was wandering back around the edge of the pit. I tried to scream that she was too close to the edge, but I made no sound. She fell in and drowned. Time flipped into a future where a legend spoke of a red demon that lived that in this lurid water. A track had been worn down to its edge by pilgrims bringing flowers as offerings. A young man dressed in a suit carried a poesy to lay by the water when the flash of something huge and red broke the surface of the lake and dragged him under.

I awoke. Took a few minutes to regain myself. The Artist made us tea and sat on the bed beside me.

What?

I explained the dream.

He thought for a minute.

You know, I've never seen an old woman anywhere here.

That's peculiar, me neither.

Later in Sheena's office we asked why.

They're all widows, she said.

What?

The sea took most of their husbands. They don't go out.

That's terrible.

The way of this coast.

In the evening we were buying groceries and a man came into the shop with a tiny old woman on his arm. At a guess she was ninety. Dressed all in black. She stopped, stared for a moment, then came at me like a raptor and stood right in front of me, smiling.

I'm lookin' at de look, she said.

Okay.

Do you mind if I'm lookin' at de look?

No, not at all.

She walked right around me, studying.

I'm likin' de look o de look.

Thanks.

The following day old women were everywhere.

On the drive towards the ferry that would take us to Inish Mór and the Black Fort, Sheena pulled up beside an ancient stone wall with a stile leading to a field and a distant copse of woodland.

You'll want to visit there, she said to me.

What?

The next field past the trees is where the battle of Cath Maige Tuired (Moytura) happened. I'll be back for you in half an hour. I've to pick up Grace.

Cath Maige Tuired is where the Tuatha Dé Danann fought the Fir Bolg. I leapt the stile, followed by the Artist and we traipsed to the further field. A stone circle was surrounded by an iron fence erected so long ago that the bars sagged like old drunks. Ample space for me to fit through. The circle was overhung by the branches of a huge, sprawling grandmother yew, her lower arms adorned liberally with clouties. I walked the circle sunwise, touching each of the stones in turn before squatting at the raised hummock in the center, the burial place of some unrecorded warrior. I spontaneously broke into the Dire Straits song, Brothers in Arms. The temperature that day was easily thirty degrees and I was in the sun in a shoestring top. As I sang the sensation of wet silk softly wrapped itself, firstly around my left arm, then across my back and down my right arm raising all the hairs on my body. Likely a thousand years or more had passed since a warrior had paid homage there. I discovered much later that one of my bloodline taproots is sunk deep in Connemara, tendrils perhaps knowing what and who lie buried in the surrounding bogs.

On Inis Mór I was introduced to twelve year old Fionn, named for the legendary warrior, and several of his friends. We battled in a scene from the mists of a thousand years gone. The Artist and I picked wild strawberries along the narrow lanes. In the shadow of the Black Fort I ate a packed lunch looking out over the navy blue western sea towards the legendary drowned land of Hy Brasil, then ran the ankle-breaking island's strange and shifting pale grey rock terrain so as to not miss the last ferry.

I caught a train to Cork to attend a launch of my book at what I thought was going to be in the town there. That's not what happened.

I was told to get off the train at a place called Dún ar Aill. I was met by a man named Bev, an Irish gypsy (an lucht siúil). Tavellers. A bard with long white hair and a braided beard. He and his wife Del had seven sons and a daughter, all born in wagons on the road. The Irish government ended countless generations of traditional nomadic life. Bev and Del had acquired the land near Caisleán anPhuca. The castle of the faerie horse just outside the village and named Pook Castle Pook, for the Caisleán. A moss and lichen covered dark stone ruin of a five storey Norman castle, the ground inside littered with owl regurgitations, originally an ancient Celtic stronghold built atop a sídhe mound.

The Synan family who built the castle, forfeited it in the time of Queen Elizabeth I. It and the surrounds given to her pretty boys, Walter Raleigh and the poet Edmund Spenser who toyed with living a pastoral lord in the Irish countryside. For a while. They were warned off venturing near the castle because the puka were not nice. The Good Folk held their revels there on the eve of Midsummer. Doom, the consequence to any mortal crossing the path of their trooping horses.

Spenser and Raleigh were ill-made of the stuff of landed lairds returned to the royal courts of England. Spenser wrote a poem, called Epithalamium, in which he mentions the name Puck. Legend tells that the two young men were in an ale house one evening, in the company of Willy Shakespeare and Spenser read his poem aloud. Shakespeare, inspired, goes home and writes A Midsummer Night's Dream.

Bev knew nothing about any book launch. Only that Sheena had said I was coming. He and Del were nonplussed and suggested I stay and enjoy their hospitality for a week. They made me a bed in the shed.

Their seven sons came round that first evening, piled into the one car. I was out in the yard practicing the kata sequences I would perform at the festival. Four of the lads were taekwondo practitioners and as they rounded the side of the house and saw me the youngest, around fourteen, came at a run. He made a grab for my sword case and I hit his hand with the bo staff, just hard enough to bring him up short.

You don't touch a lady's weapons without asking, I explained.

A woman with weapons, he grinned. What da fook?

Want me to show you?

They all crowded around as I unzipped the sword bag and went through a series of maneuvers.

When I was done I handed the sword to the boy and showed him how to make air sing with the slice of the blade.

You want me to teach you some tricks?

We all agreed we would gather in the late afternoons and train while I was there.

At tea that evening Del suggested my visit was destiny. I said I figured so too.

Back in Galway, alone, sitting in the sun and drinking coffee outside the pub on the corner of two cobbled streets. I watched anxiously as five men strode intentionally in my direction, eyes on me. Shaved heads, black T-shirts, denim jeans, steel-capped boots, their hands shoved into their pockets.

I'm dead, I thought.

Can we buy you another coffee and join you? Asked one of them.

Sure. Ah— Why?

Give us a story about your tattoos.

Sure.

It's alright, he smiled, we're poets.

Menstruation ceased for me then. Menopause. The remainder of that trip was a succession of tarot reading after tarot reading and I returned to Australia with my wallet bulging. Once back in Byron Bay Serenity moved to Melbourne. I now had no children living with me for the first time since I'd been twenty.

CHAPTER 42

The Iaido school was scuppered. It had been big and thriving for years but there were two problems. I was traitorous to myself because I was on my knees. Many kata requirements. When I understood that religion is a crock of shit I had made a promise to myself that I would never bend the knee to anyone or anything. I was justifying my practice because of tradition; because bowing and kneeling were different in Japanese culture. The second problem was the man in charge. He attempted to sabotage the school for the purposes of taking over through his chosen sensei, because we were the biggest dojo in Australia. There was a great deal of money to be made.

Everything came to a head one weekend when grading the students was due. He committed such treachery. He sent us, the senior practitioners, out for a break while he conducted a so-called seminar with the newer Iadoka. Five women and one man. He sexually insulted every woman present and I wasn't told until after the class. He had been staying in my spare room but when his misogynist infamy was exposed by the students later in the day I quit, followed by Karla. The school and its representation in NSW dissolved.

As well as witch I was now a warrior. Like Scáthach in the legends of Cú Chulain. To redress the balance, I completed an advanced first aid course, learning to resuscitate, treat snake bite and prevent an individual from bleeding to death. I then joined the Road Rescue Squad. We trained most weekends in everything from how to suspend a ladder in thin air depending on where one anchored the ropes, knots, ratios and star picket placement, to the point I could ratchet the fire-truck-sized rescue vehicle up a hill on my own. I learned about hydraulic machines, the mathematics of rope and pulley, to work the Jaws of Life to cut a car open, to abseil down a cliff and to securely strap a person into a body basket.

The first emergency call-out I was twenty minutes drive away, during the Blues and Roots Festival. I wore my white squad coveralls, with relevant patches and identification, halfway up at my waist, a pair of kick-arse heavy duty black boots on the seat beside me and a rescue squad sticker on the windshield. I drove my shiny black four wheel drive with my hand on the horn because I didn't yet have a siren.

The roads at the Bluesfest were packed with people and security was at maximum. I arrived at the barricades and the security guys tried to wave me away. I had one hand on the horn and pointed to the sticker with the other. As though the god of emergencies had given the order the staff parted a sea of people and moved all the barricades to let me through.

When I arrived at the crash site there was nowhere to park. Abandoning my truck in the middle of the road, intentionally blocking any oncoming traffic from adding to the emergency rescue. I ran, pulling my coveralls all the way on and hippity-hopping into my boots.

Elbowing my way through a mass of onlookers I ran to a cop who handed me the edge of a blanket, relieved. I would never have experienced this as an outsider. Together we blocked the view of the rescue from the rubber-neckers. A young teenaged boy was being driven home from school when the vehicle had been sideswiped. His legs were trapped between the passenger door and the dashboard. The ambos had strapped him to a board in case of back and neck injuries and were talking to him in soft, buddy voices. My crew cut away the side of the car. When the boy's mother arrived on the scene one of the squad nodded my way. I pulled her gently to the grassy verge where I soothed her with mother-noise until her son was freed.

Maintaining what I now knew to be false masks, outmoded ritual and pomp became a stifling skin I itched to shed. Not all the initiates liked this progression into simplicity and raised many objections and challenges. Some needed consistency even if that consistency is exposed as being someone else's idea of what witchcraft is. I rejected anthropomorphism and deification. I felt this genuine connection. I deepened my questioning of magic and mystery that had begun years ago. I now understood life and the objectified as an animist. I'd even brought back seven spirit coyotes from Ojibwa country, all in bright vivid colors. I'd sense them behind me when reading really bad news to a tarot client. They fall over each other laughing. A great leveler.

What I'd been teaching and these covens full of pomp and theatre were just another trap of perpetuating a modern-day dualistic ideology. One step from monotheism. There was soil to dig deeply into, dead beliefs to compost and feed back into life as nourishment. To allow buried seeds and selves to rewild in a mythscape of deep ecology and ethnicity. New food to add to this stale revolution. So when was this taken out of my hands? Without even the hint of religious idiom remaining in my vocabulary after years of assiduously weeding the brain-tongue synergy. Was the mystery now prepared to take me seriously?

Helen, Cuckoo's partner, was the last person I initiated. On a deep night in autumn, in the studio converted to a cave in the garden of 76 Shirley Street. She'd been in our lives for years but had come to the choice of initiation not long before. We didn't learn until much later that her partner was a cuckoo because his mask was super-glued with the practice of a true parasite. She was a well-educated woman and was seduced by his young, hippy facade and fashionable dreads, the persona of a sexy holy man. In Melbourne, where she'd grown up. She fell in love and travelled with him to a commune in our region and he had slowly, inexorably turned on her, depressing her sense of well-being. He kept her isolated. Owned. But I also didn't know she was an alcoholic and would one day lose her mind to the toxin and develop wet brain. She's dead now. She was forty nine.

People can have the ability to hide their real faces so well that sometimes, utilizing great effort, ages go by before they expose themselves. For the skin to molt and the bones to bare themselves. Inevitably that they do. Billy Joel's The Stranger is appropriate. I've met person after person to whom this happens. A seemingly endless line of confused refugees from the insidiousness of Little Golden Books and promises of forever.

CHAPTER 43

Then came my birthday in 2006. The abortion clinic. The yelling of my two intelligent adult children. Certainty that I was actually dead. I had crossed the Threshold into the next initiation cycle. Down I went, into the heart of that bleak and daunting forest with no track, no gingerbread cottage, no woodsman and no light to guide me. The dark night of the soul.

I no longer listened to music. That new and manufactured, thin, tinny sound. I sometimes attended live gigs, mostly to film for the artists, even though the loudness of amplified music had become even moreso over a decade. I always came away from those nights with my ears ringing and painful, not able to hear properly for days. The deep velvet of silence had become my lover. When I write, music is noise. Voices are noise. Butcherbird song, ocean roar, thunder rumble, the rustle of batwings at dusk, the bark of the skink behind the painting and the sheesheesh of cicadas in summer soothed. Jungle had died in my arms two years before, a tragedy from which I will never recover. The bones in his neck calcified around his spinal cord. The vet came to the house, gave him the green dream. He wept as I wept, carrying my dead love to the back of the garden, placing him gently in the hole I'd already dug. Covering him with earth and singing to his spirit before howling to the night. I planted papayas over him and the following year when they fruited, we plucked them when ripe and ate the sweet flesh that was also him and strewed his seeds through the mountains behind the bay so he would live everywhere. Pyewacket died the following year because she was such an ancient woman. Arrow was hit by a speeding car whilst taking himself for a walk one morning, a brutal and tragic way to die. All were buried in the garden of that potent piece of mythworld at the very edge of town.

In 1997 a tarot student had arrived at the house with a two year old black female cat in a cocky cage.
What's this about?
I fly out tomorrow. Moving to Zurich.
And?

I thought you might take my cat because you're a witch.

I gave her a dirty look.

Whatever. I'll take her to the vet to get put down. I'm out of options.

Leave her then. Go on. Fuck off.

We named her Mars and she was the only four-legged left alive in 2006.

In February and sweat-drippingly hot, the air as thick as soup, I cleaned out the last of the old cupboard at the very back of the studio. Dead paint cans, antique packets of rat poison, murderously sharp paint brushes and unused floor tiles, all hidden behind a cloth curtain and ignored. For the past twelve years. Now there was nothing left undone, no detritus from before I moved in.

A few days later that lifelong copper talisman spun again. I was given three months to find somewhere else to live. The development application had been passed. Was this the dream I'd had of cleaning that house and becoming lost at the railway station? Maybe. And the twelve year cycle of Pluto in the sign of Sagittarius that began when we first moved into 76 Shirley Street in 1995 had just ended. All things are connected.

I'd often fantasized that if that house had been mine to renovate every window would be replaced by French doors and verandas would be her skirts all around, exotic walled and secret gardens with ponds and fountains everywhere.

But she was not mine. Had never been. In the weeks before closing the door for the last time family and clan came together to dig up what plants we could for redistribution. We took hundreds of cuttings of Bran and Flidias and planted them up in the hinterland at the back of town. Except one of Flidias that I planted in a terracotta pot and kept with me wherever I moved. She held the magic and the memory of that earth-home and all the magic that happened there.

Next would be chainsaws and bulldozers.

And their roots will remain deep beneath the razed and flattened ground.

CHAPTER 44

Jarrod and Juniper moved to Wilson's Creek with me. Where Tattoo Dany had lived. The man who had once been her partner had renovated the old house and then done the same with the cattle bales, the latter transformed into a Balinese villa in which he now lived. The old Queenslander, empty.

This house was almost the same as Shirley Street. Weatherboard, same layout, but with the French doors I'd imagined and verandas all around, like skirts. Just as in the dream the house faced out over a valley between two towering escarpments. But not destined to be home. By now I was deep into the liminal space and this was the place that broke me. Where my spirit was flayed raw of any final artifice. And I was clueless.

I was taught to pursue non-attachment. To allow myself to love utterly, to rage against injustice with no god to deny my true feelings. To ultimately, let things go. To live the magic in the world as a flowing, transient thing. I thought I had that down easy and that I'd worked through all my glitches decades ago. I did—cope—for a while.

But I was lost. My soul-rend was slow to expose itself like something I cannot describe. I slid daily, by increments, into despair. No one noticed and I told no one. I didn't know what was wrong with me. I was anxious, depressed, still reading tarot but otherwise not functioning. Yes, I was. No, I wasn't.

That year just ground on and on and I was finally able to write Tarot Theory and Practice, a thing I thought I'd never do because the art of learning this technique properly is an oral one. Hands on and malleable.

The Muse also wanted me to write the screenplay of the Eureka Uprising and to call the story Bakery Hill.

That's not going to happen, I thought, almost laughing at how ridiculous the concept was.

Write it, Ly.

What? A couple of blokes in shirts and hats standing up to the queen's man at a goldfield? Hardly.

Oh my, I thought, I sounded just like the rat voice.
Give me the story, please?
No.
Silence.
Fine then, I will.

I took a long time to research. But that's not what the Muse was actually teaching me. I was learning to be a more proficient hunter. It wasn't until my hidden documents were released that I learned that my grandmother's grandmother was from, at some times in her life, the same village as the Lalor clan. At least one of her known haunts. I have a book written about her called From Ireland to Oz.

In 2007 clients came thick and fast from all across Australia and from all around the world and I kept secret despair after despair, that what was happening to me was affecting countless others. Something inexplicable. I was hearing the same story everywhere to the point I wrote To Whom It May Concern on my webpage (see Appendix 2). I received emails from around the world from people who also suffered. I experienced similar sensations of loss and despair but was unaware that aspects of that were from an encroaching deafness. The thickening fog of birdlessness.

When I thought I was going mad I wasn't. I suffered mercury poisoning. One wrong fish (and I ate a lot of fish). That didn't make the sickness any easier to deal with and I accepted the doctor's suggestion of antidepressants until the neurotoxin leached out of me. Three months later I was able to wean myself off them.

Friday night Chloe phoned. Daughter of Fairlie, the owner of that first gym and later a friend who trained with me in a tarot collective. She had inoperable lung and brain cancer. Would I call and talk to her mum? She gave me Fairlie's mobile number and I phoned her right away. She was in the Nerang Hospital and asked me to visit. She'd always been a hard living, hard loving woman and when we spoke she'd just come inside from smoking a joint. She was sitting up in bed with a glass of red wine.

You're the only person I can talk to about death without a drama, she said.

We talked for an hour about what might or might not happen when her body decomposed. Though she still felt fine and the doctors thought she had many months to live, would I read her tarot? I said I'll come Wednesday.

Chloe phoned the Sunday before. Her mother had gone into a coma, was in intensive care and the doctors didn't think she would last the night.

We have a date for later this week, I said.

But she's dying. Now.

Your mum wants a reading.

She's in a coma.

That doesn't matter, she'll wait. Go and tell her to keep our date.

On Wednesday I asked Jarrod to come with me as I had an unnerving feeling I would be too affected by the visit to drive home. The hallway outside her door was crowded with people waiting for me and they pushed in after me. I had no idea what would happen. When I took her hand she spoke through me. She had things to say to many in the room and conversation for some. I relayed the messages to whomever, with one exception.

What the fuck do you want? To a man seated by the door. Go home. Get the fuck out. Tell him.

No.

Tell him he's not welcome here.

I didn't. I ignored her until she changed the subject, all the while seemingly unconscious, flat on her back, an oxygen mask over her face and a life support monitor blipping beside her head.

Get the boys to sit me up for a minute.

She wants you to sit her up, I said to two young men closest to her. When they lifted her into a flaccid sitting position her eyes opened exposing startling azure blue irises. For three seconds she stared through me before falling back onto the pillows, comatose again, freaking the entire room out.

Hey Faith, she said to her sister at the foot of the bed, go home and get some sleep, you look deader than me.

Faith had not slept for several days, driving for three hours and holding vigil by the bedside. Faith smiled and shook her head so Fairlie turned her thoughts to me.

Read my cards, please Ly?

I pulled my tarot pack from the pouch and placed them under her hands.

Well, you're useless, I said, knowing she could not shuffle.

She chuckled. Johnno can. He's the only one qualified.

Who's Johnno? I asked.

A man lifted his hand.

She said you're the only one qualified to shuffle.

The room erupted into laughter.

What?

I've been dealing blackjack in a Nevada casino. Just flew in.

So I handed him my worn old pack and he shuffled them.

Lay out the top three cards please Johnno.

Nine of swords, death, four of swords.

Yeah, well, that's all pretty obvious. Yes, you're sick, yes you're going to die. And in four seconds (I waited) No? Okay, four minutes, four hours, four days or four weeks because I don't think you've got months or years. You okay with that?

I packed my cards away and went to kiss her goodbye, but I took her hand one more time and she said furiously; desperately. Look at all the pretty horses! So I told the room.

She says to look at all the pretty horses.

Frowns. People asking each other, shrugging their shoulders and shaking their heads.

Again please, Ly?

She wants me to repeat that last comment: Look at all the pretty horses.

Makes no sense, said Faith.

Fairlie's mind was like the silent gavel of a southern white baptist judge when a Black woman is found not guilty of anything.

Well, I don't know.

I kissed her on the cheek, saying, Catch you on the flip side.

I was shaken and so Jarrod and I drove home in silence. The following morning, I woke with a shattering pain in my left lung that turned into something very nasty before the week was out.

I've got lung cancer, I thought.

I was so spooked I stopped smoking the same day. I had an X-ray, but the results came back negative. I'd been a smoker for forty years, so I figure Fairlie did me a favor. Gave me more years to live than I'd perhaps earlier been destined.

Months later Faith phoned to tell me they were scattering Fairlie's ashes at sea and would I come? I told her how invasive the previous experience had been. She began to apologize but I said don't be silly.

She did die like you said, four hours later. When I read the doctor's report she'd also been diagnosed exactly four months before. That you could do that was liberating.

I didn't intend to. I'll be very careful not to do that again.

But Ly, the killer?

What?

Booking the crematorium for the funeral the coming week the receptionist asked that everyone take extra care.

Why?

The horses' birthday was that day. A parade passes by at the same time as the mourners will be due to arrive.

Look at all the pretty horses. Fairlie had known.

I won't come, but that man sitting by the door, who was he?

Oh, him.

I gather they didn't get along.

Did she say something about him?

No, I just knew, I lied.

He was awfully critical of her way of life and that she claimed to be a witch; said she was a bad mother.

I figured. Thanks, Faith.

Fairlie had set that up, I was certain. She knew she could do that.

I had tried to convince myself I had not been attached to 76 Shirley Street. Even after I'd driven by several weeks later to see squatters had hung an Australian flag beach towel over the front window. I assured myself I was fine. The trees still pennanted from the back garden, their topmost branches higher than the roof.

Then gone. Sold. I heard my house had been cut in two, loaded onto a massive truck and taken to another town to be re-stumped and bolted back together.

The next time I passed everything else, trees, caravan, house next door, old service station, all razed to the ground. Gone over and over with bulldozers. Nothing left. Rammed earth surrounded by ten foot high cyclone fencing.

I sat in my car for ages looking at that blight, feeling the confusion of a field blasted by warfare. I should have left well enough alone but no. Compelled, I drove from Byron Bay back into the hills and loaded the shovel, a pitchfork, the mattock, wire cutters and hessian sacks into the boot of my car. Fully intent on digging up the bones of my friends—dogs and the cat—and taking them deep into the forest where they would not be covered in asphalt. There was nothing now there to inform coming generations that there had ever been love on that land. So I cut the wire and dragged my tools through and when I was certain I was in the right place I struck the clay with the mattock. The ground had been compacted to the consistency of concrete.

I worked. Hour after hour. A grubby, forlorn and tragic sight to the constant passing traffic. Dusk set in and the mozzies came out and I had no repellent. I decided. I knew the alternative. I went into trance. Time separated and unraveled and I was able to be in the place that is not a place, where the spirits of things swirl and pattern in almost an indescribable symphony, and I called them. Jungle and Arrow, Pyewacket. Only the dogs came as though they had been down the lane somewhere. Barreled around me, their spirits leaping onto the back seat. I drove back up the hill, opened the door and they raced off in search of something to kill.

I went to the local café the following Saturday to meet a colleague and drink coffee and read the weekend stars. She and her partner Kon had already found a table and as I made my way there a man, a stranger, joined them but watched me.

You've got two spirit dogs with you, he said.
You can see them?
A big one and a little one.
The rat-voice was defeated.

I planted an organic garden with the help of Andy Pandy. He was staying with us for a while, hiding out from someone or something. He hated gardening.

Watching them grow from seemingly nothing is the closest you'll ever have to giving birth, I suggested.

He helped me plant, despite opposition, and was filled with wonder when the seeds sprouted and grew. I moved Flidias into a larger pot because her clone had struck roots. I dared not plant her out or I'd have nothing of the earth that had been my only real home.

I painted the entire house distressed white then pretended everything was fine. Convinced myself I was whole. A delusion. A goodly chunk of my soul was somewhere else. Fled. No longer trusting me to be honest with myself.

Soul healing is prodigious within indigenous cultures. Shamans of Siberia and the Midewiwin of Ojibwa know that in a crisis, or at other necessary times, aspects of self can break away and need to be found and coaxed back. This often happens when a person is ill. They will not heal until a retrieval is done. I didn't know where to start and there was no one I knew who could do this for me. I had only myself to rely on. I set to hunting, month after month, finally achieving hints. A sensory trail of clues. I smelled kelp when I was nowhere near the sea. Tar and linseed oil and maritime fuel. I smelled wood smoke from a fire that was nowhere in my world and I sensed mist, fog and beaches I had never been to.

I continued to pursue and hunt when the guy who owned the Wilsons Creek property went surfing in Bali. He returned to his own defeat. I wandered to the bales the afternoon he got back, and he asked if he could come down to my house for a cup of tea. Of course, I said. Of course I knew what was coming.

What am I supposed to do? He almost begged. Whipper-snip for the rest of my life?

I felt for him. I had my own tragedy, but he didn't have to hear because he didn't want to. I shut myself down.

The Cuckoo finally went crazy. This happens when one's real identity is hidden for too long. It warps like Dorian Gray's picture. He was an adult cuckoo pretending to be a chick. We were just the current reed warblers feeding him as though one of our own. But he could not help himself and he inexorably exposed an extreme narcissism. He'd turned forty two, was still smoking weed and required followers and adoration.

That time of life, astrologically, is known as the Uranus opposition. Common term: midlife crisis. The often unconscious knowledge that a person is only a minute from their own grave. Men seem to suffer more than women. I've never understood why unless, as Robert Bly, author of Iron John points out, this is inescapable suffering. In an interview Bly explains that up until the Industrial Revolution boys worked alongside fathers, uncles or other members of a male community. Men would talk. Sons learned the ways of men. The Industrial Revolution changed all that and fathers left their homes. Went away to work. Now, commonly, children only get the man at the end of his day. His moods. His afterwards. And that's nothing. Maybe ten minutes, maybe not even that. Not a woman's role to raise a son, truth be told.

So when the non-initiated male gets to forty two years old and he's still not the man he was never going to be? He usually fractures. If he does not understand himself in mythworld he remains in the shallow world of commerce, advertising, insurance, technology, war, bitterness at not achieving his dreams and blaming everyone else. Conspiracy theorists. Still doing drugs. More booze than ever. Losing compassion and gaining vitriol and venom. What then? Get a red sports car? Leave the partner of twenty years for a younger woman? Hurt? He realizes that his ambition to be an axe-wielding rock star is not going to happen.

If he's wise or meets a wizard within the dense woods of his lostness he will be shown his place within mythworld. Then he will possibly survive, even thrive. Otherwise he will probably sicken. Many men kill themselves during their forties.

Why am I always broke? Cuckoo would demand, lighting another cigarette from the money he got from the government, ordering another latte.

People are easily corrupted and brainwashed in a culture of confused identity. Politics does that. Religion. The need to fit in. The need to be a celebrity. To lead. To control. This clashes with what witch is because being witch is hard work, anarchist, heretical, feral and feminist. Inevitably outside mainstream culture. Many pretend. Dress up. The reason mainstream culture think that occultists are nuts. But then most mainstream people are brainwashed into belittling or burning anything that either frightens them or seems a tad too alien.

I do love you John and George but bringing the hindu religion to the west was a silly idea. This was supposed to replace the crustiness of the white christian monopolization of morality, reality and so-called spirituality. What followed was the introduction to a new generation of previously unknown cults and even more monsters of corruption. New Age corporate empires spruiking liver cleanses, aura rebooting and colonic irrigation (supposedly spiritual shit).

The Cuckoo had been after whatever pack gave him an identity.

Helen finally worked up the courage to leave. She moved into the Wilsons Creek house with us.

This was the year of the big wet when the rain never stopped. Sheets of grey, straight down veils, all the way beyond the end of that valley, swelling rivers to monsters, the trickles over the escarpments to white and thunderous waterfalls. We were crazy. We ran through the house, along the verandas, back through the house, over and over so that at least we would not go moldy from sitting all day.

Time came to leave. Jarrod and Juniper were pregnant. A son, due to be born next February. They wanted a place of their own.

In Mullumbimby, the nearest town, several miles from Byron Bay but still within the shire, I was drawn intuitively along a street I'd never walked before. A way I'd never explored. To Heritage Park. To a massive ficus rooted deeply beside the creek. Bigness and strength that took my breath away. Grandmothers and grandfathers of Flidias and Bran. I nestled between the walls of the above-ground roots of one of them just to get a sense of family. I was enfolded with love. I slept the afternoon away. They whispered to me that the next house was near, very near. Within days a client heard I was looking for a place and would I pay to live in her house while she was abroad? She was going to Canada indefinitely. Chasing some man. The house was five doors away from the park.

Of course, I said when I'd wandered through with Helen. She asked an outrageous amount of rent, but no other choice presented itself. This house also wore verandas all around. I was getting a hint of the Maze I was in. The false turns that only seemed true. Serenity, her friend Zhourelle (Mechonan of Rocky Horror's sister), Helen and I moved in. With Mars and Flidias. Zhourelle's family mostly lived around the corner and her brother Kym hung out watching television or dancing and drinking tea. He had been diagnosed with schizophrenia years before and was always embarrassed by the effects of heavy medication.

The winter solstice, celebrated in that house, that year, brought together everyone from sax players and other musicians to schoolteachers, artists, acupuncturists, witches, actors, scholars and all the children. Piles of food. The neighbors were invited. Live music on the back porch, Kym playing with the children on one of his better days.

Josh and his companions ordered the newly-famous Red One digital movie camera from overseas, as an investment and to film their work. Gone were the days of the cut and splice of the silver reel around when I was a girl. This was 2008. Josh suggested I write a short film. The trio would produce, shoot and edit, and all I had to do was cast and direct.

The story came rapidly because at some time during the previous year Virginia had said she was invisible, and I hadn't understood.

What do you mean?

People look at me and see an old woman.

You're joking?

She wasn't.

Byron Bay and the surrounding towns are filled with people suffering mental illness, much induced through early drug use. Most of that being marijuana before the age of puberty. Modern culture laughing at the concept of criminality because didn't everybody smoke weed? Over the decades since the sixties, however, mass production and economic pressure had all but bred out the CBD (one of the cannabinoids, an anti-psychotic, the body active compound) leaving mainly THC, the mind active component. Many people who used the medicine earlier developed schizophrenia or other personality disorders as young as twenty. Many parents and siblings in the Northern Rivers actively encouraged this practice amongst the very young, even producing documentaries and staging annual festivals honoring the plant. I have no doubt of its medicine, but what else can also happen. Microdosing was still a long way off my radar.

Who wants to see the man in the street leaning over and drooling and talking to someone only he sees? No one else knew to whom an indigenous kurdaicha hand gestured. No one wants to see old people because they are no longer important and pretty in the way of current consumerism and consensus. And still, after fighting for rights for over forty years, who wants to notice the bruises on a woman's face? We lived in paradise. There was no such thing as domestic violence, child abuse, rape, drink-spiking or gang bangs by Gold Coast weekend invaders. Hidden in the shadows. Was there? People weren't warned. There was no public discussion. When a well-loved local woman had her throat cut the news was hidden under the Byron Shire rug in case of an adversely affected tourism.

Why were all these people consigned to a life sentence of schizophrenia and the straight jacket of pharmaceutical oblivion when I see things and people that others don't and get paid adequately to do so and am not considered mad?

I remember James Valance getting the first of the major arcanum of tarot tattooed into his skin in 1985. After studying with me. I suggested he stop with one. James's problem was that he always had to consume the most magic mushrooms or drink more booze than his friends. A big man, this was his pattern. Several tattoos later he told me he was hearing voices predicting world events. The mysterious part is that they did happen. On the nightly news. Within days. More and more information kept being whispered to him with each subsequent inking. He lost control of his identity. He eventually had to be dragged from his home by several police after destroying the joint while ranting at the top of his lungs in response to countless unseen voices.

There is something so mystical about schizophrenia. Until it becomes terrible. Something occult. The shamanic alternative to medication has been explored in Odette Nightsky's book Bridge Between Two Worlds.

In 2008 I wrote The Redemption of Joe Frame. The story of a young man who could see people others could not and thought he was from off-world. Mother and the doctors considered him delusional. Diagnosed him as suffering from schizophrenia when eleven years old. Not sick though. Different: a savant living in the world in a state of joy at the wonders of the universe. A story of the things he knew.

We agreed the shoot would go ahead in August because that's when the Red would arrive. I asked Virginia to play the mysterious woman from Joe's other world, a twist to co-star her in a film about being invisible.

The production crew met at the Film Artists' Co-op to pitch the story and see if anyone had suggestions for casting. After I'd spoken we were approached by Ghofar Burke.

That part's mine, he said of Joe.

Trained in drama at the Victorian College of the Arts, his father had been diagnosed with schizophrenia at the age of eleven. We cast Zhourelle and Mechonan as Joe's invisible friends, Kym and Virginia as two members of Joe's very large off-world family that roosted at night around one of the giant strangler figs. We rehearsed for weeks. Josh informed us that there'd been a delay in delivery. The camera wouldn't arrive until September. This made me nervous. We kept preparing and rehearsing.

Then Josh said there was another delay and we'd have to shoot in October.

No, I said.

Why?

If we don't shoot earlier the movie won't be made. I know.

Josh had been around me long enough to trust my intuition so he and his team discussed alternatives. They agreed to use another camera.

We filmed in August. The Red One never arrived. The global financial crash happened instead.

I had only ever directed live theatre before, so I was unaware that down the other end of the lane or across the other side of the park the sound man was saying plane, truck, lawn-mower, chainsaw and sundry other interferences.

We can fix everything in post, Josh responding each time. He was wrong.

They tried everything until finally, with a deadline set for our first film festival, the footage was sent to a sound technician who assured us any audio problem could be fixed. The film returned a day before mailing was due. With reverb on everything.

Dead, I said to Josh.

I know, he replied, defeated.

And that was, we thought, the end of that.

Within days Mechonan and Zhourelle's brother Nakana jumped off the three hundred foot high cliff that is Minyon Falls. He'd also been ill with schizophrenia for a long time, prescribed heavy medication and was in and out of mental facilities. But this system, like most, was broken. He'd been released into his mother's care two weeks before his death.

Dressed only in a pink singlet and underpants he'd approached a woman packing away the remnants of a picnic into the back of the car.

Do I look really fucked up to you? he'd asked.

No darling, you look fine, she'd lied. She and her husband watched on in helplessness as Nakana strode to the edge of the falls, raised both his arms and dove. The act and gestures identical to the final shot of Joe. Nakana was twenty four years old.

I was visiting Victoria Sullivan a year later. We'd met a few years previously. Vic is in the film industry and we'd been introduced by a mutual friend at a cafe downtown. The mutual friend had mentioned The Quickening and that the rights to write the screenplay had been sold. Vic had gone off to Sydney to work but hadn't been able to get the name of my book out of her head. She bought both that and The Shining Isle and when she returned to Byron Bay she phoned me and asked if I wanted to write it as a movie, with her, even just for fun. We did so and she taught me how to think and write in the medium of film. To see my stories on screen.

She had set up a phone conversation between me and her friend, an award-winning sound man.

C'mon Ly, he said, you're a storyteller. Short film often uses voice-overs.

We were back movie-making. The film won a jury prize and was shown in Australia, Canada and Tahiti.

I taught myself to edit. The first footage I took in training was at a Wild Zinnias gig at the Railway Hotel in March that year. I shot the performance on one hand-held mini cam, Victoria shot on another, a third woman on her own, more professional camera. At the close of the gig Vic gave me the mini DV from her camera. Next day I powered up my laptop, opened the editing suite and stared at the screen as though facing an alien. The instructions beside me on the desk morphed from simple English to hieroglyphics. I phoned Jarrod and asked what was wrong with me. He calmly and patronizingly assisted me to read him the instructions. Nothing.

    Mum, it's simple.

    You told me that already.

    Then what?

    Nothing's working.

    Can you read?

    Of course I can read.

    Okay, I've got the program open here. Let's do this step by step. First thing you have to do click capture.

    Where's that? I've got two cameras here and one DV tape. Mine's a fixed hard drive and the other is Josh's old camera that I've put the first mini DV into.

    Are the cables plugged in?

    What?

    This went on for two days. Zero. Void. I engaged in other work for two weeks, and when next I opened the editing suite I had, without intention, invoked Einstein. Completing the task as though second nature. Years on I read Norman Doidge's book, The Brain that Changes Itself. Neurons need time to link along different pathways finally made sense of what I had previously thought an affliction.

CHAPTER 45

The case manager allotted to me at the post adoption agency emailed. She had found my mother and did I want to meet her. She suggested I write her a letter. Did I want to meet her? Burst the bubble of my illusions? Discover that I wasn't the secret, illegitimate daughter of the king of the gypsies or a changeling sent to live in the mortal world by my real mother, the equivalent of Titania? For fuck's sake, I did. I wrote that letter.

This womb-woman then contacted my case worker suggesting a meeting. Her name was Shirley. We spoke on the phone. I had a sister and several brothers. Surreal. What if this, what if that. Unknown variables like goldfish in a pond. I then had a phone call from someone introducing herself as a sister.

Our mother is very ill, she said. She has emphysema from smoking and is on oxygen. She might not live much longer.

"Our mother"? What defines this when you have never met the person who birthed you? Wikipedia is full of definitions, none of which answer the question of concept.

She and Shirley had houses in the snow country, and would I come? I had a discussion with my puppies. I decided, for all our sakes, to meet her. I flew to Canberra and hired a car. I drove to the remote address.

Both the woman and her daughter met me as I pulled up at the gate. They hugged me. I was uncomfortable. This was all a mistake. I looked nothing remotely like them. Again, I was a stranger. Stay overnight. Anything could happen. What if the caseworker people were wrong?

The front door entered straight into the kitchen and three plates of food sat on the sideboard of the bland and tastelessly decorated kitchen. Each held a lamb chop, a mound of mashed potato and a small pile of flaccid beans. Surely not, I hoped.

Once I'd settled in, the three of us sat in a lounge room, Shirley—my mother—in her lazyboy, in the corner near the door, as though to see her enemies approaching; her escape planned in secrecy. I wanted answers, of course, about who I was. So I could tell my children. So we had a history.

Shirley's daughter was younger than me by two years but the lines on her face were etched so deeply she had the appearance of having been scored by knives. Her story was one of life-long tragedy. Sexual abuse by her own father from early childhood, followed by that of the woman's second husband some years later. He'd paid her, of course. Oxycontin, heroin.

For the first and last time my bastardy and rejection evoked a deep, shuddering sigh, waking the slumbering Bone Woman from her cave of not belonging, having her gather her string bags and climb to the surface world to hunt the carcasses of long-dead wolves. Time to clothe them in new skin and fur. Time to live again.

She could have given birth to a watermelon for all she cared, my flesh-and-blood sister said when I'd asked Shirley, now mute, her eyes expressing something terrified, how she'd felt about my birth.

Who was my father?

He was a Frenchy.

What was his name?

Ed de Villa. But he never knew about you.

Oh, I'd smiled. And what of my brothers? When will I meet them?

I'd be so ashamed to have them think I'd been a slut. I could never tell them. You understand.

No, I said. I don't.

I switched off. I went to the bedroom and packed. At dawn I drove away.

CHAPTER 46

Since as early as 1987 tarot's predictions of world events usually began occurring three years in advance. In 2008 it/she/he/they started talking about an unprecedented year to come. What I heard, every time 2011 came up, was that it would be a calendar year of unprecedented world events. In every second person's cards was the prediction of environmental devastation. Volcanic eruptions. Earthquakes. Wild weather and the worldwide disruption to air traffic. Revolution that would not end in my lifetime. Nuclear disaster.

The new year's eve of 2009 my six year old grandson and I hung out together while his parents went out for the first time in ages. He was sleeping over. We watched Solar Max, a documentary about the sun and we learned that spent magnetic particles were transferred by a conveyor-belt-type current much like the Gulf Stream on earth, from the surface of the sun to the center where they were revitalized and returned to the convection zone and, eventually, the corona.

Was that interesting for you? I asked when the movie ended.

Oh, yes!

Will we research the internet in the morning?

Yes.

I knew all the hype about the Mayan Calendar ending in December 2012 along with the world and I was also aware of tarot's prediction, so I typed solar max 2012 into the search engine. The first thing popping up was a NASA storm warning, 2011. Supposedly massive solar storms were on their way. Notably, 2011 was unprecedented in our known history. Volcanoes blew their tops in Iceland and Chile filling skies with ash clouds and downing air traffic around the world. Earthquakes took out large chunks of New Zealand and resulted in the tsunami and the Fukushima nuclear reactotor meltdown that still continues to threaten earth. The deadliest tornado in U.S. history devastated parts of America along with record-breaking snowstorms. Norway, ordinarily a peaceful country, experienced its first mass execution: with a crazy man killing seventy seven children.

The Jasmine Revolution erupted in Saudi Arabia demanding social change. While what began in Cairo that year was the first of a non-stop wave of upheaval and devastation still occurring as I write. Turkey and Brazil. Bahrain, Sudan and Libya. Iraq and Syria. The exodus of war-ravaged refugees flooding Europe by the millions. The Roman catholic church has been brought to its knees with overwhelming numbers of sexual abuse and torture cases that continue to be dragged from beneath that monstrous rock, not yet including mine.

A pope resigned for the first time in six hundred years, revealing their infallibility doctrine as a farce. The Occupy Wall Street Movement, the 99%, sparked a groundswell of global protest in nine hundred and fifty one cities over eighty two countries.

Before that, on January twenty-first, 2009 Barack Obama, a black man, was inaugurated as president of America. Significant? Americans had hung black men for loving 'white' women, battered to death for disobeying a 'white' man's order, stoned for attempting to go to school, tarred with the brush of hoodlum and sentenced to prison for crimes that would hardly rate a mention amongst pale-skinned people. Killed by cops. Dragged behind moving cars. Slavery receiving no apology.

The same travesty of bigotry is in Australia. Black and white photographs of people in chains, not supposed to be here, needed to be taken from their families if they had even a touch of the usurpers blood. Put to work as servants and laborers. Denied their language and their culture. Forced into christianity.

Yes we can, said Obama.

Elected into government, in a country in tatters, inherited from the years of George W Bush's stark imbecility. Over six thousand mostly young service men and women slaughtered in battle. The official figures. The injured, disfigured, mutilated or mentally destroyed never tallied. Millions of Iraqis and Afghanis were killed, maimed, or took refuge in other countries, their lives devastated. Dirty bombs and the lies of weapons of mass destruction, the rumor of Al-Qaeda now Daesh ISIL, an ever-present propaganda for military action. A whole new marketplace of fear.

More will come. Pluto went into the sign of Capricorn in 2007, Capricorn being the sign of institutions, traditions and time while Pluto, utterly pissed off at no longer being a planet and known, astrologically, as the Universal Solvent seems determined to bring down the edifices that began with the Greek Empire and have, tragically, seen that country reduced to financial ruin in a domino effect with seemingly no end.

What has this to do with witchcraft? Everything. What happens in the shallow world affects the mysteries in the deep. Causes confusion. The shallow world draws magic and awe into a trap of pointlessness. The tune is loud and brash and thoughtless. Casually but intentionally cruel. The upholder of loneliness and shatterer of beauty. The shallow world smothers poetry with the ash and the rubble of broken places. Drowns song with the cheeriness of advertising and ersatz talent shows.

Was that all for that day of Obama's inauguration? No. Victoria was with me for dinner when Jarrod phoned. Juniper was in labor and they had rushed to the hospital, the baby not due to be born for another month.

I asked a nurse to let the couple know I was there if they needed anything, just as Jarrod popped his head around the door. He gestured me in.

Juniper, in a little bra top with a sarong around her hips, and as large as could be, was on her feet, leaning her upper body on the bed, rocking and moaning through a contraction. Jarrod's fingers were turning in small circles on her lower back.

What are you doing? I asked.

Massage.

That's not massage.

His face spoke volumes.

Here, I said compassionately, handing him a hand towel. Go wet that with hot water.

I grabbed the oil from the bedside table, poured a hefty amount into my hands and went to work on her back and bum.

Will you stay? she asked, turning, turtle-like.

I nodded.

The midwife provided by the hospital was sitting on a window bench with the occasional threatening glance from my son hinting that she had somehow disgraced herself. I was later told that she repeated, You're doing fine Juniper, doing fine, over and over until Juniper had banished her to her corner.

How regular? I asked of the contractions.

Not very, said Jarrod. Sometimes seventeen minutes, sometimes three.

Sometimes three?

Yep.

Oh. Okay.

I looked at the wall clock after her next contraction and after three minutes I said, you're coming up for another.

Oh, said Juniper, okay. And she did. Women are amazing. Historically having been suppressed, corseted, had our feet bound, had acid thrown in our faces, burnt, raped without surcease. Our daughters have had their genitals scraped with stone, had them sewn shut, been veiled for I don't know how many thousands of years, been forced to wear chastity belts causing sepsis and death. Sold into slavery or marriage. Fathers walking their daughter's down an aisle to give them to some man. Like possessions. Brides actually smile and think this is a loving act. Women are expected to cook, clean, keep offspring alive, serve the husband, do the shopping, get old, look after the grandchildren, be gracious enough to be happy when relegated to a nursing home. The end. Slave. The word hysteria was named for us. The weaker sex. Slaughtered, some estimate by the millions, for witchcraft that never was. Even today in some countries on the African continent, New Guinea and Haiti. Women are still hounded and persecuted for wanting to have our babies born at home. For all the activism, the women's movements have progressed little.

After three hours Juniper delivered a tiny boy. Jarrod cut his umbilical cord and finally the midwife had something to do. After sufficient cuddling and bonding with his parents I left them to their bliss.

I wept all the way home, my arms and hands covered with the sweet smell of vernix. I woke Helen, proffering both my arms, and said, Smell me! She did. She also cried. A month later Adam and his partner were pregnant, and they asked if I'd film the birth.

Tattoo Zak died of cancer.

We organized to thank the countless people who had helped with The Redemption of Joe Frame with a showing on the big screen at the Byron Bay community center but a nine minute film did not make an entertaining evening. So I wrote a series of questions challenging the health system, victims, survivors, the addicted, youth in crisis, those who had experienced loved one's suicides or overdoses, the community; to discuss all the harm occurring the beneath the tourist light. I broke my own rules of anonymity with clients, inviting death workers, a social anthropologist, psychiatrists, shamanic-style soul retrievalists, depression sufferers, schizophrenics, indigenous wisdom holders, doctors, sociologists, welfare workers, a psychiatric nurse, the heads of two regional rehabs and Mechonan. Watch the film and then decide if they would also participate in an interactive forum with anyone who came. That it would be filmed. They all said yes.

I asked Alexandra Kennett, tattooed and pierced and beautiful, who had roosted around the tree that Joe called home, to be the host for the evening. To be the one to ask the questions. She agreed. I spoke about this event on local radio, and the event manager in the community center was panicked because her phone was ringing off the hook with worried locals. She had, on the night, closed the doors to anyone who came late, turning way too many people away. That was in November that year. I called the documentary Nobody and four camera people and two boom mike operators joined me. That night Kym sat behind a psychologist, jittering and pale, the result of new and confusing medication.

Within a month he too took his own life.

The audio man promised to get the best sound to me by January the coming year. He lied.

The Mullumbimby house then closed its doors. Serenity moved to Melbourne with Zhourelle. The Historian, Helen and I took a six month lease on a shoddy house directly opposite Virginia in an outlying beach suburb. We only lasted three months because of the appalling conditions that only home builders with drug money could manage to cobble together illegally. Before we abandoned that house

Mars, the last of my four-legged family, died crazy, fighting herself as though she was in mortal combat with another animal. She had been stuck inside because the area was renowned for men who killed cats. She'd been seen eating her crystallized kitty litter.

Helen also moved to Melbourne, the Historian to Queensland and I took up residence in a building that had once been a shop. In Brunswick Heads. With Flidias, now four foot tall but sparsely leaved no matter what I did. I developed a love affair with cuisine that I shared in common with Kezza upstairs. The soundtrack to Nobody arrived much later than had been promised. In two pieces. No matter what I tried there was definitely nine minutes missing. I phoned the sound man and asked what had happened.

Naughty me, he mumbled. I have to remember to bring my good equipment when I work with you.

Huh? But the booms went through the desk.

Um, I was late. I plugged them into my computer and it crashed for nine minutes. Really sorry, Ly.

Virginia and I regularly sat by the seashore eating fish and chips and talking of the past and speculating on the future. And I feared. I didn't ask if the place I was living in was asbestos. I breathed shallowly, still unknowingly lost within the liminal space.

The call came through that Adam's partner was in labor. I filmed the process, and hung out with my grandson. We were in the birthing unit at the local hospital, as close to a home experience as one can get. A massive contraction. Adam's partner moaning and holding onto him. My grandson disturbed.

Hey?

Yes?

You know that women can be fighter pilots like men?

Yes.

And we can be police officers and drive huge trucks and be architects and scuba divers same as men.

Yes.

Well only women can do this.

He looked at me with those eyes.

So we okay?

The contraction passed and Lydia chuckled at Adam, who smiled the way he does because he loves that much.

Okay, said my grandson. I'll just go back to my computer game then.

His sibling was born in the birthing pool.

Later I edited the footage down and laid Seal's Kiss from a Rose under the visuals. My son cried.

CHAPTER 47

Numerologically 2009 was a seven personal year, one of teaching and learning, introspection, analysis and self-analysis. In actuality it was a blur of loneliness, pretense, self-certainty, self-doubt and feeling nothing like myself. I had no idea who I was or where I was supposed to be. I reflected on the weirdness of my life and how unlike I was to that demanded by mother-culture. I dabbled in self-pity for a few days. Oh, I was learning alright.

I wrote a poem, I Never Should Have Moved to a Holiday Town, for the revised edition of The Feast of Flesh and Spirit. And that's when the spell broke that had me bound and powerless within the by now decadent, greed-driven, festive shire.

One afternoon, somewhat nostalgically, I played the Filippa Giordano CD. The following morning every one of Flidias' branches insinuated towards the CD player. I was devastated. What was I doing? I dragged the pot through the shop, across the expanse behind the building, and into the back garden where she was sure to get real rain and real air. Within days her leaves curled and browned. I thought here we go again. So I phoned Adam.

Let everything go. Set her as free as the others.

He took her and planted her in the grove with Bran and their kindred. When next I visited he showed me that wide garden and that family of trees. The others were lush, their leaves glossy as they caught the sun, seven foot tall. Flidias had little left and was dwarfed by them. I was confused I had not heard her.

I travelled more and more often to Melbourne for tarot and a steadily expanding clientele. That bubble of excitement was in my body again. Change.

When, I thought. To what?

In the eight personal year everything and everyone went into the appropriate email folder: hundreds of letters, most written by possible strangers.

How do I know you? I asked in over a thousand emails.

Eight is concerned with organization and fiscal skill. The plan was to get my finances in order. Then, as the second half of that year unfurled Sydney columnist Sarah Wilson, the I Quit Sugar advocate, requested a tarot session and an interview. I agreed and asked that she not put my website or email address in the article as I thought I well and truly had enough clients.

After the article came out in the Sydney Morning Herald and the Age my inbox went nuts. Despite Sarah's suggestion that I was dangerous, several hundred people tracked me down, all wanting me and my cards. After the panic attack I got savvy. I scoped around for friends (not clients) in Sydney who were willing to put up with strangers passing through their home for a week and I requested Serenity's help. She took over the bookings.

In Melbourne again. At Milo's house for the first night of this particular trip. Due to drive down to the Mornington Peninsula with Helen, to work from her mother's beachside house. My chest hurt. Not internally, rather like the bone was bruised but when I went to bed I slept really well. The pain was there again the next morning with a vengeance and I sat in a lounge chair while Milo took her daughter to little school. When she came home nothing had changed.

What's happening?

The sensation of having been smashed in the chest with a blunt force instrument.

I laughed but Milo didn't.

I'll be alright, I said. I don't think this is the time for me to die. Besides, I'm working this afternoon.

She went into her office and came back a few minutes later with a printed sheet of information.

You're having a heart attack, she said.

No I'm not. I'd know that.

You're having a heart attack and I'm driving you to emergency. Right now.

I grumbled as she bundled me into the car.

At the hospital I was hooked up to an ECG machine and blood samples were taken.

There was no indication of heart attack on the monitor and the doctor asked if I'd been on a long flight recently and I had. Just six weeks before I'd been in England editing someone's book.

Could be a thrombosis, he said. We'll keep you monitored.

I have to be down the coast this afternoon, I complained.

You're here for at least four hours until the blood tests come back. One way or another you're stuck with us.

Milo phoned Serenity to tell her what was going on but Serenity had news of her own. Another of Zhourelle's brothers had gone to Brisbane the night before and killed himself. He'd been witnessed jumping intentionally onto the train tracks and raising his arms in welcome. The train struck him front on.

Mum, you're not sick, Serenity said.

I know. Nobody believes me though.

Two hours later the blood tests came back normal. The pain had also dissipated.

We drove down the coast in time to read for my first client.

Back in Byron Bay I sat on the grassy mound outside a café with a colleague when a lightning bolt of understanding struck.

I'm moving, I said.

When?

Not sure.

Where to?

Couches. I'm hardly here anyway.

You can sleep on my couch. When?

Um... Now?

The plan?

Go home, phone the sons, pack.

And that's what I did. I put most of my possessions in storage or gifted friends and family. I recycled most everything else. I didn't have to keep holding the central space in case one of the kids came home. I was fooling myself with that idea. My intelligent adult children had their lives with other people.

I caught another plane the day I shut the doors to the Brunswick Heads studio when I got back two weeks later somebody gave me a bed in their spare room. That became the norm. Over the next several months I was constantly between Sydney and Melbourne in an incessant bombardment of emails largely redirected to Serenity. I stopped putting my phone number on my business cards.

My nine personal year—the numerological year of endings, completions, even death—began on my birthday of 2011. I still travelled, but I also had so many clients from all around the region, from Brisbane to Dubbo, so I rented a studio above the Circus Arts building in Byron Bay. Life like this was better than for many women I know, dying in increments and desperation, in confusion because they still cooked for their husbands or hoped they might still get one if they didn't have one. And others still sitting in the passenger seat of the family car because the man is the appropriate driver in a partnership.

I moved into a small studio in Byron Bay for a while. I had bed, broadsword, red silk Persian rug, locked ritual box full of grimoires and artifacts, some paintings for the walls, heavy-metal-deaths-head cane and the full length, hooded, black leather cloak, made by hand for a wearable arts performance a few years before.

I drove a four wheel drive station wagon because the potholes in Byron Bay were legendary. If you hit one out along Left Bank Road your car was fucked. They were like roadside bombs in reverse.

I slept a lot.

I'd discovered the paperback-on-demand business run by Amazon. I had the rights back for The Quickening and The Shining Isle and I also worked on Genesis | The Future, a science fiction book, for a 2012 release. And Magdalene, that interstitial work I'd researched back in 2000 while directing Jesus Christ Superstar. I made contact with several creative designers from around the world on new, exciting covers. They were all released or re-released in 2012.

But nothing new. There was nothing new. I readied myself for whatever came

PART THREE

Into the perilous deep you dive. Trusting yourself. There's no one to see. No one to suck back a breath in fear for you. You have faith. Know. You are seal, an otter, salmon. Whale breaching. You are in the womb and buried in earth. Nothing are you not and these depths are the true reality. They are the ocean and the way of the well. You are a cave that has no bottom so we may be sure there is no center to this earth, only space. I yearn from my place of sleep. I love you for guiding me to this edge. I feel your bones in my bones. You are a line a million strong. Your lovers of a million years watch. Warrior bright. Old. Old and brazen. Young and sinewy from the long hunt. Banging their shields as this she-bear passes, fearless of them, your cubs following you into the forest. Into the future. Into the bloodline of the unborn. Into the wild woman who shakes the world off. Into the wild man who walks on all fours by your side, his hide the color of the snowline, for yet you are still winter, his eyes black as the wings of ravens, catching light. Taking flight.

You are the silence. No one sees you dive.

BECOMING BONE WOMAN

CHAPTER 48

The circle is almost closed. The journey of initiation through that forest in which every part of me was stripped clean. Where no one else could see. I was still hiding. I did not know what I had become. Kon sat at the cafe table, head down, reading an article appropriate to the PhD he was writing. His partner and I joined him for our coffee date. The June of 2012.

So, Ly, what's happening with Bakery Hill, he asked, looking up from his work.

I've written the next draft and undercut the genre. Rather a gothic western style now, at least visually. And a website.

No takers yet?

Alex gave the link to a director's agent and he got straight onto her wanting the script.

And?

Asked where the money was. I sipped my coffee. And there isn't any. It needs to be written as a book first. I'll get to that one day.

Okay. Do something else then. You should go and meet Alison.

And she is?

My PhD supervisor in Hobart.

And why would I do that?

You two would really get along.

The conversation went from there, somehow, to the indigenous Celts again.

You should teach Celtic history and mysticism at some uni.

I can't.

Why not?

I'm secretly dumb.

What?

I explained about dropping out of high school and the drugs I'd been prescribed and that I'd only just concluded in the past year or so that I'd been subverted. I'd never told anyone before. Why was I releasing this now? Telling them?

Here's Alison's phone number. You need to speak to her.

I flew to Hobart with Serenity for her birthday. To MONA. The Underworld.

I also met Alison McConnell Imbriotis, Gatekeeper. It was she who showed me the path of the Return. That time. I am, of course, still alive. I suspect more will come.

Why were the people sent to the colonies of a rapacious and arrogant empire called convicts? As far as I know the common people of Albion were living in squalor and abject poverty, even as the aristocracy, government and commercial enterprise robbed the world of other people of self-sovereignty and culture in the eighteen hundreds at the arse end of the money spectrum was so dire that workhouses were the norm. Prostitution endemic. No contraception. Stealing to survive or to support a family would have been nothing short of necessary and yet even those stolen from were impoverished. Agrarian reforms had displaced so many Scots and Irish people that political dissidents were often exiled, set to work as servants, makers of roads and railways, maids and housekeepers. Slave labor. Children were removed from families or stolen off the street. Shipped to this, or another alien land, enslavement to one despot or another.

Some people I know glean a kind of masochistic pleasure that their ancestors were chained and maimed, sent thousands of miles across the ocean in deplorable conditions and collared into servitude all in the name of a queen who, while condemning homosexuality did so only for men because she could never comprehend that women could be sexually attracted to other women. It was institutional abuse and neither the English government nor the reigning Saxon monarchy have yet to apologize.

Alison and I discussed all of this during our afternoon together.

Entire cultures can go through the organic process of initiation. Death and sometimes rebirth.

Some come through the dark night of the collective soul, others are still lost. None are ever the same as before that impenetrable and unchartable forest.

I applied to Deakin University for post graduate studies and was accepted. I prepared to relocate to Melbourne. I flew Helen to Byron Bay in November of 2012. She had agreed to ride shotgun with me in my challenging and slightly deadly clapped-out Subaru station wagon. We shoved in the few possessions we could carry and the remainder was back-loaded onto a truck. I read for the last of the local clients, bumped out my Circus Arts studio, kissed everyone important goodbye and summoned the dogs and whichever of the little mysteries still kept me company and we took off.

In the blasting oven of the summer of that December with no aircon and a fan that did nothing, adding yet another near death experience, this time through heatstroke. We trusted the spirits of all the countries we crossed to get us to Melbourne alive.

CHAPTER 49

Helen and I took on the lease of an old, peculiar Edwardian house that we named Leticia. She has a linoleum hallway, like something out of One Flew Over the Cuckoo's Nest, and a parlor that is a riot of bohemian color. I completed my post graduate degree and was accepted into a Masters by Research program.

I gained new ways with words even though the content was not what I'd envisioned in my romanticized Dead Poets' Society idea of university. Different stories came to me and I also learned to research the attic and cellar out of everything and then challenge the validity of what I uncovered. Hunting with purpose.

A first cabal studied natural magic in that house once a month, then another in 2015. None knew each other's names and they didn't discuss their personal lives so that no one (as so often happens) could create a pecking order.

I wrote a short story, Comeuppance, a hardcore crime thriller, out of sheer curiosity about a genre I had never considered. That was published in The Crime Factory and went on to win a prize in Canada at the Hamilton Writers' annual GritLit Festival.

Pi, a coal black kitten I found online at a rescue cattery came to live with us followed not long after by the Historian who swept the leaf litter from the forest path and forged before me into the Maze of the past, finding me a history.

Once I learned that I am the direct descendent of Caradoc ap Cunobelin I was able to put years of disconnected study and research together in one document.

Every book I had read on the subject said "the Celts were—" intimating an extinct people, a dead way of life. But here I am. In just a few months I was able to put my metaphorical hand through the mouth of a balloon, reach to the very back and pull an entire culture from the deep past into the present. I am Celt. I'm also Norse, Irish Breizh and Sami. It's eye-watering.

Initiation is an altering. An arc on an ever-expanding Golden Ratio.

You are drawn out of the burrow and onto the field, your ears pricked for danger. But you are that danger and you are the field and the red fox that sniffs the air and catches your scent. You are the hunt and the terror and the breathlessness. You are the fear and the adrenalin, yours the teeth that snap the neck of what you have been, that drags you home to feed your young. Within your own burrow.

I have no regret that I was blind to the experience of this life initiation. Why? If I'd been given answers would I have done what I'd been told? What answers? That's the point. None of us living or dead has anything to achieve. Nothing to prove. No reason to live, just to explore and wonder and strive for art and heart, to love and laugh and learn exquisite things. The poetry and the shade of that one tree when the desert seems to be all there is. The salmon muscle in the heartbeat of a yet unborn infant.

Words like success and failure are someone else's delineations. Nothing can corral eternity and we have been here for that long. Everything has. We all will be here or somewhere and something, like air or particle or the string in string theory. We are such a captured animal. Bound about with chains of false security and so often lonely, laughing over cheap and trivial small talk or the seeking of riches, for fear of being cast out or attempting to prove to the world that our identities matter. But we need to break concrete. Turn over ancient turf and return dormant seeds to the sunshine and rain. And be patient until they reveal who they are.

I was as responsible as anyone for wallowing in safe waters, allowing memes to define me. And all the while I knew. But I hadn't learned this deeper language of bedrock and lynx spoor or the hunt or the howl, so I had to agree to the drama, the theatre of the human. That's changed now. The whole point is to take everything so much further, to keep looking for the questions. Ripping at the throat of seeming absolutes, glibly said to be facts, to close us down and cause us to agree. I rage against that.

When I die, my body will be food for the future and so I know I am immortal. I also know that to consider anything inanimate is not only unscientific but arrogant and crude. I don't know how slowly communities of lichen covered stone move, but I do know they move. We have always known that place contains spirit. That certain trees— a thousand years old—have knowledge of the seasons of our lives far greater than any history book. That ravens have a language we don't understand unless we listen without human ears. Most of what is read in books is the repetition of something written before, or mimics religion and carries morality.

Some people have hung with me through drought and flood and grass fire. We have walked deserts and wandered countries of heather and shaded beneath paperbark. Dug up the gravel and composted the forsaken soil. Planted forests of food and thought.

2016 I condensed the book, *Priteni*, into a trance experience for others. Nila, once a student and now a knowledge holder of our mysteries, was with me to guide the people through the sweet ogham smoke. Matty Connolly, initiated in 2001 who brought the music. He invited Fingal. Between bodhràns, guitar, flute and uillean pipes we summoned ghosts who thought themselves forgotten. Mourning for a language not littered with objects and any need other than to be ourselves. To live our way.

Color and gold, bright streams. Mists and fog hiding druids and their spells. War and confusion. The symbiosis of flesh and iron. Warrior and hunting eagle, hound and horse. Blood in the water.

I took over eighty people on a two day journey into the ancientness of their flesh and bones. Some First Nation people came. They wanted to know who they are in the long ago, before colonialism. Before take.

To complete the wheel. To heal those who thought themselves nobody. To clothe memory in art.

I won't second-guess what unfolds next. That's what this has taught me. There is now, however, a seemingly endless winding, weaving passage grave to explore, the path trod by the feet of the ancients. Those still within us. Fortresses of carved stone beneath the roots of the trees of long-dead forests. The treasure of the owl mask and the cloak of raven feathers worn upon that isle while the world was still safe, where Flidias will thrive for a thousand years, her children dotting an eventually pristine landscape. The wilding of words and the stories that I will learn so that I can be their messenger when I am stardust.

I am the cave in which my mother's body lies

I am the soldier who cries, and packs of hunting dogs
I am the dance within the secret games of children
And the storm wreck on the shoreline of a bay
I'm the hammer and the clay
I am the wild host and the midden
I am here and I am somewhere other than.
I am never known to linger and yet I stay
Who am I?
Who am I not?
I am the Bone Woman that reminds dogs of the snowline
That gathers the long dead and forges a terrible beauty
The mote in that bright shard of light that once was a forest
That forms the tundra
Upon which the future aurochs thunder.

APPENDIX ONE

SLAUGHTERHOUSE CREEK
From The Feast of Flesh and Spirit

1816 Appin Massacre, 1824 Bathurst Massacre, 1828 Cape Grim Massacre, 1830 Fremantle Massacre, Convincing Grounds Massacre (of the Kilcarer clan of the Gunditjmara people only two survive), 1834 Pinjarra Massacre, 1838 Slaughterhouse Creek Massacre, 1838 Faithful Massacre, Myall Creek Massacre, Gwydir Massacre, Waterloo Creek Massacre, 1839 Murdering Gully Massacre, Campaspie Plains Massacre, between 1840 and 1850 the Gippsland Massacres, 1840 Konongwootong Massacre, 1841 Rufus River Massacre, Lake Minimup Massacre of men and boys, 1842 Brisbane Valley Massacre, Kilcoy Station Mass Poisoning, Skull Creek and Gipsland Massacres,1843 Warrigal Creek Massacre, 1846 Cape Otway Massacre, 1848 East Ballina/Evans Head Massacre, 1849 Hospital Creek Massacre, Butchers Tree Massacre, Avenue Range Station Massacre, 1857 Hornet Bank Massacre: extermination of the Yeeman People, 1861 Medway Ranges Massacre, 1865 La Grange Bay Massacre, 1867 Goulbolba Hill Massacre, 1868 Flying Foam Massacre, 1873 Battle Camp Massacre, 1874 Barrow Creek Massacre, 1874-5 Blackfellow's Creek Massacre, 1879 Cape Bedford Massacre, 1880s Florida Station Massacres, 1884 Battle Mountain Massacre, 1887: the massacres of the Djara, Konejandi and Walmadjari in Western Australia plus a few more up there in the Kimberley, 1890 Speewah Massacre, 1890 to the 1920s the Killing Times in Western Australia, 1906 Canning Stock Route Massacres, 1915 Mistake Creek Massacre, 1918 Bentick Island Massacre, 1926 Forest River Massacre, 1928 Coniston Massacre of 38 people by one sick fucker.

Full list never compiled. Neither were your names. Or all of your tribes.

No school ever taught me about this.

I am so very, very sorry.

APPENDIX TWO

2007 – THE YEAR YOUR SOUL FLED YOU

I write this to all of you who lost yourselves, or someone else, in 2007. Who have yet to fully recover, cannot fully recover because you don't understand what happened so have no way to make sense of your condition.

Some of you are self-medicating, some of you are on anti-depressants, many of you do not know why you stay alive and yet you do not want to die. You simply want to understand, and to have a reason to continue living; to once again be comfortable in your skin.

But you did die. And you have yet to learn to live again. Most carefully because your skin is still very thin and your sanity is still very fragile. You must keep away from those who would take too much of you because you exhaust, still, so easily. You are restless all the time and you don't know where or what home is anymore.

My luck is that I have met, and continue to meet, vast numbers of you. Many years later and I still meet you every day. This level of insight is important for two reasons:

1. That you don't take this event personally
2. That you know you were not the only one struck down.

Knowing will keep you growing. Only knowing this will liberate you from your isolation.

You have been inoculated from a despair that could decimate you later. Continue to be creative even though at times you fear the Muse has fled. Relearn the beauty of things that no longer taste or smell as vividly. Things must again matter.

This will be hard work but an altered way of things is dawning; the outcome of which we may not see in our lifetimes.

Teach yourselves new things. Reach out to others. Remember the slower ways. Love each other. Strive for personal excellence. Prepare for the new Renaissance.

ABOUT THE AUTHOR

Ly de Angeles (Lore) is a writer, anarchist, teacher and practitioner of what is termed druíwit: witchcraft, and has been in print since 1987. She is an award-winning author and filmmaker, director and producer of stage and screen, mother, scholar, deep ecologist, mythographer, feminist, warrior-trained and psychic, and rewilder of language; a linguist. In 2020 *Ly* became *Lore* as her identity, thought terminated through an unquiet and caged childhood, was overturned in a supreme court.

Two years later, upon being contacted by relatives through ancestry.co.uk she finally took the last name of Whitehorse. The story of her quest for authenticity, however, is incomplete.

De Angeles Whitehorse' story is not unique. She is involved with others whose mothers were shamed, whose heritage was thought permanently erased. She has a habit, in all things unjust, of suggesting one "follow the money". She learned—only as recently as 2022—that she is a high functioning neurodivergent. She learned to mask so young that she can't recall when she first learned. She remembers events as snapshots and can become manic in the heart of trauma. She has wondered if she is crazy or touched. She has remained alive despite several attempts to have her erased. She is not wired like others and has suffered, sometimes seemingly malevolently, through misdiagnosis. She maintains it is how and why she is psychic.

This memoir is only part of her life.

www.ingramcontent.com/pod-product-compliance
Lightning Source LLC
Chambersburg PA
CBHW051936290426
44110CB00015B/2005